Russia's Gamble

Russia's Gamble

The Domestic Origins of Russia's Attack on Ukraine

Vladimir Gel'man

polity

Copyright © Vladimir Gel'man 2025

The right of Vladimir Gel'man to be identified as Author of this Work has been asserted in accordance with the UK Copyright, Designs and Patents Act 1988.

First published in 2025 by Polity Press

Polity Press
65 Bridge Street
Cambridge CB2 1UR, UK

Polity Press
111 River Street
Hoboken, NJ 07030, USA

All rights reserved. Except for the quotation of short passages for the purpose of criticism and review, no part of this publication may be reproduced, stored in a retrieval system or transmitted, in any form or by any means, electronic, mechanical, photocopying, recording or otherwise, without the prior permission of the publisher.

ISBN-13: 978-1-5095-5942-8
ISBN-13: 978-1-5095-5943-5(pb)

A catalog record for this book is available from the British Library.

Library of Congress Control Number: 2024946045

Typeset in 10.5 on 12.5 pt Sabon
by Fakenham Prepress Solutions, Fakenham, Norfolk NR21 8NL
Printed and bound in Great Britain by TJ Books Ltd, Padstow, Cornwall

The publisher has used its best endeavors to ensure that the URLs for external websites referred to in this book are correct and active at the time of going to press. However, the publisher has no responsibility for the websites and can make no guarantee that a site will remain live or that the content is or will remain appropriate.

Every effort has been made to trace all copyright holders, but if any have been overlooked the publisher will be pleased to include any necessary credits in any subsequent reprint or edition.

For further information on Polity, visit our website:
politybooks.com

CONTENTS

Preface   vii

1. February 2022: Why Russia Fails   1
2. The Personalist Trap   33
3. The Well-Oiled Machine, Out of Control   59
4. The Great Self-Deception   85
5. The Victims of Previous Successes   115
6. Lost Illusions, Dashed Hopes, and Unlearned Lessons   142

Notes   158
Index   213

"Whoever exalts himself will be humbled" (Matthew, 23:12)

PREFACE

In the early morning of August 19, 1991, a telephone call woke me in my parents' Leningrad apartment. During the conversation, I learned that the conservative leaders of the Soviet Union had launched a coup d'état aimed at restoration of the political order established by the Communists over seventy years earlier. At that time, I expected that they would easily reach these goals after the declared deposal of the Soviet president and the announcement of a state of emergency. In the most far-reaching scenario, the potential success of the coup could, in my view, result in the full-scale restoration of Communist rule, with its worst institutions and practices. However, I was completely wrong – the coup was poorly prepared, and the resistance led by the Russian President Boris Yeltsin ruined the plans of the putschists over the next three days. Instead of the restoration of the previous Soviet political, economic, and societal order, the coup had quite the opposite outcomes. The Communist Party was eliminated and the Soviet Union dissolved,[1] although most probably such eventualities could have happened anyway due to the multiple changes initiated under Mikhail Gorbachev's rule of the Soviet Union since 1985, regardless of the failed coup.

More than thirty years later, early in the morning of February 24, 2022, another telephone call woke me in my St. Petersburg apartment. During the conversation, I learned that the Russian President Vladimir Putin had announced the launching of a major assault, a "special military operation," aimed at "denazification" and "demilitarization" of Ukraine, and at placing this country, which had gained independence during the Soviet collapse, under the full-scale political, military, and international control of Russia. At that time, I expected that the Russian leadership would easily reach these goals after a massive assault through the extensive use of arms, and probably take over the Ukrainian capital, Kyiv, during the next three days or so. In the most far-reaching scenario, the potential success of the "special military operation" could, in my view, result in the restoration of the Soviet-style empire, with its worst institutions and practices. However, I was completely wrong – the "special military operation" was poorly prepared and implemented, and the Ukrainian resistance, led by the President Volodymyr Zelensky, ruined the plans of the Russian leaders over the following weeks and months. Instead of the restoration of the Soviet-style empire and imposition of the Russian political, economic, and societal order onto Ukraine and beyond, the "special military operation" had quite the opposite outcomes, and it is still very far from its conclusion. The highly risky venture of the restoration of a Soviet-style empire looks unfeasible, and since February 2022, Russia has faced enormous domestic and international problems, although most probably such problems could have arisen due to the multiple changes initiated and endorsed by the Russian elites under Putin's rule, regardless of the assault on Ukraine.

The fateful decision to launch the highly risky "special military operation," which soon turned into a full-scale protracted war, provoked many responses and reactions both domestically and internationally. Apart from numerous statements by politicians, policy-makers, activists, artists, writers, and ordinary citizens, political analysts, scholars, and experts also expressed their views on the ongoing changes in Russia, Ukraine and beyond after February 2022. The large-scale assault on Ukraine was largely unexpected, and not predicted by most international scholars and experts. The very research sub-field of Russian studies (and Ukrainian studies, too) faced a major exogenous shock.[2] Initially, the first reaction of many scholars of Russia to this exogenous shock was very emotional, and contributed to numerous petitions, op-eds, interviews, and the like. However, now the time is ripe to transform these scholarly responses to current events into more in-depth research into the causes, mechanisms, effects, and implications of the Russian assault on Ukraine. This is the primary task of my book.

The core of this study is an analysis of the domestic origins of the Russian assault on Ukraine and an explanation of why this "special military operation" has not achieved its goals. As often happens in the study of any complex phenomenon, these questions have no simple and unidimensional "correct" answer: the study of global politics presupposes the coexistence of different competing explanations for the same processes. I do not claim that my approach to these issues is the only possible way of explaining the Russian military assault on Ukraine in February 2022 and its aftermath. What is presented in this book is an approach based upon three cornerstone principles unlike those of other possible explanations. First, it is less oriented around normative ideals and mostly related to positive analysis. I believe that for an understanding of the political processes, in Russia and elsewhere, it is important to discuss less how things should (or should not) be, but to concentrate more how they really are. This is the essence of the framework of analysis offered here. Instead of blaming anyone for wrong ideas and/or destructive deeds, I ask the question "why?": why did Russian elites and leaders propose, prepare for, and implement the assault on Ukraine in February 2022 in such a poorly prepared, outstandingly inefficient, and heavily destructive way? The second principle is an almost exclusive focus on Russia as the key actor in the ongoing international conflict, which emerged well before February 2022 and dramatically developed after that to a new stage of violence. It is obvious that other international actors, such as the United States, the European Union and its member states, China and, of course, Ukraine, played important roles in this conflict. However, it was Russia that launched this assault, and this is why explaining its motivations and performance before and after 2022 is essential for our understanding of the ongoing military conflict; at least, this is a necessary, though probably insufficient, condition for any in-depth analysis. Third, my book is addressed to domestic political developments within Russia: following the approach developed by George F. Kennan during the early years of the Cold War,[3] I aim to explain Russia's behavior in the international arena through the lenses of an analysis of its domestic politics. This is why I focus on the ideas, interests, and identities of Russian elites and the logic of their expectations, perceptions, and misperceptions, which formed before the launching of the "special military operation" and greatly affected its preparation, elaboration, and implementation. Readers may judge from this book to what extent these cornerstone principles are useful for a convincing explanation of the Russian assault on Ukraine in February 2022.

The impetus for writing this book emerged almost immediately after the launching of Russia's "special military operation," as it

PREFACE

became clear that a swift Russian takeover of Ukraine was not feasible. However, the development of the argument and turning my ideas into a book took a while, and several individuals and organizations contributed to this venture in one way or another. First and foremost, John Thompson from Polity Press persuaded me to formulate a book proposal, enthusiastically endorsed it from the very beginning, and supported my plans through its long journey. The Center for International Studies at Sciences Po, Paris, thanks to Emilija Pundziute-Gallois, offered me an opportunity to present an early draft of the first chapter at the international seminar in May 2023, and this discussion encouraged me to pursue this project further. My home institution, the Aleksanteri Institute at the University of Helsinki, was and remains the main venue of my research, and the discussion of the key ideas of this book at the INREES summer school it organized in August 2023 was a milestone for its further development. Other seminars, held by the European University Institute and Malmö University, were very useful in terms of discussions and development of ideas. The exchange of ideas with numerous colleagues in various countries allowed me to develop my arguments and support them with the use of various sources. In particular, I would like to thank Luca Anceschi, Sergei Guriev, Mark Kramer, Tomila Lankina, Dmitry Lanko, Alexander Libman, Andrey Makarychev, Kirill Rogov, Andrey Scherbak, Gulnaz Sharafutdinova, Konstantin Sonin, Anne de Tinguy, Dmitry Travin, and Pavel Usanov for sharing their thoughts and offering their comments on various occasions. My Aleksanteri colleagues, especially Kaarina Aitamurto, Sari Autio-Sarasmo, Markku Kangaspuro, Markku Kivinen, Katalin Miklóssy, Katri Pynnöniemi, Veli-Pekka Tynkkynen, and Margarita Zavadskaya, as well as many others, provided a highly productive environment for the exchange of ideas, some of which were used in this book in one way or another. Irina Busygina, Ilia Nadporozhskii, and Evgeny Roshchin carefully read the early version of the manuscript and offered me their outstandingly important suggestions and recommendations. The friendly, detailed, and nuanced linguistic assistance provided by Alexei Stephenson was essential for making the manuscript readable. Last but not least, my wife Oxana is the main and outstanding source of support in everything I do. I could never have completed this book without her love, patience, and encouragement.

PREFACE

The process of writing of this book unfolded against the background of the ongoing military assault on Ukraine, which has caused many military and civilian casualties among Russian and Ukrainian citizens. The vast number of such casualties is one of the tragic consequences of the processes that are analyzed in my book. I dedicate this book to the memory of those who fell victim to this assault.

Helsinki, July 2024

Chapter 1

FEBRUARY 2022: WHY RUSSIA FAILS

Early on the morning of February 24, 2022, Russia launched a major military assault on Ukraine, officially declared a "special military operation." This move, initiated by the Russian President Vladimir Putin, further extended the Russian assault on Ukraine, which had started in 2014 with the annexation of Crimea and the de facto takeover of parts of the Donetsk and Luhansk regions in southeast Ukraine. It was a follow-up to the previous episodes of Russia's conflict with Ukraine (since the Orange Revolution of 2004) aimed at keeping Ukraine under Russian control in terms of its domestic politics and foreign policy, and at preventing its political, economic, and international integration with the West. Russia's previous attempts to impose political control over Ukraine brought only temporary and limited successes to the Kremlin.[1] Its various levers of influence on Ukraine weakened over time, and the new round of attacks in February 2022 was supposed to provide a decisive solution for Russia's Ukrainian problem. In essence, this "special military operation" aimed at the violent overthrow of the Ukrainian authorities and the imposition of a new government in Kyiv that would be loyal to Moscow: alongside military occupation, it was intended to make Ukraine a dependent client state of Russia for a long time, if not forever.[2]

Undoubtedly, the Russian military assault on Ukraine became one of the greatest exogenous shocks in international politics since World War II. Unlike the two world wars, it was not driven by structural contradictions between major global powers. Rather, it emerged as a side effect of the approach to domestic and international affairs taken by Russia's political elites and leadership, which promoted outsized international aspirations for the country, thus undermining the international order of the twenty-first century. However, soon it became clear that the "special military operation" had not achieved its goals, at least, not yet.[3] Instead, the Russian military assault on Ukraine turned into a protracted full-scale war. This fateful decision had and continues to have a devastating impact on Russia, Ukraine, Europe, and the whole world. While the military assault is still ongoing, and its outcomes and consequences are very much uncertain, it leaves no doubt that the launch of the "special military operation" in February 2022 was probably the worst decision ever made by Russia's rulers in the country's long history.

This decision led to major disasters for Ukraine, which became a heavily wounded victim of military assault, as Russia continued its attacks against Ukraine over and over again, seized part of its territory, eliminated and injured numerous soldiers, officers and civilians, and destroyed residential buildings, industrial facilities, agricultural warehouses, schools, and hospitals across the country. Furthermore, the Russian military assault has proved to be outstandingly harmful for Russia. The "special military operation" has resulted in the greatest losses of Russian lives on the battlefield since World War II, the greatest emigration from the country since the Bolshevik revolution, serious economic problems, major international isolation of Russia, and a lack of any positive prospects for the country's development, at least in the foreseeable future. The goals of Russia's highly risky and gambling-like offensive were unrealistic from the beginning, and it is no wonder that they have not been achieved and are highly unlikely to be achieved any time soon. Russia's further adaptation to the new realities of ongoing military conflict, including increasing domestic political repressions, major international sanctions, capital flight, military mobilization, problems with import substitution, have only aggravated the country's problems. Meanwhile, the chances of Russia's military victory in the war – including but not limited to takeover of major cities and overthrow of the Ukrainian political leadership – have declined over time, and for these reasons the "special military operation" against Ukraine should be considered a major failure.

Political leaders in the contemporary world have rarely made fateful decisions that have produced such profoundly devastating effects for their own countries. Of course, one may note some incredibly poor decisions to launch military assaults in the twentieth century, such as Hitler's attack against the Soviet Union in 1941 and the Argentine junta's invasion of the Falkland Islands in 1982. Both decisions proved to be disastrous, and in the end, they greatly contributed to the collapse of both the German and the Argentinian political regimes. However, such instances of highly risky military adventures are very much uncommon in today's world: moreover, they may often serve as lessons for future generations of leaders of how one should not behave in the international arena. The Russian elites and leadership, however, not only ignored these lessons, but also made many other crucial mistakes, which included initial major overestimation of their own strengths and major underestimation of the strengths of their adversaries.[4] While Russia's plans for the "special military operation" were poorly designed and prepared, Russia was also not ready for a protracted full-scale war in military, political, and economic terms. Meanwhile, when the failure of the initial plans for the "special military operation" became clear, Russia further aggravated these mistakes, declaring occupied Ukrainian territories a part of the Russian Federation, making military victims and devastation much greater and culminating in the virtually endless continuation of the "special military operation" at any cost.[5] In a way, Russia's approach to pursuing the "special military operation" was quite similar to certain kinds of gambling behavior: instead of accepting the hard reality of modest losses in the game and quitting at a certain point, the addict raises the stakes over and over again, in a cycle that becomes virtually unstoppable.

These moves were in sharp contrast to Russia's previous international behavior. Under Putin's leadership, the Kremlin became very cynical and brazen, yet much more cautious and risk-averse. This was the major reason why, until the beginning of the assault, many observers did not expect that Russia would launch a large-scale military attack on Ukraine. Even those politicians, policymakers and experts who hated the Russian leadership for various reasons considered Russia's previous steps within the international arena reasonable and largely predictable. Before February 2022, Russia largely aimed at increasing its international influence by various non-violent means, ranging from economic projects (especially related to oil and gas diplomacy)[6] to covert interference in the domestic politics of certain countries, including the US,[7] and promotion of Russia-friendly European politicians such as Marine Le Pen in France and Viktor Orbán in Hungary.[8] Instances of large-scale use of military force, such as the Russian five-day war against Georgia in August 2008, the annexation of Crimea and the separatist conflict in Donbas since 2014 (see chapter 5) were relatively limited and at that time considered exceptional episodes. The full-scale assault on Ukraine and further escalation of the conflict despite increasingly high costs for Russia went far beyond these expectations. It was difficult to believe that political leaders could change their behavior on the international arena so dramatically even though there were no credible threats to the existing international status quo. Russia under Putin could have continued its deception of the "collective West" by building its image as a viable alternative to the global political order based upon US domination, reaping further benefits for the Kremlin in the process. Russian elites could continue buying new yachts and estates in the most luxurious parts of the world, whitewashing incomes and status for themselves and their families and cronies. Russian big businesses could continue their expansion into international markets by bribing foreign state officials and politicians. Russian intellectuals could continue their lofty discussions on the inevitable decay of the West and the forthcoming international leadership by Putin's Russia. All these Russia's perks were "annulled" or, at least, put into question after the launch of the military assault on Ukraine. The compensation that the Kremlin offered to the Russian elites for these losses turned out to be insufficient, although it did allow the elite to remain loyal to the Kremlin. Still, one can assess Russia's heavy losses of money, status, and credibility as major sunk costs without any benefits.

As the outcomes and consequences of Russia's military assault for Ukraine, Russia, and the entire world are still uncertain at the time of writing, the time is ripe for a critical reassessment of the sources of Russia's mistakes in the process of preparing and implementing its "special military operation." While the condemnation of Russia's assault on Ukraine and of its consequences is nearly universal among scholars, pundits, and policymakers in the West, the goal of this analysis is different. The question is what the roots of this failure are, or – paraphrasing the title of the oft-cited book by Daron Acemoglu and James A. Robinson, *Why Nations Fail*[9] – why Russia fails. Answering this question will be the focus of my book.

Before turning to the answers, four important disclaimers are necessary. First, this chapter is entitled "Why Russia Fails," rather than "Why Ukraine Endures." Even though Russia's failure in 2022 would never have occurred without major Ukrainian resistance (as well as support for Ukraine by a large coalition of supporters from various countries), the analysis in this book heavily concentrates on Russia, and Ukraine is mentioned relatively briefly. Such an approach reflects my experience and expertise in research on Russian politics, and that is why this book is driven by a Russian rather than a Ukrainian perspective. Ukrainian and international scholars have conducted many deep and detailed analyses of Ukrainian political developments, which contributed to the resistance against the Russian assault.[10] I hope that my book will be complementary to their research rather than competing with them.

Second, being a scholar of Russian domestic politics, I do not consider myself an expert on global international relations and/or on military affairs, and when dealing with these matters in this book, I rely heavily upon secondary sources rather than upon my own research. The goal of this book, however, is different from the research conducted by scholars of international relations[11] and military experts.[12] I aim to explain the failure of the "special military operation" as a political phenomenon, driven by the domestic political regime and mechanisms of governance in Russia, as well as by the perceptions and previous experiences of the Russian elites.

Third, in this book I will not discuss the Russian people as actors of Russian politics towards Ukraine and beyond, irrespective of their preferences and attitudes vis-à-vis the "special military operation" (which are widely discussed in the literature).[13] Ordinary people rarely matter much in foreign policy in various political contexts: even in established democracies, this is largely the business of elites, and in certain circumstances the mass public may support military assaults (such as the US invasion of Vietnam in 1965–7 or of Iraq in 2003). In autocracies (especially in "spin dictatorships," which rely heavily upon lies as a tool of dominance),[14] mass attitudes are strongly affected by state propaganda,[15] while mass political behavior, including but not limited to public protests, is constrained by state repression.[16] This is why one should not be overly surprised that the Kremlin quickly, decisively, and pre-emptively suppressed open public resistance to the "special military operation" well before and immediately after February 24, 2022, and that most Russians have remained loyal to the regime since, irrespective of the changes on the front lines.[17] In a broader perspective, elsewhere I consider the place of the mass public in politics mostly as a tool of the elites (or of counter-elites),[18] as ordinary people, both in Russia and beyond, lack political agency,[19] although I acknowledge that this view could be criticized as overly elitist.

Fourth, the very statement of Russia's failure might be premature amid the continuing battle, and ongoing attempts to achieve the Kremlin's goals at any cost. However, one should not deny that the initial plan of the "special military operation" has failed, and achieving the Kremlin's goal of placing Ukraine under Russia's control sounds unfeasible at this book's time of writing – irrespective of the ever-changing situation on the front lines.

In this chapter, I discuss the book's central argument that the Russian assault on Ukraine in February 2022 was the logical outcome of the evolutionary trajectory of Russia's political regime after the Soviet collapse, driven by the increasing status-seeking ambitions of Russia's elites and political leadership.[20] I elaborate this argument vis-à-vis other existing theoretical frameworks and scholarly explanations for this phenomenon. The focus of the chapter is on the rationale behind Russia's aggressive behavior in the international arena long before February 2022 amid limited domestic and international constraints. The major vices of the Russian political regime, such as personalism and bad governance, alongside the elite's misperceptions and feeling of their limitless impunity, became more and more destructive over time, especially after Russia's annexation of Crimea in 2014 and constitutional plebiscite of 2020 (which aimed at de facto extension of Putin's term in office until at least 2036). These vices contributed to the weakening of political and institutional constraints on the Kremlin and paved the way for Russia's "special military operation" in February 2022, and to its subsequent failure.

The Sources of Russian Misconduct

Since the famous article by George F. Kennan, "The Sources of Soviet Conduct" (published in 1947 under the pseudonym "X"), scholars and experts have tended to explain Soviet and Russian international behavior via systematic analysis of its domestic sources.[21] Kennan, whose approach laid the foundations for US foreign policy in relation to the Soviet Union for decades, rightly argued that the aggressive militancy of Soviet leaders stemmed from their ideas and interests, while their irresolvable hostility towards the West resulted from the recognition of the Soviet Union's multiple vulnerabilities and the attempt to overcome them through audacity and assertiveness. To summarize, Kennan argued that the aggressive Soviet foreign policy that resulted in the Cold War was driven by the country's domestic problems, such as the dubious legitimacy of Communist rule, the poor performance of the Soviet state, and the lack of confidence the elites had in the regime's stability. From this perspective, a long-term international conflict with foreign enemies legitimized the domestic status quo and allowed the Kremlin to diminish risks to the regime's stability coming from within the country.

In many ways, Kennan's analysis is still relevant with regard to present-day Russia, even though its international behavior is now driven by ideas and interests very different from those of Soviet predecessors at the beginning of the Cold War. Nevertheless, Russia's domestic political trajectory after February 2022, with the rise of repression and the tightening of state control over the media, the economy, and societal activism, serves as a vivid illustration of Kennan's comments on the role of domestic factors in the Kremlin's foreign policy, and his argument regarding the instrumental use of international conflicts as a tool for maintenance of the domestic status quo.[22] One can go further and argue that while Russia's assault on Ukraine resulted in many heavy losses in the international arena, domestically the attack on Ukraine became a sort of victory for the Kremlin in relation to real and/or imagined domestic challenges to Putin's rule. At least, from a short-term perspective, the potential sources of such challenges, resulting from major discontent among Russian elites, have diminished because of the use of repression and/or threats thereof. At the same time, the lack of domestic discontent with the assault among Russian elites (despite the fact that the goals have yet to be achieved) is driven by the lack of plausible alternatives to the indefinite continuation of the "special military operation." To put it bluntly, even in the eyes of anti-military Russian elites and masses alike, Putin is domestically considered to be the only actor who can put an end to the "special military operation" in one way or another. Thus, the ongoing assault further consolidates his undeniable dominance, undermining the Kremlin's incentives to end it: rather, the hypothetically endless continuation of war could make Putin nearly invincible.[23] However, the costs of the Kremlin's short-term victory over these risks and challenges may become prohibitively high for Russia, especially in the long run.

At first sight, the global political context of 1947 was different from that observed in 2022. The framework used in analysis at that time is often considered outdated and references to the Cold War themselves find little welcome after the Soviet collapse. However, the practice of Russia's international behavior in 2022 mimicked Stalin's approach after World War II to a great degree, imposing Russia's domestic political and economic order onto the Soviet (today Russian) sphere of influence and countering its rivals, "the collective West," elsewhere on the globe. By the standards of the international politics of 1947, this kind of international behavior was considered a familiar routine, and nobody was surprised that the Soviet Union used international aggression and the threat of brutal use of force as major tools of its foreign policy (similarly to Nazi Germany or Imperial Japan just years before). Furthermore, if one were to place Kennan's analysis into a comparative historical perspective, one might say that such international behavior was typical for various rulers across the globe over many centuries. The present-day Russian approach to international politics and the use of military assault merits significant reassessment in light of these considerations.

Indeed, while in the contemporary world military aggression and large-scale wars are perceived as the exception rather than the rule, global history until the end of the World War II was largely a history of military aggressions and wars.[24] The answer to the question of why aggressions and wars were frequent in the past and have become rare nowadays is linked to constraints on such modes of behavior – constraints, which have greatly increased over time. First, they increased within the international arena, as war-driven destruction is incredibly costly in the nuclear age. Second, they increased domestically, as massive war-related losses (which may increase over time in the case of protracted military conflicts) are unwelcome in the eyes of elites and masses alike. However, what might happen if these domestic and international constraints were considered weak or did not exist at all? Most probably, without major constraints, many political leaders and their subordinates across the globe would be free to seize more territory and/or resources previously belonging to neighboring (and not only neighboring) countries, thus increasing their power, status, and wealth, in both the domestic and international arenas. Judging from this perspective, one might argue that historically war was a norm of international behavior and peace was an exception, not vice versa. In other words, one may wonder not why Russia launched the military assault on Ukraine but rather why such international behavior is not so typical for other countries in the modern age.

Constraints on military aggression and wars can be divided into military, economic, and human aspects. Military constraints are caused by the simple fact that the military aggression can result not only in victory and subsequent seizure of territory and/or resources of other countries but also in major defeat with excessively heavy losses for the aggressor. The probability of such an outcome greatly increases if a potential target of the military aggressor can rely upon major support from its powerful allies. This is why less militarily strong countries tend to avoid military aggression against mighty and well-protected rivals, and episodes like Argentina's attack on Great Britain and attempt to conquer the Falklands Islands in 1982 are outstandingly rare. As many countries tend to protect themselves against foreign aggression by military force, these constraints often become unsurmountable. Meanwhile, economic constraints are caused by excessively high costs of large-scale and long-term wars, which often took decades in the past.[25] The continuation of such wars could cause impoverishment, if not full bankruptcy of states and their citizens: this is why military aggression could result in heavy economic losses irrespective of potential victories on the battlefield. Finally, human constraints are caused by combat and collateral losses during the fighting, which may result not only in military incapacitation, but also in increasing domestic political risks for militant rulers. Protracted and particularly bloody wars may contribute to a major decline in political support for the status quo among elites (who may even violently overthrow regimes via military coup) and the masses (who may engage in revolutionary actions, as the experience of the Russian and German Empires during World War I reflects). The rational choice theory of democratic peace developed by Bruce Bueno de Mesquita and his coauthors demonstrates the effects of human constraints on the probability of wars: when the extension of the size of the selectorate reaches the point of virtually all adults, countries tend to avoid major wars because of the unacceptability of human loss of life.[26]

However, what if the potential aggressor expects that:

(1) the potential target country of military aggression is weak enough and has little chance of long-standing military resistance and military aid from abroad;

(2) the benefits of prospective victory and potential seizure of the target's territory and resources after the war outweigh the war's economic costs;
(3) and combat and collateral losses during the war can be overlooked given the limited size of the selectorate?

In that event, constraints on military assault may become relatively negligible, and the probability of war may dramatically increase because incentives for seizure of foreign territory and resources are sufficiently strong. Imposing one's control over other states and nations may increase the wealth, power, and prestige of aggressive rulers and their countries. At the same time, aggressors tend to invest effort into diminishing the costs of their military actions and minimizing war-related losses. Instead of protracted battles with extensive involvement of armies, they prefer one-off decisive attacks by special military forces, which aim at quick deposal of adversarial rulers and taking the target country under their control without major violent resistance. Such an approach, labeled the "small victorious war" (a term, supposedly attributed to the Russian Minister of the Interior Vyacheslav von Plehve in the early twentieth century), is the most attractive option for a number of potential aggressors. The problem is that successful implementation of this strategy (such as in the case of the violent suppression of the Prague Spring in Czechoslovakia by the Soviet Union and its Warsaw Pact allies in August 1968)[27] is not always guaranteed. Very often, such wars proved to be not so small and not at all victorious, even if such an outcome was hardly predictable at the planning stage. A clear example of such a failure is the Soviet invasion of Afghanistan in December 1979: it soon developed into a ten-year-long full-scale war, which caused numerous victims and became incredibly unpopular in Soviet society. The Russian "special military operation" in Ukraine was also planned as an instance of "small victorious war," but its implementation became much more devastating than the Soviet invasion of Afghanistan.

In sum, I would argue that if and when potential aggressors expect that they would be neither deterred by military force nor constrained by risks of major economic and/or human losses, they might prefer to plan the format of assault as a "small victorious war." Under these conditions, their decision to launch attacks against target countries cannot be blocked by anyone until the implementation stage. This was exactly the case with the Russian military assault against Ukraine in February 2022, and explaining this decision is the primary task for further analysis.

The logic of George F. Kennan's approach to understanding the aggressive militancy of the Soviet (now, Russian) leaders through the prism of their ideas and interests within the context of domestic politics is still very relevant more than seventy-five years since its publication, but it needs to be updated for present-day conditions. Following the title of his 1947 article, one may summarize the arrangement of these ideas and interests as sources of Russian misconduct. One must admit that these ideas and interests did not just emerge from scratch immediately before the assault. Rather, they emerged and were gradually elaborated since the Soviet collapse, as this event and the subsequent decline of Russia's international role caused many grievances among significant segments of the Russian elites that constituted the country's ruling class. As there are many definitions of "elites," for the purposes of this book I understand "elites" to roughly mean domestic actors who systematically affect major political and policy decisions in a given country by enabling or blocking them.[28] In functional terms, for further analysis I will primarily focus on certain major segments of Russian elites, namely the top civilian state bureaucracy, the coercive state apparatus or *siloviki* ("the men of force," representatives of military and security circles), and big business, bearing in mind that their foreign policy visions, perceptions, and preferences change over time.[29] To various degrees, these segments of elites, especially *siloviki* (whose influence has greatly increased over time), shared the feeling of being losers in the international arena after the end of the Cold War.[30] Especially after the Russian annexation of Crimea in 2014, their desire to exact major revenge against the "collective West" and for the restoration and further expansion of Russia's global great power status was further inflamed, and by February 2022 became unstoppable. Moreover, they increasingly believed that Russia could actively use military means as an instrument for achieving these foreign policy goals.

According to the Survey of Russian Elites, a longitudinal study of foreign policy attitudes of Russian elites conducted by US-based scholars (in cooperation with a Russian polling company) from 1993 to 2020,[31] the militarism of Russian elites was low in the 1990s, dramatically increased during the 2000s and 2010s and reached its peak by 2020 (see figure 1).[32] By February 2022, the ideas and interests of the Russian elites were fairly consistent and developed, and they were ready to achieve their goals via military means. In a way, the ideas and interests of the Russian ruling class formed the Kremlin-led vision of Russian foreign policy (shared by major segments of the Russian elites) that stands behind the Russian assault. Such a vision included the following cornerstone principles of Russian foreign policy.[33]

First, the Russian ruling class considers the international arena to be the equivalent of a global oligarchy. According to this view, the international order is based upon the dominance of several key stakeholder countries, who act as major veto players and control other countries via various political, economic, and military levers. The international order is stable as long as key stakeholders formally and/or informally agree on their zones of control over other countries and do not breach these agreements. Countries other than the stakeholders have no major impact on the distribution of global power. At best, these countries may exert some regional influence, but in the global arena, they are doomed to be the stakeholders' puppets. Within this vision, for example, the major European powers are not considered important players in international politics, being submissive and subordinated to the US. At the same time, the European Union is perceived as a weak and indecisive body because of the complicated nature of its decision-making and the diversity of interests of its member states. Regardless, the agency of puppet states should not be considered seriously, as their deserved place in the world is somewhere near the latrine (in Russian criminal slang, *mesto vozle parashi*). Due to the Soviet collapse, Russia lost its deserved place as a global stakeholder, and restoring its status and expanding its zone of control over other countries as much as possible are priority national interests.

Second, Russia, a personalist autocracy,[34] is perceived as a country which is not only able to restore its place as a global superpower but which also has strong potential to overtake its rivals because of the strong and efficient leadership of Vladimir Putin. Such a regime developed its capacity for quick and powerful decision-making without domestic checks and balances, which only weaken the leadership and make its policies inconsistent and concessionary. As unconstrained leadership has greatly contributed to the wealth, power, and status of the Russian ruling class, this domestic political

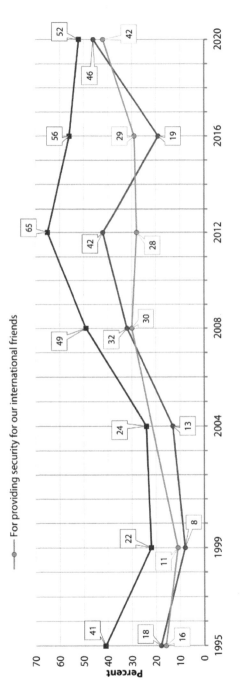

Figure 1. Russian Elite Approval of the Use of the Russian Military (%) (from Rivera, 'The Views of Russian Elites on Military Intervention Abroad', 3).

n = 180 (1995), 240 (1999), 320 (2004), 241 (2008), 240 (2012), 243 (2016), and 245 (2020).

Source: Data from the Survey of Russian Elites, 1993–2020.

Notes: The figure displays the percentage of all respondents (the total number including those who answered "don't know" or refused to answer) who responded yes to the question.

Question wording: "In your opinion, for which of the following purposes is the use of the Russian military permissible? [Defending the interests of Russians [*rossiian*] living in the former republics of the USSR] [Defending the interests of Russian citizens in other countries] [Providing security for our international friends] 1. Yes, 2. No."

order should be maintained and strengthened further for as long as possible despite its imperfect domestic policy performance. Even though Russia has limited resources for becoming a global stakeholder, its increasing military might, assertiveness, and decisiveness may compensate for these deficiencies and flaws, as other countries, frightened of Russia, will be unable to resist its aspirations.

Third, Russia, the US and China are the only international actors worthy of being global stakeholders, while other countries and regions are areas of their struggle for control. Using various means, Russia should "decolonize" other countries and regions, which are justly placed near the latrine – this "decolonization" would mean that these countries should move from the US's zone of control to Russian control, either directly or indirectly. A new zone of Russian control should include many client states in various parts of the world. However, the core zone of control will embrace not only post-Soviet Eurasia but also Europe, which should not remain under the control of the US (which was unjustly imposed after the end of the Cold War). As the European Union is weak, fragmented, and lacks a centralized hierarchy, the EU member states (or at least some of them) will inevitably fall under Russian control. In addition to this general picture, some regional powers such as Turkey or Iran are considered to be potential Russian allies whose drive to regional leadership may undermine the US-led hegemony, according to the logic of "the enemy of my enemy is my friend."

Fourth, the US, Russia's main existential rival, will inevitably lose its leading international positions despite its powerful status, wealth, and resources because of a deep and irreversible domestic and international crisis. This crisis of the US should be aggravated by every possible means, including (but not limited to) building major anti-American coalitions across the globe, again based on the principle of "the enemy of my enemy is my friend." Further weakening of the US and provoking significant conflict between it and China will contribute to the strengthening of Russia because of the *tertius gaudens* principle. In the end, conflict between Russia's major rivals will result in it imposing its international dominance.

These cornerstone principles of Russian foreign policy developed over several decades since the Soviet period. As Sergey Radchenko has convincingly argued, after World War II the drive for global dominance at any cost determined Soviet foreign policy, despite the fact that the Soviet Union's resource endowment was clearly insufficient for such a bid.[35] To some extent, this drive was a side effect of the feeling of domestic and international vulnerability among the Soviet elites and leadership,[36] and seeking global power and status compensated for these perceptions in one way or another. In the post-Soviet period, the same status-seeking and drive for global dominance at any cost was actively promoted not only by top state officials like Putin and his foreign minister Sergey Lavrov, but also by major Russian think tanks such as the Council for Foreign and Defense Policy, and discussed in major forums like the Valdai Club. Moreover, certain previous episodes of Russian foreign policy, such as the annexation of Crimea in 2014 and the continuing Russian military engagement in the Syrian civil war since 2015, were perceived as proof of the validity of these ideas and interests. At the same time, the many failures of Russia's rivals, ranging from the Capitol attack in Washington DC in January 2021 to the fall of Kabul and the failure of the pro-Western government in Afghanistan, seemingly demonstrated their irreversible decay in contrast to a rising Russia. It is no wonder that the increasing military might, assertiveness, and decisiveness of the Russian leadership are considered key ingredients in Russia's success before the beginning of the "special military operation" in Ukraine. In all probability, these ingredients are still favored by the Russian ruling class even now, but in fact, the gap between the overly high expectations of a coming Russian triumph and the overly devastating effects of Russia's aggressive actions has become insurmountable in the wake of the "special military operation."

What Went Wrong?

In essence, the Russian assault on Ukraine became a logical extension of the growing appetite of the Russian elites. Initially, the Russian plan for the assault on Ukraine entailed a prompt military conquest of its major cities – first, the capital, Kyiv, and also the second major city Kharkiv (located only forty kilometers from the Russian border). It also included the deposal of the Ukrainian authorities, led by President Volodymyr Zelensky, either by means of physical violence or because of their forced emigration. The imposition of pro-Russian Ukrainian politicians (such as former president Viktor Yanukovych, who fled to Russia in 2014, or Putin's personal friend

Viktor Medvedchuk) as puppet rulers of Ukraine was considered to be the turning point in placing Ukraine under Russian control. These goals, however, were officially presented in Russian political discourse as "demilitarization" and "denazification." The Kremlin expected that Ukrainian military would be unable to organize any serious resistance to Russian troops, and would surrender or be eliminated by force. Ukrainian officialdom, staffed by Russia loyalists, would switch sides and actively collaborate with the Russian authorities and their allies or at least would not oppose such a course of events. The majority of Ukrainian citizens (at least, among Russian-speaking Ukrainians) would simply accept the new status quo, similarly to most of the residents of Crimea after the Russian annexation in 2014. After that, Ukrainian assets would be taken over by the Russian state, state-owned companies, and private businesses loyal to the Kremlin, which would receive great opportunities for rent extraction at the Ukrainians' expense. At the same time, the response of the US and its European allies to Russian attacks would be loud but not particularly powerful. Because of the quick and decisive regime change in Ukraine, they would not be able to encroach into this process, while their possible sanctions would not inconvenience Russia too much. This is why sooner or later, the "collective West" would be forced to recognize and accept the new reality of Russia's control over Ukraine and give Russia free rein for future expansion of its zone of control over other parts of Eurasia, ranging from Moldova to Georgia, thus paving the way for further expansion into Europe and elsewhere.

It is difficult to say to what extent the Kremlin could implement these plans in practice, but in fact, they were not implemented at all. From the very beginning, Russian preparations for military assault were anything but unnoticed. Moreover, in December 2021, Russia announced a kind of ultimatum, addressed to the "collective West," which included a long list of strong demands including the renouncing of previous NATO decisions on territorial enlargement and its return to pre-1997 borders. Unsurprisingly, these demands were ultimately rejected by the Western leaders, but they provided a telling signal of Russia's military intentions. Further, US and British intelligence efforts easily recognized the major buildup of Russia's troops near the Ukrainian border and openly shared this information as well as analysis with the media and with Ukrainian authorities. The Russian assault came as no great surprise to most players involved.

FEBRUARY 2022: WHY RUSSIA FAILS

The beginning of the Russian military assault on February 24, 2022 was largely perceived as the launching of a "small victorious war." Some observers expected that Ukraine was doomed to fail shortly after major attacks by the Russian army.[37] However, in the event, the massive advances of Russian tanks and airborne attacks by Russian troops were countered by the Ukrainian military and stopped at the suburbs of Kyiv. Ukrainian troops also held Kharkiv and other key centers in the early days of the war. The Russian military was, however, able to push deep into Ukrainian territory in the south and southeast of the country. It crossed the Dnieper River and captured Kherson, and was able to surround Mariupol. Later, this large city was completely destroyed by Russian troops, who managed to seize it and establish control over land routes to the territory of Crimea. However, the initial plan of *blitzkrieg* had failed, and the "small victorious war" became neither small nor victorious. Russia was not able to break the resistance of Ukraine soon enough, and was not prepared for a decisive response at the front and beyond.

Faced with the Russian assault, both Ukrainian elites and Ukrainian society-at-large did not abandon hope, and collaboration with the occupants was not widespread. Rather, the assault was rejected sharply and there was furious condemnation of Russia's actions, which became a trigger for severe resistance in various parts of the country. The rally around the Ukrainian flag greatly contributed to anti-Russian mobilization of Ukrainians (including Russian-speaking citizens). Despite massive emigration of millions of Ukrainian residents to Europe (mostly to Poland and Germany, but also to other European countries), the Ukrainian authorities were able to organize a relatively efficient resistance to the assault and maintain it over time. The international response to the Russian assault was also fairly quick and decisive. The US and its Western allies not only condemned Russia but also imposed a number of sanctions on sensitive sectors, froze some Russian assets abroad, and organized not only humanitarian and financial aid to Ukraine but also, later on, extensive supply of arms. By late March 2022, it was already clear that the early plans for the Russian military assault had no chances of success. Russian troops were forced to retreat from the suburbs of Kyiv, thus turning the assault from a "small victorious war" to a protracted military conflict. Meanwhile, attempts to initiate peace negotiations between Russian and Ukrainian representatives, which started soon after the attack and were held in Belarus and later on in Turkey, did not bring any meaningful results. According to some available documents, Russia demanded Ukraine's neutral status and guarantees of non-alignment with NATO as a requirement for a ceasefire, but did not promise any security guarantees for Ukraine (including third party enforcement), so Kyiv was afraid that Russian assaults would soon resume.[38] This is why negotiations failed, and the war continued in a fully-fledged fashion.

The second wave of Russian attacks in May–July 2022 pursued less ambitious goals in military terms. Russia aimed to expand its zone of control to the entire territories of the Donetsk and Luhansk regions. These areas in Donbas, largely perceived by the Kremlin as belonging to the self-proclaimed Donetsk and Luhansk "people's republics" (hereafter DNR and LNR, respectively), had acted as Russia's proxies since 2014 and served as a bargaining chip in previous negotiations with Ukraine. Just before the beginning of the assault, Russia officially recognized their independence, but in reality, merely used them as a foothold for preparing the military attack on Ukraine. Using a massive concentration of military troops and arms, Russia took over a number of cities and towns but was not able to occupy these regions entirely. Moreover, in August 2022, the Ukrainian military launched a counter-offensive in the northeast (where it liberated some of the territories near Kharkiv) and in the south, restoring its control over the right bank of the Dnieper River. The final episode of this counter-offensive wave occurred in November 2022, when Ukraine took over Kherson, the only regional capital of Ukraine previously occupied by the Russian military.

The most important consequence of these episodes was the crucial fact that Russia did not acknowledge its failure. Instead of withdrawing its troops and turning to peaceful negotiations with Ukraine, Russia strategically opted for the endless continuation of its "special military operation." Moreover, Russia's rulers attempted to profit from the first stage of the military conflict by legitimizing Russian control over the territories seized from Ukraine both in 2014 (when the "people's republics" in the Donetsk and Luhansk regions proclaimed their independence from Ukraine) and in the first months of the 2022 "special military operation." In September 2022, the Russian authorities organized a plebiscite on the accession of four Ukrainian regions – Donetsk, Luhansk, and the Zaporizhzhia and Kherson oblasts – to the Russian Federation. These plebiscites were mostly fake, as voting was almost entirely manufactured by the local occupational authorities and/or by Russian proxies. Furthermore, parts of these territories remained under Ukrainian control during this time, and the plebiscite did not take place in those areas at all. Officially, all plebiscites brought the expected results, and the Russian Federation claimed an expansion of its territory as it absorbed four new regions. In fact, however, Russia did not fully control these regions at the time of writing. Moreover, the plebiscite itself took place in the middle of a Ukrainian counter-offensive, when parts of these regions were controlled by Ukraine. It is quite indicative that Russia, even as it loudly proclaimed that Kherson was part of its territory, could not resist its liberation just six weeks after the plebiscite.

At the same time, the Ukrainian counter-offensive prompted Russia to respond in order to prevent further liberation of territories previously taken by Russia and/or its Donbas proxies. In September 2022, Putin announced a campaign of mobilization for the Russian armed forces. Although many thousands of young Russian men (mostly educated residents of large cities) responded to Putin's decree on mobilization with their feet and fled the country, the plan for the draft was implemented amid a lack of serious resistance in the impoverished peripheral areas of Russia, in its small towns and villages, including some ethnic republics. Although the Russian draft in 2022 demonstrated inefficiency and poor performance by the state machinery (nobody was prepared for such a large-scale operation in organizational and administrative terms), in the end it contributed to stabilization of the front lines. The Ukrainian counter-offensive was stopped after the liberation of Kherson and did not advance further. At the same time, Russia's potential for new military advancements was all but exhausted despite the inflow of new recruits. Even the large-scale campaign of mobilization of prisoners (and, later on, volunteers) conducted by the private military company Wagner[39] brought Russia no major victories in 2022 and early 2023. The major battle over the small Ukrainian town of Bakhmut took several months, during which the town was completely destroyed by Russian artillery and then proudly taken over by Wagner troops. In turn, the new wave of Ukrainian counter-offensive during the summer of 2023 did not bring any major changes to the front lines. Overall, by the end of 2023 the protracted military campaign became a war of attrition: both Russia and Ukraine lacked the resources for a decisive victory. Some observers draw parallels with World War I, with the German military's endless and unsuccessful attempts to defeat France on the Western Front. From this perspective, the further developments of the Russian "special military operation" are very unclear and unpredictable. However, Russia initiated a new wave of large-scale military attacks on Ukraine after Russia's 2024 presidential elections (aimed at a new landslide victory over Russian voters by Putin), which suggests new attempts to conquer Kharkiv, as well as other key Ukrainian cities and attempts to impose full-scale control over the Donetsk region.[40] Irrespective of the relevance of these plans to the reality and the chances of their implementation, expectations that the military conflict will continue endlessly as long as Putin remains in power[41] undoubtedly dominated the international landscape by the spring of 2024. At least, no real prospects for achieving stable peace and security in Ukraine and beyond are visible on the horizon at the time of writing.

Although it is too early to discuss the outcomes and consequences of the Russian assault on Ukraine, the statement that it has failed is not far-fetched. Regardless of further developments in this ongoing conflict, which may last even decades from now, it is highly unlikely that Russia will ever achieve the initial goals of the "special military operation." This is why the question of "Why Russia Fails" seems appropriate despite the continuation of these attacks so far. Since February 2022, Russia has faced its heaviest human losses since World War II. Not only have dozens of thousands of Russian soldiers and officers been killed or wounded on the battlefield, but hundreds of thousands of Russians – mostly educated professionals and other representatives of the urban middle class – have fled the country, either out of moral protest against the Russian assault, or to escape the danger of military mobilization. International sanctions against Russia (which were previously not overly wide-ranging) have become much more severe and comprehensive, and affected Russian exports of oil and gas as well as its supply of dual-use goods and technologies. Russia's international reputation as a reliable and respectable country have not only been heavily damaged in Europe and North America but also put into question in other parts of the world. The fact that in March 2023 the International Criminal Court in Hague released an order for the arrest of Putin and one of his associates for alleged kidnapping of Ukrainian children from Russia-occupied territories is probably the most vivid illustration of this reputational damage. Yet the Russian economy survived the initial shock of sanctions, severance of access to Western capital markets, and freezing of Russian assets abroad. The prudent macroeconomic policy of the Central Bank of Russia,[42] alongside large-scale state orders of military procurements, prevented a huge recession, contrary to many expectations of observers and analysts. However, import substitution in Russia is still very imperfect to say the least, the technological lagging behind the West remains insurmountable, and increasing economic problems are becoming more and more serious for the country. These major failures – in human, military, economic, and international terms – are extraordinary for a developed country, which demonstrated advancement in all of these respects during the post-Communist decades.[43]

This is why one must shift from the question of "what went wrong?" to the question of "why did the 'special military operation' go wrong?" Indeed, Russia was not doomed to all of these failures before February 24, 2022. Rather, these failures were side effects of the crucial decision to launch a military assault on Ukraine made by Vladimir Putin and his entourage – and Russia and Ukraine, as well as many other countries, are paying the price for this pernicious decision. Such decisions are exceptionally rare in the modern history of the world. This is why understanding the roots of Russia's decision to attack Ukraine, its causes and mechanisms, requires a close examination from the perspective of research in comparative politics. The Russian assault on Ukraine can be considered not only as an outlier from the general trends of the contemporary world but also as a "hypothesis-generating" case study, which may be useful for explaining the roots and mechanisms of major political failures in a broader context. The rest of this book will concentrate on the in-depth analysis of these issues.

The Essence of a Pernicious Decision: The Argument in Brief

Political decisions on major issues taken during certain critical junctures of history often attract the attention of scholars.[44] Revolutionary episodes, military coups, and international conflicts have served as focal points of many scholarly analyses because they enable the use of these cases not only for explanation of certain trajectories of states and nations, or of the entire world, but also for building theoretical arguments, which focus on particular accidents of history while aiming to explain the general logic of political development. In this respect, the critical juncture of the Russian decision to attack Ukraine in February 2022 is important not only for the study of Russian and/or Ukrainian politics and history. It is important as a case of a rather arbitrary and poorly prepared political decision, based on inadequate assessment of the information available and a lack of consideration of viable alternatives. Individuals, too, often make decisions of this kind in their everyday lives, becoming victims of unsuccessful marriages or fraud. However, contemporary rulers, unlike individuals, are at least in theory usually better prepared for decision-making – their decisions are based upon the expertise of the state apparatus and/or independent analysts, as well as on intelligence reports. Moreover, Russia under Putin successfully adopted and implemented many political and policy decisions on certain very important issues, ranging from the response to the major global financial crisis of 2008–9 to the extension of Putin's terms in office in 2020. The well-developed and highly professional technocratic expertise and efficient performance of some state agencies, such as the Central Bank, served as a shield, which blocked major political and policy failures in Russia during this long period.[45] Still, these previous "success stories" did not protect Russia from a major failure in case of the 2022 assault on Ukraine, and, to some extent, even contributed to this failure.

To summarize, the question of "Why Russia Fails" with regard to its military assault on Ukraine may be useful not only from the perspective of Russian studies, but also as a contribution to research on political decision-making in theoretical and comparative perspectives. It may be considered as a crucial case of a major pernicious political decision made by the rulers of a developed and relatively successful country without any serious compelling circumstances. In other words, answering the question of "Why Russia Fails" may shed some light on answers to the greater question of "Why Nations Fail," previously addressed by numerous scholars, from Niccolo Machiavelli to Daron Acemoglu and James Robinson. In essence, why do rulers of modern states sometimes behave so incredibly wrongly? What are the factors behind their pernicious decisions? Indeed, why do some rulers lure themselves into the trap of destructive decisions while others do not?

A classical study of foreign policy decision-making, *Essence of Decision* by Graham Allison, offers us a possible approach to solving this research puzzle.[46] Allison analyzed the case of the Cuban Missile Crisis of 1962, and offered several competing explanations of the same chain of events observed during this crisis – the deployment of Soviet offensive missiles to Cuba, the US response to this move with a blockade of Cuba, and further negotiations, which led to the Soviet withdrawal of missiles. His original study, published in 1971, was based upon the limited, imperfect, and incomplete information presented in open Western sources, as classified sources (including tape recordings of the US government proceedings) as well as Soviet documents and other sources were unavailable at that time. Later on, some of these materials were used for a new edition of Allison's book, written with Philip Zelikow and published in 1999.[47] However, the additional sources and the new evidence did not shatter the frameworks of analysis and conclusions, but rather enriched the original study with many important facts and details. The major theoretical and methodological contribution made by Allison was his offering of three different and competing perspectives of analysis, or "lenses" of research, through which he addressed the research questions. These three scholarly lenses – the "rational actor model," "organizational behavior," and "governmental politics" – were not mutually exclusive, despite certain contradictions. Rather, these lenses complemented each other, and only a winning combination of all these three competing explanations of the Cuban Missile Crisis gave a comprehensive answer to the questions of the causes and effects of the US and Soviet decisions, which prevented the further deterioration of this crisis into a possible World War III.

In this book, I will follow some of the insights offered by Allison, and employ a fusion of several complementary rather than competing perspectives to analyze the Russian assault on Ukraine. Even though, as Allison noted in his quote from John F. Kennedy, "The essence of ultimate decision remains impenetrable to the observer – often, indeed, to the decider himself," this does not necessarily mean that a political decision is a black box which cannot be opened due to limited, imperfect, and incomplete information. Indeed, we know enough to propose certain complementary explanations for the essence of Russia's destructive decision. These explanations are based upon my central assumption that this fundamentally wrong decision to launch the assault and the inefficient way in which this attack was conducted were not predetermined by Russia's previous developmental trajectory over the entire period since the Soviet collapse in

1991. There is no evidence that Russia was doomed to initiate the military assault on Ukraine in 2022 for whatever reasons. Instead, I argue that Russia's military attacks were an effect of an agency-driven phenomenon heavily affected by a combination of four main factors, considered in this book to be the four traps of the pernicious decision:

(1) *the personalist trap* – the building and consolidation of a personalist authoritarian regime in Russia[48] has greatly contributed to the arbitrariness and poor quality of decision-making,[49] and its further aggravation over time;[50]
(2) *the bad governance trap* – the establishment and maintenance of a politico-economic order of bad governance in Russia, aimed at rent-seeking as the goal of governing the state, has resulted in gross corruption and major misconduct in the state apparatus and beyond;[51]
(3) *the trap of misperceptions* – systematic distortions and misinformation in major policy fields, including foreign and security policy, contributed to misperceptions by Russia's political leadership and elites about both the domestic and the international arenas[52] and about global dynamics in the twenty-first century;
(4) *the trap of impunity* – Russia's rulers were overconfident in the belief in their impunity and heavily relied upon the previous experience of successful achievement of domestic and international goals; this is why they considered the "special military operation" in Ukraine as a logical continuation of this chain of achievements, irrespective of potential risks.

The consequences of the four traps were as follows. The personalist trap contributed to poor policy-making institutions, which played a key role in the decision to assault Ukraine being made by only a tiny group of Putin's trusted closest allies under a veil of secrecy (even Lavrov, according to some sources, received the information about the launching of a military attack just several hours before it started).[53] This mode of decision-making paved the way for an overly selective and heavily biased approach to the planning of the assault, which resulted in an inadequate assessment of its possible benefits against its potential costs. The bad governance trap contributed to the inefficiency of the Russian state machinery, which was not able to cope with the preparation and implementation of the "special military operation," while state officials and managers pursued their own self-interest, sometimes different from that of the Kremlin. Moreover, the quality of the Russian military troops and security apparatus was heavily misrepresented before the assault, as they were incapable of achieving the goal of seizure of power in Ukraine and taking it under Russian control. Misperceptions as part of overall inefficient processing of information flows (to some extent, driven by bad governance) played a major role in Russia's misunderstanding of politico-economic, societal, and security developments in Ukraine and underestimation of the global West (as well as non-West) in terms of their possible responses to the Russian assault. At the same time, Russia's top state officials greatly overestimated Russia's own capabilities despite warning calls from some top military officers just before the assault. Finally, the Russian leadership and elites became victims of their own chain of successes in domestic and international politics due to their previously established feeling of impunity. They considered the "special military operation" to be more or less just an extended version of the 2014 annexation of Crimea, which could bring the Russian leadership great benefits at relatively low cost. In other words, the approach of Russia's rulers was similar to the behavior of a gambler who raises the stakes every time after winning a previous round of the game.[54] However, as often happens with gamblers, raising the stakes in an unrestrained manner turned into a trap.

The same traps that contributed to the beginning of the Russian "special military operation" played an important role in its further development. The personalist trap not only prevented cessation of the military assault and a possible turn to peaceful negotiations, but also resulted in Putin's personal engagement in the conduct of military actions, which was of little use for their implementation. The trap of bad governance caused messy adjustment by the Russian state machinery to changing conditions, and its chaotic conduct of various actions, ranging from import substitution in industries to military drafting. The trap of misperceptions deeply affected the worldview of the Russian elites and society-at-large and precluded their recognition of the hard realities not only before the assault on Ukraine but also after the failure of the early stage of the "special military operation." Instead, propagandist narratives and conspiracy theories became the main tools for Kremlin's understanding of the international and domestic agenda. Finally, the trap of impunity prompted Russia's rulers to raise the stakes in the military conflict with Ukraine further and further (similarly to heavily addicted gamblers), including the use of nuclear blackmail against Ukraine and the "collective West." The Kremlin considered alternatives to a full-scale Russian victory over Ukraine to be undesirable outcomes and so did not seriously consider them. The persistence of these traps meant that once Russia failed during the early stage of the "special military operation," Russia's rulers preferred to let Russia fail further, at least as long as they were still alive themselves. At least as of yet there are no major signs that this endless failure will stop any time soon. This is why, most likely, the "special military operation" will continue at least until the very end of Putin's rule.

Alternative Explanations and Scholarly Perspectives

My argument and the focus of analysis on Russian elites are juxtaposed with two very popular approaches, which dominate the scholarly literature on contemporary Russia. Scholarly assessments of many recent and historical developments elsewhere often fall between excessively shallow and excessively deep explanations, and the case of Russia's assault on Ukraine is no exception in this respect. One pole is excessively shallow, as it revolves almost exclusively around the personality of Putin and his previous trajectory in the Soviet security apparatus, experience at the St. Petersburg city hall during the 1990s, and the like.[55] Analyses of this type consider the many destructive developments in Russia to be induced only by Putin and his entourage, and the Russian assault is perceived as a projection of the preferences, misperceptions, fears, and grievances of one man in the Kremlin. Such a view on Russia surprisingly corresponds with a statement by Putin's top official, chair of the State Duma Vyacheslav Volodin, who once proclaimed: "if there is Putin, there is Russia; if there is no Putin, there is no Russia."[56] Such a view, while it may be factually correct, is certainly insufficient for a full-fledged explanation, as it is too focused on a particular figure. Scholars rarely equate the Bolshevik Revolution of 1917 with just Lenin and Trotsky, or the Soviet collapse in 1991 with just Gorbachev and Yeltsin. In a similar way, consideration of contemporary Russia just in terms of "Putinology" is rather unproductive.[57]

In real terms, the foundations of the Russian military assault were elaborated not only by Putin but also by major segments of the

Russian political class. The Survey of Russian Elites quite convincingly illustrates these dynamics in the preferences of Russian elites.[58] After a brief period of pro-Western orientation, since the late 1990s Russian elites have been subject to major disillusionments, paving the way to the increasing revanchist, revisionist, and anti-American attitudes which developed in the 2000s, driven by both international and domestic developments.[59] It is no wonder that these dynamics of elite attitudes were later successfully transmitted via "Kremlin cues" to the hearts and minds of the Russian mass public,[60] which initially largely endorsed the military assault on Ukraine within the framework of a rally around the Russian flag (similarly to the previous annexation of Crimea).[61] As the Survey of Russian Elites data demonstrate, the cornerstone principles of Russian foreign policy outlined above were shared by a significant part of the Russian elites well before the February 2022 attack on Ukraine.[62] Without denying Putin's pivotal role in the conversion of these cornerstone principles and visions of foreign policy into military action, one must admit that Putin was not alone. His destructive ideas about the possibility and desirability of the military assault, in a way, reflected the visions, preferences, and desires of the Russian elites. At the same time, the Russian mass public played a secondary role in this process at best.[63]

Quite the opposite of the excessively shallow view is the excessively deep view, which tends to comprehensively condemn Russia – both the state and society – for its inherent and irreversible imperialism, militarism, and anti-Westernism. Thus, a military assault on Ukraine is perceived as a side effect of Russia's past, its imperial and/or colonial legacies, of real and/or imagined features of Russian culture, of its geo-political and geo-economic determinism, of its eternal drive to anti-modernization, and the like. However, this approach, deeply embedded in many historical[64] and contemporary[65] writings, is misleading. It not only ignores or downplays many successful episodes of Russian liberalization in the past – both pre-1917[66] and in the late twentieth century – but also assumes that Russia as a country cannot be improved by any means and is worthy only of total elimination in one way or another. The perception of Russia as a quintessential and eternal global evil is understandable today due to the fury of many observers after Russia's violent attacks on Ukraine. However, this approach should not be considered a reliable analytical tool because it aims at accusations instead of explanations,[67] and impartial scholarly analysis should not be replaced by emotional punditry.[68] Speaking in a more comparative way, no serious analysts today blame Germany for Nazism or believe that Germany could not have been improved after Nazism in any possible way, even though such a view was fairly popular during World War II and immediately after it.

Overall, the dichotomy of excessively shallow and excessively deep explanations for Russia's military assault (and, in a broader sense, for its international behavior) to a certain degree reflects the fundamental gap between structure-induced and agency-driven approaches to the analysis of Russian and Eurasian politics that developed in recent decades after the Communist collapse.[69] However, the fruitful integration of these approaches remains a major weakness in the research agenda, and this book will attempt to strengthen it. Instead of focusing on blame – either Putin is guilty, or Russia is guilty, or both – I offer a different perspective, one aimed at explanation rather than at accusation, and with an emphasis on the role of Russian elites rather than on both Putin and the Russian state and society.

In addition to these two explanations, focused on interpretations of Russia's domestic trajectory, there is yet another approach to the analysis of the Russian military assault on Ukraine, which prioritizes the logic of international relations. According to this reasoning, most comprehensively elaborated by John Mearsheimer and greatly endorsed in the Kremlin's narratives, Russia's attack on Ukraine in February 2022, as well as the annexation of Crimea and conflict in Donbas since 2014, are considered a pre-emptive response to the threats posed to Russia by the "collective West" due to the ongoing expansion of NATO.[70] Such an explanation follows the lines of Mearsheimer's powerful book, *The Tragedy of Great Power Politics*,[71] known as a core text of the "offensive realism" approach in international relations. It implicitly presumed that the attempt at military and territorial expansion of Russia at the expense of Ukraine is a norm of international domination by a more militarily-capable and assertive state over its less powerful neighbor (especially if and when constraints on such behavior are very low, as stated in this chapter). While there is no room in this book to discuss the theoretical value of this approach, its empirical validity is rather dubious, to put it mildly. Not only should NATO threats before February 2022 be regarded as rather minor compared with Russia's very high military potential and capabilities, but portraying Russia's assault on Ukraine in this light is also contrary to most observations of international behavior by great powers after World War II in general and after the Cold War in particular. Even judged from the perspective of "offensive realism," the case of Russia's assault on Ukraine in 2022 is exceptional. Despite numerous violent international conflicts across the globe over recent decades, large-scale inter-state wars with the extensive use of regular armies are rare today. Therefore, one needs to explain why Russia directed its military towards the conquest of Kyiv amid the lack of similar actions in many other international conflicts. In other words, one has to explain why other countries in the contemporary world rarely behave as Russia did in February 2022, and why Russia is so different in this respect. Without a convincing explanation for this case as an outlier in present-day international politics, the reliance upon "offensive realism" as a sole analytic tool looks like an attempt of ex post justification of the Russian attack on Ukraine rather than an example of scholarly expertise.

My idea is that Russia's predatory and aggressive international behavior is a natural strategic choice by leaders and elites in any given country, if and when they seek maximization of their control in the global arena but at the same time do not face effective deterrence from other international actors. As both domestic and international constraints on this behavior were relatively weak in the case of post-Communist Russia, the appetite of Russia's elites and leadership increased over time, fueling further assertiveness up until the very beginning of the assault. In this respect, the Russian assault on Ukraine was not only a failed attempt to reassert Russia's control over areas that were lost after the collapse of the Soviet Union. It was also a failed attempt to establish a much greater sphere of Russian influence (including but not limited to Europe), which would elevate Russia's global role to one of the key international veto players alongside China and the US. Meanwhile, the nature of the personalist authoritarian regime in Russia left no room for potential correction of errors after the initial failure of the assault.

From a broader perspective, the case of Russia's assault on Ukraine tells us that states do not behave peacefully by default or due to the goodwill of benevolent rulers. When leaders and elites in any given country meet with few domestic and international constraints, they behave aggressively and tend to seize rents and resources as much as possible and for as long as possible. In this respect, I follow the logic of Carl von Clausewitz, who argued that the war is "nothing but a continuation of policy with other means"[72] – violent and bloody, yet largely a rationalist enterprise.[73] In a somewhat similar way, foreign policy is a continuation of domestic politics by other means. This is why I tend to analyze Russia's international behavior through the analytic lenses that were used in my previous research on Russia's domestic politics.

Indeed, this book presents a continuation of the arguments elaborated in my two previous books. In my 2015 book, *Authoritarian Russia: Analyzing Post-Soviet Regime Changes* (hereafter, AR), I argued that authoritarianism is a norm and democracy is an exception, and this is why unconstrained politicians elsewhere – not only in Russia – tend to build authoritarian regimes.[74] In my 2022 book, *The Politics of Bad Governance in Contemporary Russia* (hereafter, BG), I argued that bad governance is a norm, and good governance is an exception, and this is why unconstrained rulers tend to rob their countries as much as possible and for as long as possible.[75] In this book, which constitutes the third volume of my trilogy alongside AR and BG, I would go further and argue that the case of the Russian assault on Ukraine tells us that in the international arena, aggressive behavior, violent conflicts, and bloody attacks are a norm, while voluntary cooperation, prudent benevolence, and fruitful peace are an exception, not vice versa. From this scholarly perspective, peace does not come by default but emerges as a side effect of major political and institutional constraints on the behavior of states and their elites and leaders, imposed both domestically and internationally. Thus, the Russian experience of the twenty-first century becomes a powerful reminder of the necessity of putting major pre-emptive constraints on aggressive behavior in international politics.

Plan of the Book

The next five chapters will provide an answer to the question of "Why Russia Fails" from different research angles.

Chapter 2, entitled *The Personalist Trap*, concentrates on the nature of the personalist authoritarian regime in Russia and its effects on Russia's international behavior. It will underline the arbitrary nature of decision-making in Russia, which has increased over time, and the weakness of formal and informal checks and balances within the state apparatus, especially in the fields of foreign, military, and security policy. These factors, alongside the personal concerns and preferences of Vladimir Putin and his entourage, paved the way to military assault. The chapter draws parallels between the Russian assault on Ukraine in 2022 and the Soviet military action in Czechoslovakia in 1968 and focuses on the similarities and differences between these two "special military operations" based on similarities and differences between personalist and party-based authoritarian regimes.

Chapter 3, entitled *The Well-Oiled Machine, Out of Control*, addresses the issue of poor quality of governance in Russia and its impact on policy-making. While rent-seeking and corruption have become the main mechanisms for governing the Russian state, there have been certain fool-proofing technocratic mechanisms for governing the economy, which have prevented major failures. However, the Russian state agencies in charge of foreign, military, and security policies operate under a veil of secrecy, and their performance has been dubious for many years. This is why the Russian state machinery was so poorly prepared for the "special military operation" and demonstrated its numerous flaws during the protracted military conflict.

Chapter 4, entitled *The Great Self-Deception*, focuses on misperceptions by the Russian leadership and elites before and during the military assault on Ukraine. Their beliefs and ideas were to a great degree driven by resentment among Russian elites after the Soviet collapse and Russia's partial loss of status as a major veto player in international politics. They also reflected poor understanding of political, economic, and societal developments in Ukraine, in Russia, and in other countries, to say nothing of global political dynamics in the twenty-first century. In a broader perspective, these perceptions resulted from fundamental problems of dealing with information flows in authoritarian regimes, which are often discussed in the literature on autocracies under the rubric of the "dictator's dilemma."[76] These problems are especially acute in informational autocracies, or "spin dictatorships,"[77] as such regimes suffer from intentionally distorted information on foreign policy even to a greater degree than on domestic politics. This is why Russia's rulers greatly overestimated the country's own potential and underestimated the potential for resistance to their military assault, and were not ready for a major setback.

Chapter 5, entitled *The Victims of Previous Successes*, offers an excursion into Russia's domestic and international experience from the early 2000s to the beginning of the assault. The maximization of power and control by Putin and his entourage and successful achievement of their domestic and international goals are considered a major success story. Russia's rulers were able to diminish domestic resistance from all corners of society, achieve several military victories (Chechnya in 1999–2002, Georgia in 2008, Crimea in 2014), and face few constraints on their expansion from the "collective West." This impunity was in effect expected to be eternal, and this is why they anticipated that the "special military operation" in Ukraine would be a sequel to this virtually endless chain of successes, and remain praised domestically and unpunished internationally. These lessons from the past played a major role in the planning of the military assault and contributed to the wrong expectations of a major victory.

Chapter 6, entitled *Lost Illusions, Dashed Hopes, and Unlearned Lessons*, analyzes the effects of the Russian military assault on Russia's post-2022 domestic and international politics. When the initial goals of the "special military operation" became unrealistic and hopes of successful swift conquest of Ukraine were dashed on the battlefield, Russia's rulers followed the path of further escalation of the conflict, not intending to stop the military assault. Thus, they continued the chain of previous errors without making major corrections. Domestically, amid the further strengthening of the Kremlin's rule, Russia aggravated the heavily negative consequences of its previous actions and, most probably, will continue to do so at least until the end of Putin's rule. This chapter reviews the lessons of the Russian experience of failed assault, both for a study of Russia and its prospects for the future and for an understanding of the behavior of states and nations and of the nature of war and peace in theoretical and comparative perspective. It also addresses the lessons of Russia's assault for an understanding of the global agenda and for the study of domestic and international politics in the twenty-first century.

Chapter 2

THE PERSONALIST TRAP

On February 21, 2022, the Russian Security Council met in the Kremlin. This council was a major consultative body under the president, in charge of discussing matters of national security. It included ex officio top state officials and other persons appointed by the president, but its discretion was officially limited to an advisory role, similarly to many other consultative bodies on culture, science and education. However, during the period of Putin's rule, the Security Council became a key state office.[1] Nikolai Patrushev, its long-standing secretary since 2008 (till May 2024) and a long-term ally of Putin since the times of their KGB service in Leningrad in the 1970s, known as one of the most outspoken conservatives in the Russian top leadership,[2] became one of Putin's most trusted advisors. Due to these changes, frequent meetings of the Security Council, usually held behind closed doors, were perceived by many observers as major sites of decision-making in Russia, and their agenda covered many issues in both domestic politics and foreign policy.

Contrary to the regular practices of secret meetings held behind closed doors, on that day in February, the session of the Security Council was broadcast on the major Russian TV channels.[3] It was exclusively devoted to Vladimir Putin's proposal regarding official legal recognition of the independence of the separatist, pro-Russian self-proclaimed Donetsk and Luhansk "people's republics" in East Ukraine.[4] In fact, these separatist activities had been initiated, heavily backed politically and sponsored financially by the Kremlin, and its representatives directly and indirectly controlled the "people's republics" from the very beginning in spring 2014. The Kremlin used the "people's republics" as proxies in negotiations with Ukraine in

2014–15, which resulted in the de facto ceasefire after the Minsk agreements. After that time, a fragile status quo was maintained on both sides of the front lines on the territories of the Donetsk and Luhansk regions of Ukraine, and was used by Russia as a bargaining chip in negotiations with Ukraine within the framework of the "Normandy format" under France and Germany's mediation.[5] As these negotiations were exhausted over time with no progress achieved, the legal recognition of the independence of the "people's republics" most probably could not add much to an already gloomy situation.

However, the atmosphere before the Security Council meeting was very tense. The official Russian discourse towards the US and Europe was full of hate, while the Ukrainian authorities were openly and systematically disregarded by the Kremlin as American puppets, and even Ukraine itself was considered an artificial creation of the policy on national minorities conducted by Lenin during the early Soviet period.[6] As negotiations between Russia and the US about Ukraine did not bring any results,[7] reports and expectations about possible Russian military attacks on Ukraine dominated the agenda both in the West[8] and in Russia[9] (where, despite the omnipresence of the Kremlin, some dissenting voices could be heard as well).[10] Rumors regarding potential risks for Russia, such as new economic sanctions, forced disconnection of Russia from global payment services, and the like were widely discussed at that time.[11] Against this background, the February 21 Security Council meeting was announced by the Kremlin as a key turning point in discussions about Russian policy toward Ukraine.

However, the most striking feature of this long and tedious meeting, held in the Kremlin, was a nearly total lack of any discussion. Putin's relatively short introductory speech was full of aggressive rhetoric and various invectives about many Ukrainian wrongdoings not only in regard to the Donetsk and Luhansk "people's republics" but also about Western threats, rudeness and disrespect towards Russia. However, this speech did not contain any particularly new ideas. Having made an emotive suggestion about the official legal recognition of the independence of the separatist "people's republics" in order to protect them from hostile takeover by Ukraine and its NATO superiors, Putin requested that all of the participants of the meeting express their opinions about his proposal. Unsurprisingly, the Russian state officials who gathered at the Kremlin that day enthusiastically and almost unanimously endorsed Putin's suggestion. Moreover, Sergey Naryshkin, the head of the Foreign Intelligence Service, went further and proudly announced his support for the accession of both "people's republics" to Russia[12] (this move was not suggested by Putin at this meeting; it was made much later, in September 2022). Only Dmitry Kozak, the deputy head of the presidential administration in charge of policy on the post-Soviet region, rather shyly expressed some concerns and briefly argued that diplomatic efforts had not yet been exhausted. In addition, the Prime Minister of Russia Mikhail Mishustin carefully noted that the Russian economy would face many new difficulties, but promised to cope with coming hardships. Still, there was no word of objection, nor deliberations among participants on the matter, nor even dialogue between them in any form. Everyone just individually addressed Putin and assured him of their wholehearted support of the boss's brilliant ideas. Similarly to the title of the popular 1980s BBC TV serial,[13] the contents of the meeting of February 21, 2022 could be best summarized as "Yes, President." In short, Putin's proposal was unquestioningly approved by the Security Council, and on the next day, February 22, 2022, by both chambers of the Russian parliament, the State Duma and the Federation Council.

Paradoxically, this Security Council decision, so loudly proclaimed and demonstrated before the domestic and international audiences, did not make any sense in practical terms of policy-making. Irrespective of what was actually approved during the February 21 meeting, at 4 a.m. on February 24 Vladimir Putin launched what was called a "special military operation" – a full-scale severe military assault on Ukraine. Even some participants at the Security Council meeting were completely unaware of this plan before they met on February 21.[14] At least, according to a media report, the Russian Foreign Minister Sergey Lavrov was informed about the launch of the "special military operation" just three hours before its start.[15] We do not know to what extent Putin and his entourage kept top officials unaware of their real plans for Ukraine as an intentional strategy and to what extent they simply ignored Lavrov (and, probably, some other members of the Security Council). In fact, the very presence of these top state officials on the political scene did not matter for a decision made by Putin on his own. At best, the participants in the Security Council meeting, as well as other representatives of the Russian elites, acted merely as extras in this one-man show, which had such a tragic impact for Russia, Ukraine, and the entire world. One might even say that their function as key political actors during this meeting and beyond it was reduced to submissive acclamation of whatever political decision was unilaterally made by Putin, regardless of its contents and consequences.[16]

This episode clearly illustrates the key feature of political decision-making in Russia, namely its personalist nature.[17] Although the decision on launching the "special military operation" was crucial in terms of its impact on domestic and international politics, it was a rather routine move in terms of the practices of policy-making in Russia. During the period of Putin's rule, Russia experienced a major turn to personalization of political power, which affected mechanisms of governance in two different yet interrelated ways. First, personalization of power led to weakening of many political and institutional constraints on decision-making, thus increasing both the decisiveness and the arbitrariness of practices of governance.[18] Second, it contributed to changes to incentives among elites, as their preferences shifted toward increasing loyalty at the expense of efficiency.[19] Thus, the personalist authoritarian regime in Russia became very vulnerable to major errors made by the ruler, much like a car without brakes. This personalist trap of Russian autocracy was a side effect of poor institutionalization of decision-making, typical for many regimes of this kind.[20] In sum, it became one of the major factors in the pernicious decision of the Russian assault on Ukraine and in the continuation of this assault over time despite (or, rather, because of) the devastating consequences of this decision.

In this chapter, I will consider the role of the personalist trap of the Russian political regime in the assault on Ukraine from theoretical and comparative perspectives. After analyzing the institutional framework of personalist autocracies and their impact on policy-making against the background of the personalization of the Russian political regime, I will offer a comparison of two cases of military attacks planned and conducted by authoritarian regimes, namely the Russian assault on Ukraine in 2022 and the Soviet invasion of Czechoslovakia in 1968. I will focus on similarities and differences between the Soviet experience of the one-party authoritarian regime and Russian personalist authoritarianism in order to demonstrate the fundamental flaws of the decision-making practices of contemporary Russian authoritarianism. Some implications of the impact of

Personalist Autocracies: Pitfalls and Perils

the personalist trap for Russia and beyond will be discussed in the conclusion.

To paraphrase Tolstoy, all democracies are alike, but each autocracy is unhappy in its own way. Despite the fact that the world of autocracies is rather diverse, in general authoritarian regimes often demonstrate much poorer performance than their democratic counterparts. Historical and contemporary exceptions to this rule are relatively rare. They may be summarized in a succinct statement by Dani Rodrik: "For every President Lee Kuan Yew of Singapore, there are many like President Mobutu Sese Seko of Zaire (now called the Democratic Republic of the Congo)."[21] In reality, there is a huge variation in political and policy performance among various types of authoritarian regimes due to their different political and institutional arrangements.

According to the most popular classification of autocracies across the globe, they belong to four major types: monarchies, one-party regimes, military regimes, and personalist regimes.[22] Monarchies (such as in Saudi Arabia or Morocco) are based on hereditary leadership succession in the form of a dynasty.[23] One-party regimes (such as in the Soviet Union or in China – at least, until the very recent changes under the leadership of Xi Jinping) are organized around the ruling party, which penetrates all layers of state governance and of society at large. As both of these types of regime are highly institutionalized in various ways, they often demonstrate relatively high longevity,[24] and tend to perform reasonably well in terms of government effectiveness.[25] At the same time, military regimes (such as in Myanmar) are the most problematic because of the problems with legitimacy of military rule: they often fail to institutionalize, their time span is relatively short, and their policy performance is worst among autocracies.[26] Despite the diversity of these three types, these regimes have something in common: they have to be built and maintained over time through the use of various mechanisms, which impose certain political and institutional constraints on the political leadership.[27] These constraints may include collective decision-making (in one-party regimes),[28] complexity of royal court politics and leadership succession (in monarchies), or risk of the use of arms and violence (in military regimes).[29] However, regimes of all of these three types are relatively rare in the twenty-first century. The fourth type, personalist regimes, tends to dominate the world of contemporary autocracies.

Unlike many monarchies, one-party regimes, and military regimes formed on the basis of certain institutions, personalist autocracies emerge nearly by default when individual rulers are able to seize power and consolidate their rule through the efficient use of certain political tricks. These regimes may survive for a relatively long period of time but their life span rarely exceeds the personal life cycle of a dictator, while their chances of dynastic leadership succession are often dubious.[30] This is why personalist autocracies rarely demonstrate successful institutionalization, and provide leaders and elites with short-term rather than long-term incentives for their behavior. In Mancur Olson's terms, the major actors of personalist regimes often tend to behave as "roving" rather than "stationary" bandits.[31] They aim to achieve one-off goals at any cost but do not much bother themselves about the long-term consequences of their actions. The leaders of personalist authoritarian regimes are least constrained both politically and institutionally compared to their monarchic, one-party, and military counterparts, and their dynamics are heavily dependent on the balance of forces within informal ruling coalitions of elites around leaders. In addition, personalist autocracies often rely upon regular formally competitive yet unfree and unfair elections, and are dubbed electoral authoritarian regimes.[32] Mass electoral support is considered a major source of legitimation for these regimes, while for other types of autocracies, electoral arrangements are rarely as important. At the same time, the calendar of political planning for electoral authoritarian regimes is often driven by electoral considerations, and they are vulnerable to the problem of "political business cycles,"[33] which often contribute to short-term populist policy solutions and prevent the implementation of long-term developmental plans.

The political and policy performances of personalist authoritarian regimes vary greatly, but largely they demonstrate a tendency to decline over time amid overall degeneration and decay of their rule. The reasons for this are related to the fact that personalist leaders, as they age, are often (although not always) afraid of losing power because of coups and/or popular discontent, and their fears tend to increase over time.[34] These changes produce two-fold effects. On the one hand, personalist leaders prefer the loyalty of their inner circle of elites at the expense of their efficiency.[35] Thus, the quality of policy-making under these regimes may decrease. On the other hand, increasing repressions against the opposition may empower the security apparatus and law enforcement agencies, and they may use coercion not only against the opposition but also against other segments of elites. This risk may provide strong incentives for preservation of the political status quo at any cost, while not providing incentives for serious policy improvements. Although similar tendencies are also observed in some one-party regimes (including the Soviet Union's),[36] these regimes are often able to diminish or at least postpone the related risks of degeneration and decay. One-party regimes sometimes establish certain internal mechanisms of fool-proofing, such as performance-based career promotion of mid-level officials (as in present-day China),[37] and/or a powerful and competent policy-making party-state apparatus (as in the Soviet Union after World War II).[38] Compared to personalist autocracies, they also are more flexible in terms of correction of errors, due to reshuffling of state officials (including those in the higher echelons of power) and due to developed and institutionalized mechanisms of feedback and policy responsiveness.[39] Personalist regimes rarely bother themselves with these issues and furthermore tend to avoid major reshufflings in ruling coalitions in order to protect themselves against risk of breakdown.[40]

Given these features of personalist authoritarian regimes, one should not be surprised that the effectiveness of their government on average is much lower than those of monarchies and one-party regimes, although better than that of military regimes.[41] Personalist regimes face these problems not only because of the individual traits of particular leaders but also because of their poor institutionalization. Even though these leaders may gain a greater degree of freedom to maneuver than their counterparts in one-party regimes, this freedom cannot substitute for prudence of political and policy choices. In a way, the arbitrariness and decisiveness of these choices serve as the other side of the coin of ineffectiveness. Such a difficult combination becomes one of the major pitfalls of personalist autocracies in various political and institutional contexts. Yes, exceptional successful leaders like Lee Kwan Yew may avoid these pitfalls due to certain circumstances (his family was one of the major landowners in Singapore, and he ran the small island country similarly to a family business). However, many personalist autocrats, being unconstrained, tend to behave like Mobutu Sese Seko in Congo or Robert Mugabe in Zimbabwe, who became notorious due to their corruption and inefficiency. If and when these pitfalls of personalist autocracies coincide with major ambitions and gross misperceptions by their leaders, they may become major perils for personalist authoritarian regimes. Present-day Russia may serve as a prime example of these pitfalls and perils.

Russia: The Road to Regime Personalization

According to conventional wisdom, the current personalist authoritarian regime in Russia emerged during the 2000s on the back of the failed democratization of the 1990s. This process was fueled by the difficult effects of the Soviet collapse on post-Soviet state building and the deep and protracted recession of the Russian economy. This is why Russia's leaders and elites preferred non-democratic options in major instances of political conflict, such as the dissolution of the Russian parliament in 1993, Yeltsin's presidential re-election campaign in 1996, or "the war of Yeltsin's succession" in 1999–2000.[42] When Putin came to power in 2000, Russia had already laid the major political and institutional foundations of personalist authoritarianism. The Russian constitution, adopted in a 1993 plebiscite, placed very minimal constraints on a vaguely defined presidential power in the form of term limits (two consecutive terms in office). In political terms, Yeltsin briefly summarized his vision of presidential power as follows: "To put it bluntly, somebody had to be the boss in the country; that's all there was to it."[43] Although Yeltsin rarely behaved as "the boss in the country," given the weakness of the Russian economy and of the Russian state in the 1990s, his successor Putin was able to conduct a major "correction of errors" and establish a full-fledged personalist authoritarianism in the 2000s.[44] It was not just a transition from failed democracy to personalist authoritarianism as such but also a major increase in the degree of Putin's personalist rule.

On the one hand, Putin became a beneficiary of the Russian economy's post-crisis recovery and rapid growth of 1999–2008, which contributed to the skyrocketing of his popularity and gave him free rein in dealing with the elites and the general public.[45] On the other hand, Putin initiated several major political and institutional changes (including recentralization of the Russian state, reforms of the electoral and party systems, imposing state control over business actors, media, NGOs, etc.) which made him less constrained and less accountable.[46] Some major decisions made by Putin in the 2000s, such as the abolition of popular elections of regional chief executives in 2004 or the "Yukos affair," which drastically shifted state–business relations toward the model of the "predatory state,"[47] were made unilaterally or, at best, based on informal consultations with a narrow pool of trusted advisors. At that time, Putin greatly strengthened personal control over key appointments and dismissals, and filled major elite positions with loyalists from his personal networks. In their comprehensive analysis of regime personalization in Russia, Alexander Baturo and Jos Elknik considered this early stage of Putin's rule to be "regime takeover."[48] It lasted approximately until 2008, when Putin turned to a job swap with Dmitry Medvedev, who temporarily occupied the office of the president in 2008–12. Still, at that time, Putin was not able to implement all major decisions without consultation with significant segments of the elites (most probably, this was one of the reasons why he did not initially abandon presidential term limits as the leaders of several other countries of post-Soviet Eurasia, such as Kazakhstan or Belarus, did). Some episodes of disagreement among elites were openly visible to the public at that time, and nothing like the unconditional approval of any decision by Putin, so clearly demonstrated during and after the February 21, 2022 Security Council meeting, was observed in the 2000s.

The second stage of "consolidation" of the personalist regime in Russia coincided with the period of Medvedev's presidency, when Putin, as prime minister, concentrated more power in his hands than his formal boss. This stage symbolically culminated in September 2011, when the initial plan of temporary replacement of Putin by Medvedev in presidential office was unveiled, and in March 2012 Putin returned to the presidency, offering Medvedev the job of prime minister.[49] By this time, Putin's personal power exceeded the cumulative potential of his personal networks, while some of the networks inherited from Yeltsin's period ceased to exist. Finally, in the third stage of personalization of the Russian political regime, the "take-off," Putin as a ruler became "largely autonomous from his ruling coalition."[50] According to Baturo and Elknik, this period started with the Russian annexation of Crimea in March 2014. The decision on the annexation, unilaterally made by Putin despite the numerous fears and concerns of Russian elites, brought him a major surge in domestic popularity among the general public and greatly increased his status as a powerful international player. As is demonstrated in chapter 5, the costs of the annexation of Crimea can be considered relatively negligible. Such a turn to the "take-off" stage of the personalist regime "is accompanied by increased perception of the ruler as permanent and irreplaceable." The statement by Vyacheslav Volodin, "If there is Putin, there is Russia, if there is no Putin, there is no Russia,"[51] made in October 2014, soon after the annexation of Crimea, is a telling illustration of these developments. The following step of abandoning term limits and possible extension of the presidential term in office until 2036, initially proposed by Putin in March 2020 and approved during the constitutional plebiscite in July 2020, served as a logical extension, if not a conclusion of the process of personalization.[52] Putin "became no longer dependent on support from his patronage network … As a result, loyalty in a personalist system at this stage is determined by the logic that all officials regard the ruler as their overall patron."[53]

What did the personalization of the Russian authoritarian regime mean for its practices of politics and policy-making? Baturo and Elknik outlined four dimensions, or pillars, of regime personalization in Russia: patronage personalization, deinstitutionalization, permanency of ruler in office and media personalization. Using various data and methods, including reputational analyses of the composition of Russian elites and sophisticated techniques of textual analysis, they convincingly demonstrated trends of increasing personalization of Russia's regime in all of these dimensions during the period from 1999 to 2020. For the purposes of this chapter, I will mostly focus on two of these pillars, namely regime deinstitutionalization and personalized patronage, which serve as two sides of the same coin. As "personalist rulers aim to reduce institutional autonomy by weakening the power of political institutions and relying on less formal arrangements to rule," Putin implemented several mechanisms for the reduction of institutional autonomy so clearly demonstrated during the above-mentioned meeting of the Russian Security Council on February 21, 2022. He not only increased personal control over major institutions and state agencies and placed his friends and cronies in various top positions, but also established "multiple agencies with overlapping functions [that] can also serve alternative purposes such as 'authoritarian checks and balances' and deliberate redundancy."[54] As a result, the Russian political regime's informal institutions – first and foremost, personalized patronage networks – were gradually substituted for formal institutions, while the configuration of ruling elites and their impact on key decisions became increasingly dependent upon personal ties to Putin, which remained relatively stable over time. Although episodes of poor performance and wrongdoing among elites were widespread, instances of de-cooptation of elites and their downgrading to non-elite status in Russia were relatively rare.

Deinstitutionalization affected politics and policy-making in Russia in two different though overlapping ways. Many important issues related to economic policy and public finance remained under the firm control of the civilian bureaucracy (rather than under the control of the *siloviki*), and deinstitutionalization did not affect them to a great degree. Moreover, many competent technocrats who occupied key positions in these policy areas[55] successfully performed their duties amid various crises (such as that of 2008–9).[56] As their professional expertise was often indispensable, technocrats in major ministries and the Central Bank, as well as in other state agencies, also performed a fool-proofing role, and helped the leadership to avoid major failures. According to some media reports, Putin's only concern before the annexation of Crimea in 2014 was the state of the Russian currency reserves – whether or not their amount was sufficient for economic survival after the imposition of Western sanctions. Upon receiving an affirmative answer from the head of the Central Bank, Elvira Nabiullina, Putin decided to go ahead and launch the process of annexation.[57] While top technocrats were themselves deeply involved in Putin's patronage networks, the ministries and state agencies under their auspices retained some professional and bureaucratic autonomy. These organizations mostly conducted their jobs within the framework of standard operating procedures, somewhat similarly to their bureaucratic counterparts in other countries, irrespective of their political regimes. In a sense, deinstitutionalization did not corrupt technocrats entirely. However, the role of technocrats in the informal ruling coalition of elites diminished over time. As Andrei Yakovlev argued in his thoughtful analysis, during the 2010s (the "take-off" stage of regime personalization, according to the Baturo–Elknik periodization), they became junior partners in this coalition, submissive and subordinated to a dominant faction of *siloviki*.[58]

It is no wonder that technocrats had very limited impact on many political and policy decisions beyond their area of responsibility, and did not even attempt to extend it further (especially in the process of preparation for the Russian assault on Ukraine before February 2022 and after its beginning). To put it bluntly, while avoiding the most negative effects of deinstitutionalization, technocrats were pushed (and even isolated themselves) into the narrow niches, if not ghettos, of their professional expertise.[59]

At the same time, many other political and policy domains, especially those related to foreign policy, military and security issues, were affected by the deinstitutionalization of the Russian political regime in quite a different way. Their distinctive institutional framework had been established as early as 1994, when Yeltsin took several ministries and state agencies (defense, interior, justice, security, foreign affairs, etc.) under his direct presidential control, even though formally they remained part of the government.[60] During Yeltsin's presidency, the institutional disjuncture between these two types of state agencies and tensions between the civilian bureaucracy and *siloviki*, as well as fragmentation of these agencies and many rivalries among them, fueled numerous intra-elite conflicts in Russia and greatly contributed to the poor performance of the Russian state.[61] However, during the first years of Putin's rule (the aforementioned "takeover" stage), these domains were first to come under personalized patronage, while their top officials were greatly empowered. The "Yukos affair," which launched the process of major re-nationalization of industrial assets privatized during the 1990s, became a turning point in a process that placed Russia on the path to state-directed crony capitalism.[62] The subsequent promotion of certain *siloviki* to key positions in civilian bureaucracy turned them into veto players in ruling coalitions of elites well beyond their respective domains, while during the consolidation and, especially, "take-off" stages, they increased their influence and became major partners in these coalitions. Putin's personalized patronage played the central role in this transformation.[63] While some top-level *siloviki* had been Putin's friends since the days of his service in the KGB during the late-Soviet years, the promotion of their friends and cronies (and, later on, children) increasingly became a matter of personal ties rather than of professional credentials and merit. Similarly to the spread of a cancerous tumor, these personal ties among *siloviki* became more and more important for ever new sections of the civilian bureaucracy, which were increasingly captured by *siloviki* and their allies.

According to data from surveys of Russian elites, many representatives of *siloviki* shared not only a common career background, but also a common set of attitudes – heavily anti-Western, anti-democratic, and illiberal.[64] Needless to say, a number of top officials with *siloviki* backgrounds also became notorious as the most voracious rent-seekers in the state apparatus and/or in state-led companies. Under the conditions of Putin's personalized patronage and strengthening of clientelist linkages over time, top *siloviki* officials became less and less constrained and less and less accountable and tended to turn their respective agencies into personal fiefdoms. A further increase in the personnel and budgets of the foreign policy, military, and security agencies coincided with the proliferation of law enforcement agencies, including the establishment of new organizations such as the Investigative Committee (juxtaposed with the Prosecutor General's Office) and the National Guard (juxtaposed with the Ministry of the Interior, which was in charge of police). Such a proliferation of security and law enforcement agencies is typical for autocracies as a pre-emptive mechanism against potential coups, even though it contributes to poor coordination of these agencies and their inefficiency. Still, this process did not always proceed smoothly, and rivalry between individuals and agencies in these domains continued over time. The most well-known episode of these battles in Russia was the forced resignation of Russian Minister of Defense Anatoly Serdyukov, who initiated a major military reform (described in chapter 3). He was accused of many wrongdoings and was fired by Putin soon after the latter's return to the presidency in 2012 (allegedly because of rumors of his personal disloyalty to Putin during the period of Medvedev's presidency). Symptomatically, Serdyukov's successor was Sergei Shoigu, a long-standing personal crony of Putin. Upon appointment to the Defense Ministry, Shoigu reversed many changes initiated by his predecessor, although his own qualifications as a minister were rather dubious, to put it mildly.[65] This case serves as a vivid illustration of the substitution of relatively efficient state officials with loyal personal clients of leaders under the conditions of personalist authoritarianism.

The consequences of deinstitutionalization and personalization of patronage in Russia were two-fold. The first was that these dynamics contributed to the declining performance of the Russian state over time.[66] During the first years of Putin's presidency, Russia demonstrated visible progress in major dimensions of governance such as the rule of law, control of corruption, regulatory quality, and government effectiveness. Under Putin's auspices, a number of state-directed projects and programs aimed at advancement of the socio-economic development of the country were launched and implemented to a certain extent. However, even before the "take-off" stage of the personalization of the Russian regime, all these changes were either stopped or slowed down to a great degree. Putin gradually lost interest in domestic affairs and developmental projects and shifted his priorities to the international agenda (especially after the annexation of Crimea in 2014).[67] Without top-level patronage, previously active policy reforms stalled in many areas. It is no wonder that under these conditions, the drive for the preservation of the status quo in the domestic political and policy arenas tended to dominate Russia's landscape, and these tendencies increased over time. Such a shift in priorities greatly affected the quality of decision-making in non-prioritized policy areas. Even some technocratic niches previously perceived as sanctums of well-established expertise and prudency suffered from hasty preparation and poor implementation of major policy changes, such as the significant increase in the retirement age in 2018.[68]

The most important episode of this process was the response of Russian authorities to the COVID-19 pandemic in 2020–1.[69] In the wake of a major exogenous shock, Putin's administration prioritized the constitutional plebiscite on the extension of Putin's term limit until 2036, and aversion of risks of major public discontent. While Putin himself was distanced from the everyday routines of governance during the pandemic, the government, in charge of economic affairs, mostly focused on targets related to minimizing decline in production output. These policy goals were successfully achieved at the expense of the lives and health of many ordinary Russians, as the excess mortality in Russia during the period of the pandemic exceeded 1 million people (one of the highest numbers of pandemic victims across the globe). Even though Russia fairly quickly and successfully developed its own COVID-19 vaccine, Sputnik V, it was mostly used as a bargaining chip in the international arena and became a tool of "vaccine diplomacy," while the domestic vaccination campaign received minimal government support and largely failed. These major human losses met virtually no reaction in Russia – to put it bluntly, nobody in the Russian elite cared about these matters. In a way, this sluggish reception to the pandemic amid such numerous tragedies later served as a sort of justification for continuing the military assault on Ukraine in the eyes of top state officials. Indeed, if nobody cared about the victims of the pandemic, why should one expect major public discontent due to the numerous victims of the "special military operation"?

The second consequence was that personalization of patronage had a major impact on the ideational agenda of Russian elites in terms of their role models. The problem was that none of the real-world role models existing in the present day could perfectly fit Putin's priorities and preferences. He was (and is) an aging leader deeply rooted in the late-Soviet past, who considered the international status and military might of the Soviet Union to be the normative ideal for twenty-first-century Russia. This is why the Kremlin's spin doctors invented and elaborated a complex of ideas which I label elsewhere the "Good Soviet Union."[70] This is an imagined socio-political and economic order, which somehow resembles that of the late-Soviet past while lacking its inherent flaws, but in reality, bears little resemblance to the historical Soviet experience. Elements of the Soviet experience were selectively and deliberately chosen and promoted for the sake of the power maximization of the ruling elites. They include the hierarchy of the power vertical, low elite circulation, a closed recruitment pool of elites and their formal and informal privileged status, state control over major media, and state repression toward organized dissent. Meanwhile, other elements of the late-Soviet politico-economic order, such as relatively low inequality and certain state social guarantees, were discarded without meaningful public resistance. In addition, the "Good Soviet Union" includes certain features, which did not exist in the real Soviet Union but are very important for present-day Russia: a market economy and no shortages of goods and services. For the elites, a lack of institutional constraints on rent-seeking and (before February 2022) an external interface for legalization of incomes and status abroad for family members and for themselves were included in the menu of a "Good Soviet Union." The same went for Russia's high international status and ultimate veto power in any developments elsewhere across the globe. However, one should not consider the "Good Soviet Union" exclusively as a propagandist narrative. In fact, the Kremlin also attempted to convert this set of ideas into Russia's political and policy agenda, using real or imagined Soviet-era recipes for resolving numerous post-Soviet problems. As a result, the

"Good Soviet Union" as a normative ideal has not produced incentives for Russia's successful development, even if these policy goals were officially declared by the Kremlin.

The increasing reliance upon the combination of real and imagined Soviet solutions for solving post-Soviet problems became a major driver of Russian politics and policy-making, especially during the "take-off" stage of regime personalization. Many political practices and mechanisms of governance proposed by top Russian officials in the twenty-first century imitated those of their Soviet predecessors. Large-scale "national projects" of sectoral development in certain policy areas in many ways resembled Soviet-style five-year plans. Major state-owned industrial conglomerates, such as Rostec, were modeled upon the experience of powerful Soviet-style industrial branch ministries.[71] However, copies usually are much worse than original versions, and post-Soviet replicas of the Soviet experience were often heavily criticized for their poor policy design and implementation.[72] Meanwhile, the fundamental problems were much more serious and related to greater issues than individual policies. It is not only that reliance upon greatly outdated Soviet practices as a role model for the twenty-first century was hardly productive for Russian politics and policy-making. As the institutional foundations of the political regimes in the Soviet Union and present-day Russia were completely different, their effects on regime performance contributed to diverse policy outcomes. The Soviet one-party regime was highly institutionalized and often too inflexible, while the personalist political regime in present-day Russia suffered from its deinstitutionalization. Even though personalized patronage was relatively widespread during the Soviet decades,[73] it nevertheless had certain limits, while present-day Russia has experienced many vices of personalized patronage to a much greater degree. This is why many attempts to replicate late-Soviet practices had at best incomplete and imperfect results, and, in the worst-case scenario, were completely wrong. The differences between major foreign policy decisions in the Soviet Union and in contemporary Russia are quite indicative in this respect.

A Point of Comparison: Czechoslovakia 1968 versus Ukraine 2022

The closest functional equivalent to the Russian "special military operation" in Ukraine in 2022 was the Soviet military invasion of

Czechoslovakia in August 1968, officially code-named "Operation Danube." Despite the obvious major differences between these countries in their size and political significance for the Soviet Union and post-Soviet Russia, respectively, these two cases share major similarities in terms of political and international context. Political liberalization in Czechoslovakia, known as the "Prague Spring," was perceived in the Kremlin as an undermining of Soviet dominance within its sphere of influence in Eastern Europe, with great risk of such a trend spreading to other countries of the Communist bloc as well as certain republics of the Soviet Union.[74] In a way, these fears of 1968 were similar to the Kremlin's fears of losing control over Ukraine and the risk of a spread of anti-Kremlin trends in Russia and Eurasia after Yanukovych's deposal in 2014. In both cases, the Kremlin attempted to secure certain compromises, aimed at keeping Czechoslovakia before August 1968 and Ukraine between 2014 and 2022 submissive and subordinated to Moscow, and these attempts largely failed in different ways. After that, both Soviet and Russian leaders turned from negotiations to coercion, and used military power in full swing (moreover, the Soviet 1968 invasion of Czechoslovakia was conducted in accordance with the Warsaw Pact, with active involvement of Soviet junior partners, at least, in the process of preparation of military actions). In the end, the Warsaw Pact troops occupied Czechoslovakia in August 1968. Although the immediate attempt by the pro-Soviet faction of Czechoslovak elites to overthrow the reformist leadership in response to the Soviet invasion failed, over time, the Soviet Union was able to place its loyalists in key positions in the country and launch a process of "normalization," which brought Czechoslovakia back in line under Soviet dominance. The new "normalcy" ended only in 1989, in the wake of the collapse of Communism in Eastern Europe. Meanwhile, the Soviet military, initially sent to Czechoslovakia just for a one-off action of restoration of Kremlin control, stayed there for more than 20 years to guarantee the submission and subordination of this country to the Kremlin. One can imagine that a similar outcome of the 2022 "special military operation" in Ukraine would probably suit the Kremlin's preferences and intentions.

Despite numerous similarities and parallels, the 1968 "Operation Danube" was very different from the 2022 "special military operation" in many respects. The most important difference relates to the fact that, unlike personalist authoritarianism in present-day

THE PERSONALIST TRAP

Russia, the Soviet party-based political regime was highly institutionalized, both formally and informally. It was based upon collective leadership and collective decision-making at the highest echelons of power. The Politburo, the main decision-making body of the Communist Party (which included twelve full members and eight candidate members by 1968), met regularly (usually, every week) to discuss the most important issues in domestic politics and foreign policy and to attempt to build consensus among the top Soviet elites. By the time of the Prague Spring, many discussions were held during Politburo plenary meetings. At the stage of preparation of decisions, the apparatus of the Communist Party and of respective ministries and stage agencies had seriously considered various options through the process of informal bargaining, official approvals and mutual adjustments of various positions among the Soviet leaders. Although the Secretary General of the Communist Party (in 1968, Leonid Brezhnev) had informal veto power in these discussions, he was not always able to impose his agenda unilaterally. The implementation of decisions made by the Politburo was also highly institutionalized. It was conducted through several state agencies subordinated to the Communist Party leadership. Over time, decision-making practices varied to a great degree – for example, during Stalin's decades, many key decisions were made by him unilaterally, and during the last years of Brezhnev's leadership in the late 1970s and early 1980s, the Politburo became less active because of his poor health and often rubber-stamped proposals prepared by the apparatus.[75] Still, by 1968 the practice of collective decision-making by the Soviet leadership was probably at its peak. In the case of the invasion of Czechoslovakia, this process took a two-tier form, as collective decision-making also involved negotiations between Soviet leaders and their junior partners in Warsaw Pact countries.

Mark Kramer, a prominent Cold War historian from Harvard, provided a comprehensive process-tracing account of the 1968 Soviet decision to invade Czechoslovakia.[76] The decision-making process took more than five months, from March 15, 1968, when Politburo members discussed for the first time what to do with dangerous Czechoslovak reformers, to August 17, 1968, when the Politburo at last officially approved a military operation with the agreement of Soviet satellites in the Warsaw Pact. Discussions on these matters were rather heated, as various options were proposed. The most hawkish members of the Politburo, who suggested military action from the very beginning, were Yuri Andropov, the head of the KGB, and Petro Shelest, the first secretary of the Communist Party of Ukraine. While Shelest was deeply concerned about the risk of diffusion of the anti-Kremlin mood to Ukraine, Andropov, who had been a Soviet ambassador in Hungary during the 1956 uprising, shared his bitter personal memories with his colleagues and argued for pre-emptive suppression of possible rebellions. Contrary to these hawks, Brezhnev and, to some extent, the Soviet Prime Minister Alexei Kosygin initially took much more moderate positions, and proposed negotiations with the Czechoslovak leadership in order to find a solution palatable for Moscow.[77] Brezhnev's arguments against a military solution were driven by potential problems for Soviet relationships with the United States and other Western countries (although in fact, the US government at that time was so deeply engaged with the Vietnam War that it paid little attention to Czechoslovakia). Regardless, there was no consensus in the Politburo about the invasion even in April 1968, when preparation for military action officially launched, and so discussions took a great deal of time. Soviet leaders were in close contact with their Warsaw Pact partners, especially with the Polish and East German leaderships, which also took hawkish positions because of domestic concerns. While several rounds of top-level negotiations by Brezhnev and other Soviet leaders with Czechoslovak Communist Party leader Alexander Dubček did not produce any results satisfactory for the Kremlin, an informal coalition of supporters of the invasion emerged both within the Politburo and among the Warsaw Pact leaders. In the end, Brezhnev realized that Dubček and his Czechoslovak allies would not abandon their reformist course despite pressure from the Soviet Union, and by the time of his last meeting with Dubček at the beginning of August 1968, he had finally joined the camp of proponents of a military solution. Meanwhile, planning for military action developed well before the political decision on the invasion was approved by the Politburo, and all cogs of the Soviet state machinery performed relatively well in the process of preparations.

These collective deliberations and negotiations were instrumental for better preparation of the military invasion and helped to avoid major flaws and mitigate potential risks. For example, Soviet leaders instructed that the military should avoid aggression and violence towards Czechoslovak residents in order not to repeat the experience of massive bloodshed in Hungary in 1956. They also rejected the idea of active involvement of East German troops in "Operation Danube," against Walter Ulbricht's intentions – otherwise, parallels with the German occupation of Czechoslovakia during World War II could become too apparent, possibly causing very negative reactions among the Czechoslovak people.[78] Domestically, collective deliberations and negotiations as well as engagement of top echelons of state machinery in the decision-making process prevented any hidden or open discontent within the Soviet leadership and made their actions more coherent and coordinated. Even though the Soviet Foreign Minister Andrei Gromyko was, at that time, not even a candidate member of the Politburo, it is difficult to imagine that he could have received the information about the proposed military invasion just three hours before its start as his Russian counterpart Lavrov did in February 2022.

To be fair, the veil of secrecy over decision-making in Russia in 2022 (in comparison with Soviet decision-making in 1968) was a side effect of the relative domestic and international information openness of the Russian political regime compared to its Soviet predecessors. The Soviet Communist Party and state apparatus routinely operated behind closed doors not only in foreign and security policy domains but also in all other activities:[79] heavily institutionalized and highly centralized control over information flows minimized the risk of undesired leaks. However, in Russia in the 2020s, domestic information control was not particularly centralized and institutionalized. Many official and unofficial information sources in Russia were available for legal and semi-legal use by business actors and/or investigative journalists, and information leaks from the Kremlin (often spread by competing cliques) were nearly routine. In addition, the over-secrecy of Russian decision-making in 2022 was fueled by perception of higher risk of international leaks in comparison with 1968 due to the different international configuration of actors and institutional settings. In 1968, the Soviet Union organized the military invasion of Czechoslovakia within its own "sphere of influence" and was acting on behalf of the Warsaw Pact coalition of allies, so the Kremlin largely perceived its actions as legitimate moves in the international arena. Contrary to that, in 2022 the Kremlin clearly understood that the Russian military assault on Ukraine would be ex ante perceived as illegitimate by many foreign actors, and potential information leakages could only amplify these perceptions. The relative international openness of Russia in 2022 compared to the Soviet Union in 1968 (multiplied by open-source intelligence techniques [OSINT] analytics and other technological developments) diminished the expected chances of ex post legitimation of the "special military operation" upon its (presumably successful) implementation. Most probably, the over-secrecy of decision-making in February 2022 was considered an antidote to the relative openness of the Russian regime, but in fact, it was counter-productive for planning and implementation of the "special military operation."

One should take into account that in its dealings with Czechoslovakia in 1968, the Soviet Politburo faced a similar one-party political regime, based upon similar mechanisms of collective decision-making in the Presidium of the Central Committee of the Communist Party of Czechoslovakia. This similarity, alongside deep divisions in the Czechoslovak leadership between the reformers (led by Dubček) and pro-Soviet hardliners, prompted the Kremlin to build an informal coalition with Soviet allies in Prague. They, in turn, expected that upon the arrival of Soviet troops in Czechoslovakia, the balance of forces in the Presidium would shift toward its pro-Moscow faction, and then an internal coup would become inevitable, with subsequent restoration of pre-1968 loyalty to the Kremlin without serious resistance. Vasil' Bil'ak, the informal leader of the pro-Moscow faction of the Czechoslovak leadership, sold this plan to Shelest during their secret meeting in Hungary in July 1968, and the idea was greatly appreciated by the Kremlin.[80] Indeed, military invasion and a restoration of the Kremlin's control over the Prague rebels were perceived as a one-off action with a short-term presence of Soviet troops. In fact, these expectations were ultimately wrong. Not only did an internal coup in the Czechoslovak leadership fail immediately after the Soviet invasion (a majority in the Presidium supported Dubček), but resistance to the Soviet actions in Czechoslovakia was also rather strong.[81] In the end, the Kremlin had to invest a great deal of time and efforts before Dubček was ousted from his post in April 1969, and the restoration of its full-scale control over Czechoslovakia (dubbed "normalization") was accompanied by a sizeable presence of Soviet troops in the country over the next 20 years. Even though the Kremlin achieved the goals of its military invasion of Czechoslovakia, their costs became much higher than initially expected.

One must note that the Soviet invasion of Czechoslovakia in 1968 was not the only example of collective decision-making regarding international military assault. The experience of the Soviet invasion of Afghanistan in December 1979, which launched the Soviet–Afghan War (which continued until February 1989), represented a different pattern of decision-making.[82] Despite the fact that the use of military force in order to keep Afghanistan under Soviet control had been on the table for several months, at that time the Politburo did not discuss these plans collectively. By 1979, many decisions were approved without oral discussions, via the exchange of written documents, as aging Soviet top leaders (including Brezhnev) suffered from poor health and were physically incapable of spending long hours in collective debates. The proposal for the military invasion of Afghanistan was poorly designed, based upon rather unrealistic considerations and expectations (such as countering both US influence and Islamic threats in the region of Central Asia) and did not imply any long-term consequences. This proposal, driven by the trio of hawkish Soviet leaders – the Foreign Minister Andrei Gromyko, the Minister of Defense Dmitry Ustinov, and Andropov (still the head of the KGB) – was never seriously discussed by Politburo members. Fifteen days before the invasion, the proposal was sent to Brezhnev, accompanied by handwritten notes by Brezhnev's most trusted person in the Politburo, Konstantin Chernenko (in addition, Andropov sent a personal memo to Brezhnev, persuading him to agree with this move). Later, the fateful decision was formalized in the official minutes of a Politburo meeting. Overall, however, this pattern illustrated the decay of collective decision-making under the Soviet one-party regime, which was on the verge of numerous crises that would be aggravated during the 1980s.[83]

The planning of Russian actions toward Ukraine in 2022 demonstrated a sharp contrast with the planning of the Soviet invasion of Czechoslovakia in 1968. According to media reports, the idea was initially proposed to Putin by a long-standing close friend, the wealthy businessman Yuri Kovalchuk, who had spent countless hours together with Putin in self-isolation at the Valdai state residence during the pandemic in 2020–1. Kovalchuk, known for his illiberal and anti-Western stances as well as for adherence to conspiracy theories, persuaded Putin that he should launch an assault on Ukraine soon.[84] According to him, as the United States was weakened domestically and internationally, and Europe was divided by numerous internal contradictions, they would not be able to protect Ukraine against the Russian assault, so Russia could easily achieve its goals. Shoigu, in turn, enthusiastically endorsed this proposal, as he considered the assault a great opportunity for empowerment of the Ministry of Defense and of himself,[85] despite serious warnings from certain top military officers about Russia's poor preparedness for an assault and numerous risks of such an action. In Ukraine, Viktor Medvedchuk, a personal friend of Putin and a leader of the opposition Platform – For Life Party in the Ukrainian parliament, persuaded the Kremlin of the alleged loyalty of Ukrainian elites and citizens at large to Russia and of the lack of serious resistance to a potential Russian assault. Medvedchuk, one of the key figures in Yanukovych's entourage, attempted to act as liaison between Ukraine and Russia during Petro Poroshenko's presidency. He was closely connected with the separatists in Donbas and had strong ambitions of occupying a key position in Ukrainian politics. However, Medvedchuk suffered heavy attacks on his party and TV network initiated by Zelensky in 2020, and later on he was prosecuted in Ukraine on charges of state treason. This is why Medvedchuk's expectations and claims to Putin were largely a matter of personal revenge; although these assessments were completely wrong, Putin tended to believe them.[86]

Despite many differences between Kovalchuk, Shoigu, and Medvedchuk, all three major initiators of the Russian military action were personal clients of Putin, who pursued their own self-interest, and did not base their proposals and expectations on in-depth analyses of potential risks and consequences. At the same time, the deinstitutionalization of the Russian personalist authoritarianism left the Kremlin vulnerable vis-à-vis these proposals because of the lack of fool-proofing mechanisms within the state apparatus. While technocrats were isolated and afraid to object to ideas about military assault, many *siloviki* largely endorsed them because of a combination of ideational reasons and self-interest. As a result, the preparation for a military solution easily received a green light in the Kremlin without serious discussion, as the infamous Security Council meeting on February 21, 2022 clearly illustrated.

Despite many crucial differences between Russia in 2022 and the Soviet Union in 1968, there was at least one striking similarity between the actions of the Russian personalist leadership and the Soviet Communist leadership. Both the personalist and the party-based regime faced the same fundamental information problem, typical for most autocracies across the globe. Both regimes used similar biased information sources about the situation in their target countries – pro-Kremlin politicians, linked with the anti-reformist camp in the Communist Party (in Czechoslovakia) or with the regime of the ousted former president Yanukovych (in Ukraine), who expected to benefit from the Soviet or Russian assault. Their persuasive efforts were heavily biased. Medvedchuk in 2022 and Bil'ak and his allies in 1968 poorly reflected the real state of affairs in Ukraine and in Czechoslovakia, respectively. In both cases, however, the Kremlin systematically ignored alternative sources of information and listened only to those signals that the Soviet and Russian leaders were pleased to hear.[87] From this perspective, both Soviet one-party authoritarianism and Russian personalist authoritarianism faced a similar problem of dealing with information flows. In essence, both the personalist authoritarian regime in Russia and the party-based authoritarian regime in the Soviet Union suffered from distorted information,[88] and, as chapter 4 of this book demonstrates, this problem is more acute in foreign policy than in domestic politics. However, in personalist regimes, dealing with information flows (especially in the foreign policy arena) is also a matter of clientelist links, which play a less salient role in one-party regimes because of their high institutionalization.

To summarize, one might argue that the Soviet Union was much better prepared for its military attack on Czechoslovakia in 1968 than Russia was for its attack on Ukraine in 2022, both in political and in military terms. The Soviet decision to invade Czechoslovakia was collectively endorsed by the Politburo, and its implementation was conducted by civilian and military executives in a systematic way. In addition, the Kremlin built coalitions of allies internationally (on the level of the Warsaw Pact) and within the target country (on the level of the pro-Moscow faction in the Presidium). Even though the 1968 invasion of Czechoslovakia was harmful for the Soviet Union in terms of its support in the West (especially among left-wing politicians) and put an end to domestic liberalization in the Soviet Union (launched in 1956 with Khrushchev's Thaw), it was not completely detrimental to the country. For the Soviet Union, which by that time was a stable and legitimate global superpower (although full of other problems), even though the invasion of Czechoslovakia was important, it was in fact a relatively minor episode in its foreign policy during the Cold War. In Russia in 2022, the personalist nature of decision-making amid increasing deinstitutionalization and personalized patronage within the regime contributed to heavy distortion of foreign policy-making and arbitrarily and imperfectly conducted preparations for the assault. The veil of over-secrecy, which covered these preparations, as well as poor coordination at the level of major state agencies, were also hardly conducive for successful implementation of the initial plans. Despite certain efforts, the Kremlin failed to build strong support within the target country and did not even attempt to build a coalition of allies internationally. It is no wonder that the 2022 assault faced numerous problems from the very beginning and became a major turning point in Russia's entire history as a crucial episode in its downward trajectory.

The Personalist Trap: Tentative Conclusions

Autocracies are often praised for their decisiveness. Against the background of protracted and often compromise-based decision-making in democracies, they are perceived as examples of strong leadership, which are able to act quickly and resolutely.[89] This is particularly true for personalist regimes, which are the least constrained by both formal and informal political institutions. Personalist autocrats do not need to spend time in countless discussions with domestic subordinates and international allies, and Russia was no exception in this respect. The widespread image of Putin as a powerful, decisive, and steadfast strongman, who was always able to achieve his goals because of these features, and who deserved to be a truly global decision-maker, was greatly reinforced after the Russian annexation of Crimea in 2014 and boosted his domestic support and international reputation as a major strongman. The idea of a swift conquest of Ukraine proposed by the Kremlin in 2022 was very much in line with this image and reflected many perceptions of strong and successful personalist leadership.

However, the decisiveness of many strongmen is often nothing more than the other side of the coin of their arbitrariness. Political leaders who are not constrained by other domestic actors and/or by political institutions face major risks of taking ultimately wrong decisions. These risks tend to increase over time because of the aggravated deinstitutionalization of personalist authoritarian regimes and further expansion of personalized patronage amid conditions of "degenerate autocracy."[90] The deterioration of the quality of decision-making, typical for regimes of this kind, can turn all advantages of decisiveness into their opposites. As the following chapters demonstrate, strong leaders who act with impunity are prone to great mistakes, facing no constraints and relying upon their past successes as indicators for the future. This was exactly the case with the 2022 Russian assault on Ukraine.

In light of this experience, the role of political institutions under authoritarianism is worth further consideration.[91] Most scholars concentrate on their impact on the continuity of autocratic rule in terms of mitigation of domestic risks of discontent among elites and the masses. Political institutions such as elections, parties, and legislatures enable efficient power sharing for autocrats, which is essential for cooptation of various segments of elites and satisfaction of societal demands. Apart from these important functions, political institutions are even more essential for authoritarian policy-making, especially in the very sensitive domains of foreign, military, and security policy. In a way, these institutions serve as an emergency brake, which may – or may not – prevent the most destructive decisions made by autocrats or at least diminish their negative consequences. While in the case of the Soviet military action in Czechoslovakia in 1968 this role was performed by the political institutions of collective leadership and the highly institutionalized civilian and military bureaucracy to some extent (even though imperfectly), the Russian plan of military assault on Ukraine in 2022 was developed and implemented without any such brakes at all.

As a result, the Russian personalist regime relied upon a heavily distorted mechanism of decision-making, which was not able to build barriers against major misunderstandings and poor policy planning. Putin's great ambitions, as well as the personal preferences and perceptions openly declared in his numerous public statements made before the assault on Ukraine, became the main drivers of the "special military operation" amid unconditional loyalty among the Russian elites and the lack of any serious discussions. Not only were alternative information sources and warnings not taken into account and systematically ignored by the Kremlin, but initial master plans of quick and triumphant conquest of Ukraine also met no serious doubts or major revisions. However, the clash of these master plans with the tough reality after February 2022 turned out to be too harsh for Russia, Ukraine, and the entire world.

― Chapter 3 ―

THE WELL-OILED MACHINE, OUT OF CONTROL

In June 2021, eight months before the Russian assault on Ukraine, the Ministry of Industry and Trade signed a contract with the Russian company Avtomatika regarding development of broadband satellite communication systems for Russian means of transportation, such as railway carriages, automobiles, planes, and ships, over the next three years. As similar communication systems were previously exclusively used by the Russian military and were incredibly expensive and complicated for dual (military and civilian) use, their development and adjustment for commercial purposes was considered by the state officials a serious step forward for the country. This project, among many others, was considered part of a large-scale program of state-funded import substitution, prioritized by the Russian authorities as a major element of Russia's technological sovereignty. To achieve these goals, the ministry offered Avtomatika a state subsidy of more than 400 million rubles (about $5.6 million at that time). For this money, Avtomatika promised to produce new antennas with modern domestic software, which could be applied not only for use by train and car passengers, but also for drone control and similar military-related tasks. Avtomatika, a part of the large state-owned military-industrial conglomerate Rostec, proudly announced its plan to launch these communication systems by 2023. Soon after that, the executive director of Rostec, Oleg Yevtushenko, advertised these new products as advanced Russian hi-tech solutions, which would greatly increase transportation security as well as convenience for consumers. However, in May 2023 the ministry suddenly discovered that instead of developing Russia-made technologies, Avtomatika had actually bought Chinese communication systems, which not only included imported hardware components but also used foreign-made software without access to the necessary source codes. This fraud was discovered almost accidentally because of a journalist investigation. The ministry perceived such "creative" implementation as a gross violation of the conditions of the contract, stopped paying subsidies to Avtomatika, and requested that the State Investigative Committee examine the legality of the company's actions.[1] In this case, the technological sovereignty of Russia proclaimed by the Kremlin was illusionary to say the least.

Meanwhile, in December 2022, in the midst of the Russian assault on Ukraine, the Anti-Corruption Foundation led by the major Russian opposition figure Alexei Navalny had published an investigative report about the luxury lifestyle of the Russian Deputy Minister of Defense Timur Ivanov and his wife Svetlana.[2] The couple owned expensive estates, cars, clothes, works of art, etc. (often legally registered with dummy intermediaries), and regularly rented villas for vacations on the Côte d'Azur and other prestigious locations. Ivanov, a long-term associate of the minister Sergei Shoigu, had been promoted to this important post in 2016, and was responsible for all key state-funded construction projects conducted by the Ministry of Defense. This included the major reconstruction of Mariupol, the big Ukrainian city, largely destroyed and then occupied by Russia in March 2022. Unsurprisingly, many of Ivanov and his wife's personal expenditures were actually paid for by several companies, which served as major contractors for the ministry. However, in July 2022, in anticipation of personal sanctions against Timur Ivanov (which were imposed by the European Union in October 2022), the couple officially divorced, making Svetlana essentially immune: amid the ongoing assault on Ukraine, she continued her previous lifestyle, residing in Paris and buying expensive goods for personal use. In the end, in April 2024 Ivanov was accused of bribery and imprisoned. Later on, in May 2024, Ivanov's patron Shoigu left his post in the Ministry of Defense and was appointed a secretary of the Russian Security Council. However, episodes like this are more or less business as usual, a routine practice for the top Russian state officials and their relatives.

These two episodes of corruption and mismanagement in the Russian military and military-industrial complex are hardly unique for the Russian state. These practices are widely known at all levels of authority; they have been extensively observed, reported, and analyzed over a long period of time by numerous scholars,[3] activists,[4] investigative journalists,[5] and international agencies such as the World Bank,[6] World Justice Project,[7] and Transparency International.[8] In fact, nearly ubiquitous corruption, rent-seeking, and government ineffectiveness amid the lack of the rule of law and poor regulatory quality serve as major manifestations of the politico-economic order of bad governance. In my previous book, I defined this as a distinctive mechanism of governing the state, aimed at maximization of rents at the expense of development.[9] To put it bluntly, the rulers of any given country are largely interested in stealing its resources as much as possible and for as long as possible, but they are often unable to do so because of significant political and/or institutional constraints on such behavior, ranging from competitive elections to an independent judiciary. However, if and when they face few or no such constraints, this politico-economic order may be consolidated as a long-term feature of the state. Post-Communist Russia serves as a prime example of bad governance over the last several decades, and the impact of this phenomenon on the launch and subsequent failure of the Russian assault on Ukraine was very important, if not decisive.

On the one hand, bad governance severely affected Russia's foreign, military, and security policies – most likely, more severely than many other policy fields. The veil of state secrecy, which covers related policies to a great degree in many places,[10] in Russia served as an extensive excuse for numerous instances of misconduct,[11] not so dissimilar to the above-mentioned cases of Avtomatika and Timur Ivanov. As a result, the Russian leadership systematically received distorted information about the military capability of Russia and its adversaries, about many security-related matters on the global and regional scales, and about the opportunities and constraints of its foreign policy. In other words, bad governance aggravated the problem of the poor quality of essential information, typical for many authoritarian regimes.[12] On the other hand, unconstrained rent-seeking in Russia occurred not only domestically but also internationally, serving as one of the key drivers of an aggressive foreign policy and for the use of the "special military operation" as a potential way to expand the pool of rents for the Russian elites and society at large. Indeed, Russia's elites, having extended their rent-seeking practices well beyond Russian borders in various ways[13] (ranging from the widespread use of offshore companies for legalization of wealth to the purchase of foreign citizenships for their family members and for themselves),[14] perceived a possible quick conquest of Ukraine as an easily available source of new rents. Bad governance in Russia greatly contributed to a combination of misleading information and unreasonable expectations, which paved the way for the pernicious decision of the Russian military assault on Ukraine and its flawed implementation.

In this chapter, I will consider the role of bad governance in Russia in its assault on Ukraine from the scholarly perspective of the political economy of war.[15] After analyzing the impact of bad governance on policy-making in Russia, especially with regard to foreign, military, and security policy issues, I will focus on the consequences of bad governance for Russia's performance before and during its "special military operation" in Ukraine and attempts to resolve the problem of bad governance at the cost of weakening the Russian state. Some broader implications of the causes and effects of bad governance on international politics in Russia and beyond will be discussed in the conclusion.

Introduction: Why Bad Governance?

As I previously stated elsewhere, the politico-economic order of bad governance includes several major attributes:

(1) a lack of the rule of law and/or perversion of its basic principles;
(2) a high degree of corruption, which penetrates all layers of governance;
(3) a combination of high density, poor quality and selective implementation of state regulations; and
(4) general government ineffectiveness, except for certain crucial policy areas and/or priority projects and programs.[16]

These attributes are not just manifestations of gross violations of the principles of good governance,[17] but rather, major foundations of a distinctive politico-economic order that is based on a set of formal and informal rules, norms, and practices quite different from the norms of good governance. Some countries are intentionally governed badly because their political leaders establish and maintain rules, norms, and practices that serve their own interests. These foundations are treated as de facto "rules-in-use,"[18] serving as key institutional arrangements of the politico-economic order that sets the framework and mechanisms for governing the state. Among these mechanisms, the following are of utmost importance:

(1) Rent extraction is the main goal and substantive purpose of governing the state at all levels of authority.
(2) The mechanism of governing the state tends toward a hierarchy (the "power vertical") with only one major center of decision-making, which claims a monopoly on political power (the "single power pyramid").[19]
(3) The autonomy of domestic political and economic actors vis-à-vis this center is conditional; it can be reduced and/or abolished at any given moment.
(4) The formal institutions that define the framework of power and governance are arranged as by-products of the distribution of resources within the power vertical: they matter as rules of the game only to the degree to which they contribute to rent-seeking (or at least do not prevent it).
(5) The power apparatus within the power vertical is divided into several organized groups and/or informal cliques, which compete with one another for access to rents.[20]

Bad governance is by no means a country-specific and context-bounded phenomenon of present-day Russia. Rather, it is a natural outcome of the unconstrained behavior of ruling elites, who aim at the maximization of rents. Their drive contributes to consistent building of institutions such as corruption,[21] poor regulations,[22] and the unrule of law,[23] which maintain a socially inefficient equilibrium in order to serve the vested interests of actors with strong bargaining power.[24] This is why bad governance is a functional, purpose-built, and even acceptable mechanism for many (if not most) political and economic actors, at least as a short-term solution. It is a primarily agency-driven rather than structure-induced phenomenon, and there is no reason to consider bad governance in any given country (including Russia) to be inevitable. Indeed, bad governance is created and maintained by individuals who have strong temptations to exploit their power for private purposes. If these individuals do not face insurmountable constraints, they may impose such a mechanism on society. Although bad governance has emerged and developed in various countries, ranging from post-Soviet Central

Asia to sub-Saharan Africa,[25] in Russia the negative consequences of bad governance have been especially devastating. They have not only contributed to numerous instances of mismanagement in Russian state-owned companies (such as Rostec or Russian Railways)[26] and blatant cases of corruption in the state order and procurement systems, but also played a major role in the Russian state's inefficient response to the COVID-19 pandemic. The pandemic caused extraordinary excess mortality among Russian citizens, exceeding 1 million lives, one of the highest rates among developed countries globally (despite relatively developed public health infrastructure, facilities and practices).

However, the great paradox of bad governance in Russia and elsewhere is that it does not always lead to a total decay and degradation of the state. The appointment of well-qualified technocrats and their relative autonomy in policy-making, at least in some crucially important policy areas, has often served as a major fool-proofing mechanism, which helps to avoid major state failures through prudent technocratic solutions. Such good examples, labeled in the literature as "pockets of effectiveness" or "pockets of efficiency,"[27] have been distinctly visible in Russia. The efficient tax reform in the early 2000s provided a solid fiscal basis for the Russian economy for decades,[28] while the highly professional monetary policy of the Russian Central Bank[29] diminished many negative effects of the global financial crisis in 2008–9,[30] and helped to avoid other major crises in the following period. Still, the problem of these and other "pockets of efficiency" in Russia is poor institutionalization: their performance is highly contingent on the priorities of the political leadership and its patronage. As such, these technocrats can be sacrificed at any given moment, even though their skills are often highly valued by the state authorities, especially in the wake of crises and conflicts.[31] According to media reports, after the beginning of the Russian assault on Ukraine, the presidential administration applied serious pressure on top professionals in key ministries and state agencies in order to avoid their resignations.[32] Apart from persuasion, threats of criminal cases against certain technocrats and their family members were effectively used to prevent such developments, which would have been potentially dangerous for the Russian state's performance amid an ongoing "special military operation."[33]

While it is difficult to measure and compare the negative effects of bad governance across policy areas in various states, to suggest that it has especially negative consequences for broadly defined foreign, military, and security policies and related policy areas (such as military-related industries) in Russia would not be a wild exaggeration. First, these policy areas are greatly affected by the veil of secrecy, which has enabled sectoral lobbyists to pursue their primary goals of maximization of both budgets and slack and effectively avoid external quality control by the relevant state agencies. Even the Ministry of Foreign Affairs, though less secretive than other state agencies such as the Ministry of Defense or the Federal Security Service, effectively insulated itself from political and bureaucratic accountability.[34] Second, as stated in chapter 1, during Putin's reign, *siloviki* played increasingly important roles in politics and policy-making.[35] These actors expanded their influence far beyond their narrowly defined niches and also became the most voracious rent-seekers in the country.[36] At the same time, political and/or civilian control over these sectors of the Russian state was limited, and these agencies were basically left to their own devices. Third, the top-down hierarchical institutional organization of the state agencies in charge of these policies was aimed at achieving limited quantifiable numbers in key performance indicators in their divisions and branches at any cost, and not much addressed to overall achievement of policy goals.[37] As a result, these segments of the Russian state apparatus became a well-oiled machine out of control. In the Russian context, "well-oiled" also reflects the tremendous role of oil-related revenues in Russia's economy and society,[38] including their impact on Russia's aggressive foreign policy.[39]

Several in-depth studies of coercive agencies of the Russian state (such as the police, courts, state watchdogs, and the like), conducted by the Institute for the Rule of Law at the European University at St. Petersburg, revealed a rather gloomy picture.[40] These agencies demonstrated organizational inertia, non-transparent recruitment and promotion of personnel, the ineffectiveness of both positive and negative incentives for improvement of their performance, and overall resistance to reforms. Undoubtedly, various other state agencies in Russia face similar problems. Moreover, the relatively high fragmentation of the coercive apparatus of the state and fierce competition for resources and influence between various agencies in charge of military and security policy, while serving as a coup prevention mechanism, also contribute to the inefficiency of these agencies and their poor coordination. This is why the badly-governed Russian state and most parts of its coercive apparatus aimed at preservation of the status quo rather than meaningful changes, and were poorly prepared for major challenges – including, but not limited to, the assault on Ukraine and the following protracted military conflict.

Reforms and Entrenchments of Russian Bad Governance

Although the Russian political leadership is genuinely interested in efficient conduct of its foreign, military, and security policies, its attempts to implement major changes face serious constraints. The problem is that the personalist authoritarian regime vitally needs the loyalty of its coercive apparatus, and certainly prioritizes this goal over efficiency in the wake of domestic political challenges, let alone major international conflicts. At the same time, the low rotation of powerful elites, especially within the coercive apparatus, greatly contributes to increasing the longevity of autocracies, and serves as an additional reason for state agencies to preserve the status quo. It is no wonder that this approach of "cadre stability" (the slogan initially promoted by the Soviet leader Leonid Brezhnev in his informal deal with Communist Party elites in the 1960s–1970s)[41] played an important role in further entrenchment of elites within the Russian state apparatus.[42] For example, the Russian Foreign Minister Sergey Lavrov has held his current post since 2004, and the head of the Federal Security Service Alexander Bortnikov has occupied his position since 2008. Such a practice provides perverse incentives for sectoral power verticals in state agencies, which tend to resist any organizational and/or institutional changes, even if these changes are initiated by the political leadership. These changes, irrespective of the good or bad intentions of policy reforms, are widely considered through the lenses of redistribution of rents and resources and perceived by entrenched bureaucrats in an exclusively negative light. While in socio-economic policy areas technocratic experts endorsed by the political leadership may sometimes receive sweeping mandates for policy changes, such bold moves are often taboo in the politically sensitive foreign, military, and security policy areas because the risks associated with disloyalty are overly high. This is why bad governance in these sectors, although it causes major misconduct and inefficiency, has often flourished over time against the wishes of the Kremlin.

The most vivid example of unsuccessful policy change has probably been the police reform initiated under Dmitry Medvedev's presidency, as convincingly analyzed by Brian Taylor.[43] Even though Medvedev declared the development of the rule of law and the creation of efficient law enforcement agencies to be his main priorities, the launch of the police reform in 2009 did not bring about any significant effects. This failure was caused not only by resistance from influential *siloviki* in the presidential administration and in the Ministry of the Interior and by Medvedev's inability to build a successful pro-reform coalition among non-*siloviki* officials. The rise of public protests, including rallies against the fraudulent State Duma elections in 2011, also greatly affected the political leadership's priorities and placed the loyalty of the coercive apparatus at the top of the policy agenda. In essence, the development and implementation of the police reform (including the reduction in the number of servants, personnel changes, and a structural reorganization of agencies) were performed by the Ministry of the Interior officials themselves. The problem was that the ministry's officials were the least interested actors when it came to genuine change. As a result, the only visible effect of the reform was the change of the title *militsiya* to *politsiya* ("police"). The numerous reshufflings among the midlevel officials were insignificant, and soon after its start, the reform came to a halt. The failure of the police reform demonstrates that policies implemented by an entrenched bureaucracy do not allow for provision of incentives for real change, but often support the status quo. In practice, the police remained an inefficient agency oriented around presenting appropriate statistical reports irrespective of the real situation regarding crime.

Yet not all policy reforms in politically sensitive policy areas in Russia are doomed to fail, although their consequences may sometimes turn the situation from bad to worse. The Russian military analyst Alexander Golts has presented a vivid example of policy advancement in a rather unlikely environment in his perceptive account of the partially successful military reform in Russia in 2008–12.[44] After a series of replacements of top officials who had done little to restructure the post-Soviet army and attempted to preserve the oversized, inefficient, and costly performance of the Russian military, in 2007 Putin surprisingly appointed Anatoly Serdyukov, the son-in-law of then-Prime Minister Viktor Zubkov, to be the new Minister of Defense. His tenure began with the Russian military conflict with Georgia, the episode known as the Five-Day War in August

2008.⁴⁵ This conflict demonstrated that the Russian army was not properly prepared for major ground operations due to technological obsoleteness and poor management and personnel quality. Although the Five-Day War was perceived as a Russian victory, in a sense this experience became a major exogenous shock that paved the way to serious reorganization of the military. Serdyukov came to the right job at the right time. He received carte blanche for many actions, laid off many generals and officers (overall, almost 200,000 personnel were cut), reorganized divisions and battalions, restructured the chain of command to make it more modern and efficient, and greatly diminished the number of conscripts in favor of professional military personnel (*kontraktniki*). All of this had been unthinkable for many would-be military reformers after the Soviet collapse, but the political will and patronage of the leadership, alongside perceptions of the urgent necessity of policy reforms, served as major arguments for Serdyukov.⁴⁶ In a way, such an approach followed the logic of technocratic changes in socio-economic policy domains in Russia.

To some extent, Serdyukov was able to achieve his goals despite fierce resistance from the military bureaucracy and its numerous lobbyists. However, his reform plans also included the outsourcing of many non-essential services previously performed by the military itself (ranging from construction to catering) away from the insiders of the Ministry of Defense and into the hands of external contractors. He also attempted to review the practices of state procurement for the military to combat overpricing of arms and equipment. Such bold moves would inevitably mean a major redistribution of rents and hurt the vital interests of many powerful interest groups. It is no surprise that in 2012 Serdyukov fell victim to a major scandal: an investigation against him was opened amid accusations of adultery with an alleged mistress, Evgeniya Vasilyeva, who headed a major department in the ministry. According to some accounts, however, the attack on Serdyukov was caused not by any misconduct but rather by his alleged disloyalty to Putin at the time of his job swap with Medvedev when Putin announced his decision to return to the presidential post in September 2011 and implemented it in March 2012. Serdyukov was fired, although his criminal case was closed after a lengthy process.

Although Serdyukov's military reform bore significant fruits, greatly contributing to the more efficient performance of the Russian army during the annexation of Crimea in 2014 and military adventures in Syria in 2015–16, its effects were partial and short-lived.[47] Serdyukov's core reforms were weakened and revised after he was replaced by Putin's long-term associate and unconditional loyalist Sergey Shoigu. The latter, upon his ascendance to the Ministry of Defense, not only appointed his personal cronies (such as Timur Ivanov) to key positions in related areas, but also terminated some of his predecessor's reforms (such as changes in military education aimed at major reorganization of specialized military colleges).[48] Shoigu also redirected the flows of state contracts and procurements (as well as of related rents) to a new pool of beneficiaries. As a result, personnel replacement and inconsistent policy changes turned the ministry into a conglomerate of competing cliques hardly productive for military policy. Furthermore, Shoigu was not a particularly competent manager (previously, he had served as the Minister of Emergency Situations and later as governor of Moscow Oblast) but a very efficient promoter in terms of public relations campaigns. He invested major efforts into constructing a heroic image of himself as the brilliant leader of an invincible, well-equipped and well-prepared army, which was presented to both the Russian political leadership and the general public as the "second greatest army in the world" (after the US military) – although the reality was very different from this glamorous picture. Against the background of very close and long-term personal connections between Shoigu and Putin (they often spent vacations together in some remote areas of Siberia), these efforts improved Shoigu's credentials in the eyes of the president,[49] but were hardly productive for the actual capability and performance of the Russian military. To summarize, one might argue that the partial reforms had major distortive effects on further developments of the Russian military,[50] contributing to wrong expectations and inefficient governance.

Bad Governance Goes to the Front

In the process of preparation for the Russian assault on Ukraine, the politico-economic order of bad governance affected the Russian state's performance in two different but related ways. First, it provided strong incentives for intentional misinformation of superiors within the power vertical. The above-mentioned Avtomatika case was just the tip of the iceberg, as such stories of rent-seeking and corruption were far from unusual. While the management of several companies of the Rostec holding was accused of bribery, embezzlement of funds, and other mismanagement affairs, its CEO Sergey Chemezov, a friend of Putin since their service in the KGB in East Germany during the 1980s, hid his money, luxury yacht, and Spanish villa by registering them with offshore companies.[51] Apart from that, however, the intentional distortion of information was driven by risk-averse behavior of officials who did not want to spread bad news to the top layers of the power vertical. During the COVID-19 pandemic, the Russian regional authorities systematically reported low numbers of casualties and sometimes even encouraged their subordinates to misreport. According to some accounts, this approach was driven by the Kremlin's fear that the availability of bad news about the grim number of victims of the pandemic could undermine public support for Putin (even though survey data did not demonstrate any such thing).[52] Nevertheless, in the case of the pandemic, this distortion of information was identified by independent data analysts: they compared official numbers with state mortality statistics and found striking irregularities.[53] Meanwhile, the veil of secrecy, which covered foreign, military, and security policy, helped the respective agencies to hide bad news or not report it at all. This is why the production of fake statistics (which was originally typical for the Russian police) became a nearly ubiquitous practice for Russian state agencies in these policy areas. Fitting the data to a predetermined result desired by superiors became a trademark of their policy planning.[54] At the same time, the veil of secrecy was instrumental for state officials in these policy areas, as it enabled them to hide many blatant episodes of corruption. The case of Timur Ivanov and his ex-wife became highly visible only because of her conspicuous consumption style and her boastful behavior on social media. However, many similar cases of top-level corruption remain invisible and most probably will not be disclosed until the dismantling of high-level political patronage.

Second, the top-down nature of sectoral power verticals within the Russian state amid the lack of transparency and accountability of government agencies contributed to reverse flows of information. Instead of signaling the top layers of power verticals about real or potential problems in certain policy areas, low-level officials just reproduced their superiors' official narratives. Boris Bondarev, a former Russian diplomat at the United Nations office in Geneva who resigned from his post some months after the beginning of the assault on Ukraine, vividly described these practices as parroting the Ministry of Foreign Affairs even in minor details.[55] His bosses, for instance, were not allowed to correct any typos made in documents by the ministry, while their main demands focused on conveying the ministry's official position to authorities in foreign states rather than on information gathering abroad. It is no wonder that many Russian diplomats tend to isolate themselves into echo chambers produced by their superiors. As a result, they have gradually lost their capacity for professional analysis, essential for foreign policy-making. In other words, under conditions of bad governance, foreign policy expertise was replaced by the Kremlin's advocacy, if not by propaganda. This was especially true for expertise on Ukraine, which was largely driven by the Russian leadership's numerous misperceptions about the country (outlined in detail in chapter 4), rather than by professional knowledge.

Although foreign policy expertise in Russia is based on quite a developed infrastructure, its quality and impact on Russian policy-making have been relatively negligible and rather dubious. Despite the fact that some institutions of the Russian Academy of Science had an extensive knowledge base in area studies, the primary institution in charge, the Moscow State Institute of International Relations, worked under the auspices of the Ministry of Foreign Affairs (with its graduates occupying prestigious positions in the ministry), followed its policy guidelines and avoided any criticism of superiors. In the 1990s, the Council for Foreign and Defense Policy independent think tank (modeled after the Council of Foreign Relations in the US) was established with the mission to assist the development and implementation of Russia's strategies in the relevant policy areas. However, over time the policy positions of the Council and its bosses (first, Sergey Karaganov, and since 2012, Fyodor Lukyanov) became more and more anti-Western and hawkish.[56] Moreover, since 2004, the Council has mostly concentrated on the Valdai Club project – a major propagandist show organized by the Kremlin for numerous Western experts in international affairs and Russian studies. During its annual gatherings, Russian top officials, including Putin, visited this forum and used it to publicly advance the Kremlin's narratives and recruit allies among Western scholars and journalists (the Valdai Club lavishly covered their trips to and stays in Russia and also offered them grants).[57] In a similar way, the Council's bimonthly journal, *Russia in Global Affairs* (modeled after the *Foreign Affairs* journal in the US), published both in Russian and in English, started in 2002 and initially served as a forum for the exchange of foreign policy ideas between Russian and Western intellectuals.[58] Later on, it became a mouthpiece for the Kremlin's propaganda. At the same time, Russian foreign policy experts attempted to increase their influence and increasingly offered the Kremlin the most hawkish and militant policy recommendations. Although attempts to influence foreign policy-making are typical for many foreign policy experts and think tanks in various countries (both in democracies and in non-democracies), the Valdai Club and other Russian foreign policy experts often substituted heavily-biased punditry and promotion of the most outrageous foreign policy proposals for evidence-based expertise. In June 2023, *Russia in Global Affairs* proudly published an article by Karaganov featuring a suggestion to the Kremlin to pre-emptively use nuclear weapons against Poland.[59] In essence, the Council turned into a major propagandist tool and an active warmonger of the Kremlin and lost its intellectual credibility in independent and impartial foreign policy expertise.

These practices of Russian foreign policy expertise were in sharp contrast with socio-economic policy, where open policy discussions had been quite intensive since the late 1980s and involved not only academics but also key official decision-makers (and some Russian economists, such as Yegor Gaidar or Yevgeny Yasin, combined both roles at certain times). These heated and extensive discussions, described by Joachim Zweynert as tensions between economic "liberals" and "statists," represented diverse viewpoints and policy recommendations and continued in major public gatherings such as the annual Gaidar Forum, as well as in media outlets (including op-eds in major newspapers).[60] Numerous economic think tanks organized under the auspices of the Russian state, on the basis of both universities and independent entities, were involved in socio-economic policy-making in Russia, though not always successfully.[61] More importantly, these discussions influenced important policy changes, such as tax reform, monetary policy, establishment and use of the Stabilization Fund, etc. This is why the quality of Russian socio-economic policy after the end of the protracted transformation recession in 1998 was fairly high, and it helped to avoid major policy failures during the period of rapid economic growth in the 2000s and in the wake of the global financial crisis of 2008–9. In these policy areas, there was no room for major secrecy (even though increasing military- and security-related budgetary expenditures were, and remain, non-transparent and non-observable for experts), and the pluralism of ideas, interests, and institutions, which became rooted in the field, provided a necessary infrastructure. By contrast, foreign policy has almost universally been considered the exclusive domain of the Kremlin since Soviet times, and open criticism of official foreign policy guidelines is not much welcomed in expertise and recommendations. Thus, foreign policy expertise in Russia is mostly performed as ideological framing of an official discourse full of anti-Western rhetoric,[62] rather than as independent and high-quality scholarly analysis.[63] Meanwhile, it is necessary to admit that military and security policy in Russia has rarely become a matter for public discussion at all. Policy expertise in these areas is confined to state-related organizations, affiliated with respective state agencies: the insiders of these organizations, however, largely reflect the preferences and interests of their superiors, while independent experts play almost no role in policy-making.

It comes as no surprise that reverse flows of information and replacement of expertise by advocacy and propaganda were hardly conducive for fool-proofing in Russian foreign, military, and security policy before the assault on Ukraine. Even though there was a number of technocratic-minded professionals in the relevant policy areas, over time they converted themselves into the Kremlin's "yes-men," as Bondarev put it with regard to Russian diplomacy.[64] As a result, Russian foreign, military, and security policy was mostly driven by the personal preferences of a personalist leader under conditions of poor regime institutionalization, while bad governance contributed to perverse incentives among state bureaucrats. They intended to please their superiors at any cost – by providing incorrect and/or distorted information and by thoughtlessly implementing top-down policy directives – at the expense of policy outcomes in the future. Thus, bad governance in Russia multiplied the negative effects of wrong moves by the political leadership at the stage of policy planning and preparing to assault. "Yes-men" (and women) in the relevant state agencies at best remained passive and incapable in the wake of these preparations or even prepared themselves for an easy victory over Ukraine and for increasing access to new sources of rents after this victory.

It is no wonder that during the period before the assault on Ukraine and at the beginning of the "special military operation"

Russian state agencies made extremely poor decisions in terms of both foreign policy and military planning. In the foreign policy arena, not only did Putin ultimately reject any bilateral negotiations with Zelensky (mostly because of his feeling of personal offense),[65] but he also addressed his Ukraine-related grievances to the US leadership. The Russian leadership openly denied Ukraine's political agency and perceived it as an American client state,[66] very much along the lines of the cornerstone principles of Russian foreign policy outlined in chapter 1. Furthermore, instead of any serious negotiations with the United States about policy towards Ukraine and its possible security status (including NATO membership), in December 2021 the Russian leadership presented a far-reaching ultimatum to the US, demanding numerous one-sided concessions and legally binding security guarantees for Russia. Among others, Russia's demands included a return to the pre-1997 boundaries of NATO (before its territorial expansion into Eastern Europe) and a ban on any further NATO activities in Eastern Europe, Central Asia, and the Caucasus.[67] At the same time, Russia demonstrated no willingness to offer any concessions to the US in exchange and did not even consider other contested issues as potential bargaining chips. Such an "all-or-nothing" proposal was certainly unacceptable to American state officials and did not leave room for any further negotiations, assuming an unrealistic unilateral surrender by the US as the only possible outcome. This move openly contradicted any Diplomacy 101 textbook and was definitely counterproductive in terms of its political consequences, as it only fueled preparations by the US and its allies (including Ukraine) for Russia's military attacks.

One might argue that this ultimatum, useless in practical terms, served the purposes of demonstrating Russia's toughness, decisiveness, and assertiveness to both domestic and international audiences. Such an approach was proposed by the Security Council of Russia (heavily staffed by hawkish security officers),[68] rather than by the Ministry of Foreign Affairs. This major foreign policy shift did not only indicate that Patrushev, known for his reactionary worldviews and adherence to conspiracy theories, had an upper hand in Russian foreign policy-making,[69] while Lavrov performed a subordinated role at best. It also meant that diplomacy as such was no longer considered a major instrument of Russian foreign policy; diplomats converted themselves into propagandists, and the use of negotiations was replaced with threats of use of military force. The problem, however, was that these military threats were not sufficiently credible in the eyes of Russia's adversaries (even when Russia attempted to raise the possible use of nuclear weapons as its last resort). At the same time, the Russian military, despite loud propaganda and a carefully crafted image of nearly-omnipotent might, was insufficiently prepared to defeat Ukraine.[70]

With regard to military planning, the overly high hopes of the Russian leadership were dashed after the first Russian attacks. At the beginning of the Russian assault on February 24, 2022, some Western military observers discussed whether the Ukrainian capital Kyiv would be conquered by Russian troops during the first 72 or 96 hours of attacks.[71] In fact, however, Kyiv was not conquered at all for many reasons, including poor Russian military planning and implementation. In a way, the very design of the Russian "special military operation" of February 2022 copy-pasted the Soviet "special military operation" in Czechoslovakia in August 1968 (briefly covered in chapter 2). According to the initial plan, special divisions of Russian paratroopers were to be massively deployed to the Hostomel airfield, northwest of Kyiv, where they would easily break through to the capital and soon establish their control over major targets and key locations in Kyiv (similarly to the 1968 Operation Danube in Prague). At the same time, Russian tanks should quickly approach Kyiv from the north and northeast without any serious resistance. In reality, Russian paratroopers' advance was stopped and they were surrounded near the airfield, unable to quickly break through to the city, diving only to face a protracted battle on the ground. Russian tank brigades were stretched over dozens of kilometers of roads northwest of Kyiv, where they were attacked by the Ukrainian army as they tried to advance and from the rear.[72] Not only were Russian military commanders on the battlefield unprepared for severe resistance by Ukrainians, but the top military commanders, led by the Chief of the General Staff army general Valery Gerasimov also did not expect such an outcome. They were so confident with regard to coming military success that they did not prepare a detailed "Plan B" in case of major problems with the initial plan. According to some journalist accounts, the Russian military so casually expected a swift and victorious outcome of the "special military operation," to culminate in the form of a parade of the Russian army down the major Kyiv avenue Khreshatyk, that some senior officers even took a special dress uniform with them for such a celebration.[73] The result, however, was the opposite: Russian troops were stopped at the Kyiv suburbs, the battle in the vicinity of the Ukrainian capital continued for almost five weeks, and by the end of March 2022, the Russian military was forced to retreat towards the Ukrainian borders with Russia and Belarus.

In essence, the first stage of the Russian "special military operation" failed largely because of the poor planning and inefficient conduct of the Russian military, caused by bad governance in the country in general and in its foreign, military, and security policy in particular. Unconditional loyalty among Russian officials and experts-turned-propagandists dominated over efficiency, and many vices of the Russian state agencies and their top officials, previously hidden beneath the veil of secrecy, were revealed soon after the assault on Ukraine. Only several weeks before the assault had some dissenting voices among the Russian military openly broken the silence, and sent some warning signals about the real state of affairs and the army's unpreparedness for a "special military operation" against Ukraine. In January 2022, retired colonel general Leonid Ivashov, the head of the All-Russian Assembly of Military Officers, known for his heavily anti-Western and ultra-conservative political stances, published his manifesto, *The Eve of War*, on the Assembly website. In this piece, he openly called for a rejection of the use of military force against Ukraine. Ivashov condemned "the failure of Russian foreign policy, and the unattractiveness of its domestic politics" and argued that Russia could encounter not only the Ukrainian army but also NATO troops, and that failures on the battlefield could cause major domestic political instability and even put an end to Russia as a state and nation.[74] On February 3, 2022, three weeks before the assault, Mikhail Khodarenok, a colonel of the Russian army and the former top official in the main operational department of the General Staff, published an op-ed piece with a strong criticism of the forecasts of a swift and nearly bloodless conquest of Ukraine by the Russian military. His list of counter-arguments against such optimistic expectations included warnings about the limited capacity of the Russian military, which was insufficient for one-off total elimination of the Ukrainian army, underestimation of Ukrainian military potential, prospects of extensive supply of arms to Ukraine by the US and its NATO allies, and risk of guerilla war in Russian-occupied Ukraine territory. At the end of his piece, Khodarenok stated: "military conflict with Ukraine nowadays would work against

Russia's national interests."[75] Yet these warnings came too late and had too little effect. By that time, the key drivers of the badly-governed Russian state machinery were unwilling and even unable to apply the brakes. The road to Russia's failed attack in February 2022 was paved not only by Putin (although he played a major role in the military assault on Ukraine), but by the entire state apparatus in charge of Russian foreign, military, and security policy. However, once this road was taken in February 2022 and the pernicious effects of the political decision on military assault became apparent, Russian state officials realized that there was no way out.

Circumventing Bad Governance: The Case of the Wagner Group

For a long period of time, Russian state authorities have attempted to compensate for numerous vices of bad governance through establishment and maintenance of "pockets of efficiency." These state-led projects and programs, staffed by well-qualified professionals and based upon top-level patronage by the political leadership, receive priority supply of financial and material resources and operate under different rules and regulations from the standard organizational and institutional routines of other agencies, projects, and programs conducted by the Russian state. Sometimes, when the special conditions of "pockets of efficiency" are fortunate enough to meet with good examples of policy entrepreneurship among their top managers, these ventures may become major "success stories" – bright but often short-lived advancements with highly visible performance in a policy field. Numerous instances of these success stories in Russia, ranging from the Soviet space program in the 1950s–1960s to post-Soviet development of the Higher School of Economics, the newly built prestigious state university, which became a major Russian hub in social science and humanities during the 2000s–2010s, serve as prominent illustrations of this phenomenon.[76]

From a functional viewpoint, "pockets of efficiency" under bad governance perform a dubious role. Their positioning vis-à-vis ordinary state agencies, projects, and programs appears neither like substitution nor like full-scale complementarity. They do not replace existing organizations but also do not work as welcome additions. Rather, these "pockets of efficiency" and their policy entrepreneurs compete with other organizations and their top managers for scarce resources and top-level patronage by the political leadership. Moreover, even if and when "pockets of efficiency" achieve outstanding performance, the contagion effects of transfer of their best practices to other organizations are often limited. In essence, the role of "pockets of efficiency" may be best described as a circumvention of the routines of bad governance, which may make it possible to resolve certain policy issues and avoid risks of major failures (the Central Bank of Russia may serve as a prime example here) but cannot improve the overall quality of governance beyond their niches. This circumvention may at best provide a partial and temporary solution, but in the worst case may aggravate previously existing problems.

By autumn 2022, the Russian assault on Ukraine had seemingly come to a dead end. Russian advancement at the frontline eventually stopped during summer 2022, and later on Ukrainian forces launched a counter-offensive, taking back many areas in the Kharkiv and Kherson regions. Although major mobilization of Russian conscripts in September–October 2022 made it possible to stop Ukrainian breakthroughs and close the holes at the frontline, it was conducted poorly in terms of supplies for those drafted into the army (their families were even forced to buy some ammunition themselves) and, more importantly, in terms of the unpopularity of these decisions among Russians.[77] This is why large-scale mobilization was a one-off event, and the Russian political leadership attempted to avoid repeating this experience, and instead promoted recruitment of volunteers to the front. Despite the fact that the Russian state offered volunteers rather high salaries (about $2300 per month by autumn 2022, while the average monthly salary in the country was about $730), the inflow of new soldiers was limited, while military performance at the frontline raised many questions.[78] Although no further Ukrainian counter-offensives were observed until the summer of 2023, the Russian political leadership critically needed more "success stories" on the frontline. However, it became clear that existing military units were not able to achieve these goals. Their limited technical capability and insufficient supply of arms were combined with the vices of bad governance in Russia. Top military commanders and field officers lacked incentives for further risky offensive operations and attempts at territorial advancement, and preferred to maintain the status quo on the frontline in the manner of a nearly endless war of attrition. This is why the Kremlin opted for an alternative solution and endorsed the making of a new "pocket of efficiency" on the battlefield.

This alternative solution had a relatively long pre-history. In 2014, the private military company Wagner (also known as the Wagner Group), was founded by an officer of the Main Intelligence Directorate of the General Staff (GRU), Dmitry Utkin, and the businessman Yevgeny Prigozhin. Wagner first gained visibility during the Donbas War in Ukraine in 2014–15, when it helped pro-Russian separatists, but later on gained major global recognition during several violent conflicts around the world, including the civil wars in Syria, Libya, Mali, and the Central African Republic.[79] In these conflicts, Wagner mercenaries battled on the pro-Russian sides and were covertly supported by the Russian state, which provided Wagnerites with funding, arms, and other supplies. Wagner mercenaries were accused of committing numerous war crimes but in many ways their actions were instrumental to Russia's foreign policy goals, assisting the Kremlin in countering Western influence, supporting local autocrats, and gaining access to natural resources in Africa. In effect, the Russian state outsourced its functions on the international arena to the private company, which operated beyond any legal framework and performed under the Kremlin's informal patronage. It served as a proxy for the Russian government, allowing the Russian state to have plausible deniability for military operations abroad, and enabled it to hide the violence caused by Russia's foreign interventions.[80]

While the "Wagner" title was derived from Utkin's personal call sign, used in phone conversations, the group's main driving force was Prigozhin, a key figure in many Wagner activities over a long period of time. A native of Leningrad, in the early 1980s he was imprisoned with a long sentence for robbery, theft, fraud, and involving minors in criminal activity. Upon release from prison in the early 1990s, Prigozhin founded various businesses and owned several restaurants in St. Petersburg. In the 2000s, he became close to Vladimir Putin, who was a frequent customer of his restaurants and even celebrated one of his birthdays there. These connections helped Prigozhin to obtain numerous government contracts for one of his companies, Concord, which became a major supplier of meals for the Russian military, schoolchildren, and government workers (including catering for banquets at the Kremlin). Prigozhin invested some of his profits into his media project, the Internet Research Agency, dubbed a "troll farm."[81] This company specialized in online propaganda and influence operations on behalf of Russian business and political interests. Among other things, it was engaged in numerous online and offline campaigns aimed at undermining the political foundations of the Western establishment, including organized support for Brexit in the UK and interference in the 2016 presidential election in the US, where Russia supported Donald Trump's campaign. Although assessments of the efficacy of these trolls varied greatly,[82] Prigozhin gained major domestic and international recognition and was widely perceived as a mastermind of Russian actions abroad.[83] By the late 2010s, Prigozhin had greatly expanded his media empire, and attempted to affect domestic politics in St. Petersburg: he came into open conflict with city governor Alexander Beglov (a trusted personal ally of Putin since the 1990s), but failed to achieve his dismissal or resignation.[84]

The launching of the Russian "special military operation" in Ukraine in 2022 opened a new window of opportunity for Prigozhin and Wagner. Prigozhin not only expanded recruitment of mercenaries, but also, most importantly, persuaded the Kremlin to turn Wagner into a real private army, de facto autonomous from the Russian state and controlled by its boss. This practice was somewhat similar to that of several African states, such as Sudan with its Rapid Support Forces.[85] Prigozhin received a chance to recruit inmates from Russian prisons to Wagner. In return for agreeing to fight in Ukraine, the criminals were promised a shortening of their sentences and monetary remuneration (officially, ex-prisoners recruited to Wagner were pardoned by secret presidential decrees). According to some accounts, Prigozhin himself came to prisons by helicopter, gave emotive talks before prisoners, and promised them a release to freedom after six months of fighting in Ukraine.[86] This recruitment greatly bolstered the size of the Wagner troops, which, according to some estimates, had about 50,000 fighters in Ukraine by the end of 2022 (including 40,000 convicts). As Wagner had a priority supply of funding, arms, and other resources from the Russian state, and was heavily staffed by former staff of the GRU and other coercive state agencies, it became a very powerful actor on the battlefield. Wagner operated at the frontline independently from the units belonging to the Ministry of Defense, and actively participated in several battles, including the long-lasting battles for Soledar (August 2022–January 2023) and Bakhmut (roughly August 2022–May 2023). Despite severe resistance from Ukrainian military forces, Wagner was able to claim victory in both of these battles and widely reported it as "liberation," positioning Prigozhin as a highly effective military commander in the eyes of Russian elites and the general public (even though the military importance of these victories was not particularly high). It is very difficult to measure the effectiveness of Wagner troops on the battlefield, given the fact that the number of casualties among ex-prisoners was staggeringly high, and the casualty rate among Wagner troops was up to 50%. Nevertheless, from September 2022 to May 2023, Wagner troops seized more Ukrainian territory than all of the units belonging to the Ministry of Defense put together.[87] This perceived "success story" amid continued bad governance in the Russian military further fueled Prigozhin's increasing political ambitions. In this respect, his widely advertised tours across Russia's provinces may even have been laying foundations for a future presidential campaign.

In the wake of the battle for Bakhmut, Prigozhin became a major public figure using his own media resources and Telegram channels, as well as a network of military bloggers, and used these opportunities for open criticism of Shoigu and Gerasimov. He not only requested better supply of arms from the Ministry of Defense but also accused them of misinforming Putin about the real state of affairs in Ukraine before the assault in February 2022 (indirectly, his criticism was addressed at Putin as well). According to Prigozhin's claims, although Russia was poorly prepared for the "special military operation," which was unnecessary in the first place and did not achieve its goals, it should have achieved military victory anyway. Shoigu, in turn, asked Putin to integrate private military companies (first and foremost, Wagner) under the control of the Ministry of Defense by July 2023. Prigozhin ultimately rejected this demand and continued his public criticism of Shoigu, gaining even broader public recognition and support from various segments of the Russian coercive apparatus.[88] Finally, on June 23, 2023, Prigozhin announced that units controlled by the Ministry of Defense had shelled Wagner's positions in Donbas, and asked Putin to fire Shoigu and Gerasimov immediately. Prigozhin sent his troops into the city of Rostov, Shoigu's supposed location (reportedly, he left the city just before Wagner's raid) and soon took over the city center, including the headquarters of the North Caucasus Military District of the Russian army. Furthermore, against the background of Putin's public appearance on TV, where he denounced this mutiny and appealed to the loyalty of the military and security apparatus, Wagner troops marched more than 400 kilometers towards Moscow, meeting little resistance from the military, police, and other coercive agencies. Almost nobody wanted to protect the previous status quo, while some Rostov residents enthusiastically endorsed Prigozhin's mutiny, and some top military officers, upset by Shoigu and Gerasimov's ineffective leadership, covertly endorsed it. Wagner's march on Moscow, labeled a "march for justice" by Prigozhin, stopped only after a series of informal negotiations with top members of Putin's entourage (with the President of Belarus, Alexander Lukashenko, allegedly serving as Putin's representative).[89] Afterwards, Prigozhin and Wagner received an offer to relocate to Belarus without any punishment, Prigozhin's money (including 10 billion rubles, or about $110 million, seized in cash in his office) remained untouched, and his media empire was soon destroyed by Prigozhin himself.[90] Many observers were surprised that Prigozhin received no immediate punishment for his mutiny; however, it was merely delayed. In August 2023, Prigozhin, Utkin and some of their associates died in a plane crash under suspicious circumstances.[91] Afterwards, the Wagner combat divisions were absorbed by the Russian National Guard, and its military units in Africa were taken over by the Ministry of Defense. In the end, Prigozhin's mutiny had no direct effect on the "special military operation," but demonstrated the fragility of the Russian state and of its attempts to circumvent its problems of bad governance. The very existence of the inefficient Russian state machinery was threatened during Prigozhin's mutiny, even though these threats did not materialize.[92]

One might argue that the rise and fall of Prigozhin and the Wagner Group were instrumental for the Kremlin. On the one hand, the Wagner Group relatively successfully performed the functions of a "pocket of efficiency" on the battlefield. On the other hand, the failure of Prigozhin's mutiny and his subsequent death were instrumental for the continuity of the Russian political regime, which was able to diminish risks of being overthrown via military coup: in comparative perspective, such instances are considered the most frequent cause of collapse of authoritarian regimes, especially personalist ones.[93] In essence, the case of Wagner demonstrated that the outsourcing of the Russian state's monopoly on legitimate use of violence and delegation of state functions to a private military company is a very risky game. Wagner relied upon top-level political patronage, operated within specially designed formal and informal "rules of the game" unavailable to any other state or private actors, and received priority when it came to supply of resources. Its boss Prigozhin became probably one of the most efficient and successful policy entrepreneurs in post-Soviet Russian history. The only major difference from numerous other "pockets of efficiency" in Russia was their degree of autonomy. The autonomy of "pockets of efficiency" in socio-economic policy areas is contingent nearly by definition and cannot extend beyond the room for maneuver delegated to them by the political leadership.[94] However, in the field of military policy, where "political power grows out of the barrel of a gun," as Mao Zedong put it, the autonomy of "pockets of efficiency" may go well beyond the initial plans of top state officials, and policy entrepreneurs who achieved their initial goals may extend their political ambitions considerably beyond these limits. We know from experience of everyday life that any pockets, when they become too full, can tear and become full of holes. This is exactly what happened with Wagner's "pocket of efficiency": an attempt to compensate for the numerous vices of bad governance in Russian military policy by circumventing them caused more fundamental problems.

Concluding Remarks: When War Unmade the State

The role of bad governance in the Russian military assault on Ukraine was two-fold. On the one hand, rent-seeking and corruption served as drivers for the Russian political leadership and elites, who sought seizure of Ukrainian territories as a potential new source of rents. On the other hand, bad governance greatly contributed to misinformation of the Russian political leadership about Russia's own capabilities and poor preparedness for a full-scale protracted military conflict. Moreover, corruption and mismanagement of top military officials and military-industrial complex organizations served as major impediments to Russian attacks against Ukraine. The notorious inefficiency of the entire Russian state machinery played an important role in the failure of the "special military operation," while attempts to circumvent this inefficiency through the reliance upon "pockets of efficiency" such as the Wagner Group could not resolve these issues and risked becoming a major threat to the preservation of the political status quo.

In a broader sense, not only did the bad governance in Russia influence the poor conduct of the military assault on Ukraine, but the way the assault was proposed and implemented also further aggravated numerous vices of bad governance and the decay of the Russian state. In his famous analysis of the impact of wars on state-building (and vice versa) in medieval and early modern Europe, Charles Tilly summarized this mutual connection as "war made the state, and the state made war."[95] He argued that large-scale and long-standing wars in the past contributed to building of mechanisms of regular taxation, professional military forces, technological progress, and development of education.[96] If Tilly could have witnessed the Russian "special military operation" against Ukraine, he could probably have summarized its effects as "war unmade the state." To what extent is it possible for the Russian state, which is based on rent-seeking and corruption as the main goal and substantive purpose of governance, to improve its performance in the wake of protracted and extensive military conflict with a neighboring state? In theory, one can imagine such a transformation, somewhat similar to the conversion of Saul into Paul the Apostle, but only upon observance of one important condition. The international conflicts of the past, which were productive for state-building, contributed to major rotation of ruling elites, especially in those states where political leaders did not bring about major successes.[97] However, if the preservation of the political status quo and prevention of rotation of ruling elites in a personalist autocracy[98] become the central goals of unleashing and conducting wars, incentives for improving quality of governance cannot emerge. Rather, the picture is quite the opposite: such wars provide incentives for further decay of these states. The difference is that during the wars of the past, inefficient and badly governed states ultimately became easy targets for their more efficient, capable, and successful adversaries, and were conquered by their rivals or sometimes even disappeared from the map as independent entities. However, in the present-day world such a scenario looks unrealistic at least with regard to Russia. This is why the decay of the Russian state amid bad governance may become incurable under conditions of ongoing military conflict. If so, then the Russian state may continue its mediocre, hopeless, and meaningless existence all but endlessly under these worsening conditions.

Chapter 4

THE GREAT SELF-DECEPTION

On January 6, 2021, a mob of Donald Trump supporters attacked the United States Capitol building in Washington, DC.[1] This attack was aimed at keeping Trump in power by preventing a session of both chambers of the US Congress from approving the results of the Electoral College vote to formalize Joe Biden's victory in the presidential elections held in November 2020. Outgoing President Trump, who lost this election and claimed that his victory had been stolen, called his supporters to action and encouraged thousands of them to march to the Capitol to "make their voices heard." More than 2,000 rioters, some of them armed, entered the building at the very beginning of the Congress session, then occupied, vandalized and looted offices, assaulted police officers and reporters, and attempted to capture and beat lawmakers. As the Congress session was interrupted, and members of Congress and staff were evacuated, Trump refused to send the National Guard to quell the mob, and only reluctantly suggested that rioters "go home in peace." Several hours later, the Capitol was cleared of rioters, and Congress completed its session. These events were widely considered across the globe to be a major assault on American democracy. However, the Russian establishment (which tends to endorse Trump as a lesser evil for Russia compared to Biden) perceived this attack differently. It was assessed as a major sign of weakness of American political institutions, which were on the verge of being violently overthrown because of deep divisions within the American elite and society at large and because of excessive political and civil freedoms in the country.

Less than eight months after the storming of the Capitol, in late August 2021, US troops completed their withdrawal from

Afghanistan.[2] The withdrawal ended almost 20 years of US military presence and unsuccessful attempts to impose and maintain a civilian and secular government. When these plans failed, mostly because of the lack of political will and capability of Afghanistan's governments, the withdrawal of the US became inevitable (in fact, it had been planned under two previous administrations, Obama's and Trump's) and Afghanistan was taken over by Taliban troops.[3] However, the evacuation of the last US troops from Kabul airport was very chaotic, and was accompanied by desperate attempts by numerous local residents, who were afraid of the coming of the Taliban government, to board planes that were leaving the country. Video footage from Kabul of the fleeing Americans and their supporters and of the intense panic among abandoned Afghan people surrounding this event was widely circulated around the world, causing joy in the Kremlin. In many countries in the West, the American withdrawal from Afghanistan was considered a recognition of the failure of the US-driven strategy of "democracy promotion."[4] However, in Russia it was largely perceived not only as a sign of American weakness in the international arena[5] but also as an argument in favor of the viewpoint that the Americans had betrayed their puppets abroad and shamelessly abandoned them to the mercy of stronger rivals.

The conclusions drawn by the Russian leadership and elites from these two episodes were straightforward. The American leadership is very fragile, both at home and abroad, and can be undermined by the assertiveness of its rivals; American authorities are unable and unwilling to protect their allies and even unable to keep firm control over law and order in the very heart of their own country.[6] For this reason, actions aimed at further weakening the US and assault on its client states, including but not limited to Ukraine, may go unpunished (while European countries and the EU as a whole lack agency, being merely puppets of the US, and matter little within this context). These conclusions may be considered a wild exaggeration; however, they are based not only on these two episodes but also on the Russian establishment's overall perceptions of international politics in general and the United States in particular.[7] These perceptions by no means emerged as a product of inadequate supply of information from the Russian state agencies in charge of foreign policy issues, although the quality of this information was very much imperfect due to the problems of bad governance covered in the previous chapter. The problem was not only on the level of supply of information available for the Russian political class, but rather on the level of demand. Russian decision-makers' perceptions of international politics (as well of some other political and policy issues) largely reflected their well-established worldviews, and new information was channeled to their hearts and minds only through numerous confirmation biases of various sorts.[8] Wrong signals produced as an effect of the bad governance practices of state agencies (see chapter 3) were further misunderstood and multiplied because of these misperceptions. While they played an important role in the Russian rulers' decision to launch the "special military operation," these misperceptions turned out to be deceptive. Russian plans for attacking Ukraine and redrawing the global political map in their favor were largely driven by a mix of outdated doctrines, unreasonable expectations, and conspiracy theories.[9] Why did such a combination produce such a devastating outcome and to what extent did these doctrines, expectations, and theories play a role in the failure of the Russian assault on Ukraine? This chapter will focus on an analysis of the roots and mechanisms of the Russian elites' self-deception.

The structure of this chapter is the following. After discussing existing explanations of misperceptions in politics and foreign policy in general and in Russia in particular, I will offer my own approach to this phenomenon, based on the security background of the Russian elites and their ideas and preferences, partly inherited from the Soviet and post-Soviet past. I will further explore these issues through an account of the numerous misperceptions of Russian elites regarding Ukraine. An analysis of how these misperceptions were converted into Russia's self-deception before and during the assault on Ukraine will be presented in the conclusion.

Causes of Misperceptions in Russia: Why?

Since the pioneering works of Robert Jervis, misperceptions among policymakers have been widely considered one of the key factors that often contribute to major wars.[10] These misperceptions about adversary countries and oneself are attributed to the psychological features and predispositions of policymakers, and create major obstacles for adequate processing of information. According to Jervis, "decision-makers ... tend to fit incoming information into their existing theories and images,"[11] and rarely change their views in the face of conflicting information. This is why aggressive powers (such as Russia) tend to exaggerate the hostility of status quo-oriented powers (such as the US and the EU) and to believe in the advantages of a pre-emptive attack. Thus, misperceptions often cause self-deception. This approach, further elaborated by scholars of the psychology of judgment and decision-making, such as Amos Tversky and Daniel Kahneman, tells us a great deal about the mechanisms by which misperceptions are converted into poor foreign policy and other policy decisions,[12] but little about the roots of these misperceptions. Indeed, why did Russia's elites interpret the episode of the Capitol riot in Washington, DC, as evidence of the profound weakness and fragility of the American state and the long-prepared flight of US troops from Kabul as a sign of the cowardly betrayal and humiliation of pro-Western actors across the globe?

Scholars of "Putinology" respond to these questions by looking at the personal features of Vladimir Putin and his entourage, and tend to find the origins of these misperceptions in Putin's personal biography and his experience in various roles.[13] Although it is difficult to deny the influence of personal experience on one's misperceptions, such a view tends to ignore the dynamic component of this process. In the early 2000s, soon after his ascension to the presidency, Putin did not perceive the West as a major rival, and he genuinely aimed at rapprochement with the US and European countries. After all, Putin was the first foreign leader to call George W. Bush immediately after the terrorist attack of September 11, 2001 and openly offered him Russia's support.[14] At that time, Putin was also fairly tolerant towards Ukraine.[15] It is not clear in what ways the same person's past experience gave birth to such different perceptions. Of course, one might argue that at a certain point in time before the assault on Ukraine, Putin might have gone insane, and his past experience (whatever we may attribute to it) was no longer relevant thereafter. However, such a far-fetched interpretation seems even more problematic, as this hypothetical madness could not work so selectively and cause misperceptions regarding only foreign and security policies, but not regarding socio-economic policies, which were relatively reasonable before the assault on Ukraine[16] and remained reasonable afterwards.

Another explanation, which seems more theoretically solid and better placed in a comparative perspective, assumes changing motivations on the part of aging long-standing dictators, who over time may lead their countries and themselves to gradual but irreversible "degeneration."[17] In fact, many personalist rulers fear new challenges and tend to consider a changing environment to be more and more hostile toward their regimes over time. Cases of gradual adjustment of such regimes to these challenges and improvement of their performance over time (such as in Spain during the last 15 years of Franco's rule)[18] are relatively rare. Meanwhile, accumulation of negative attitudes of rulers and elites to coming changes and attempts to restore the "good old days" at any cost often prompt their major drift toward an increasingly reactionary understanding of the contemporary world. Such a pattern is hardly unique to political elites and leaders, and is commonly observed in the everyday lives of many aging people elsewhere across the globe. Moreover, low elite rotation in Russia under Putin's rule greatly contributed to such a "degeneration" amid the aging of Putin's entourage. However, again, "degeneration" alone cannot explain the different effects of this process on Russian policy-making, namely, gross misperceptions in the foreign and security policy areas (largely managed by Putin himself together with an "inner circle" of trusted advisors) versus relatively limited misperceptions in socio-economic policies (largely managed by technocrats under Putin's patronage).[19]

A more sophisticated approach to explaining the misperceptions of the Russian leadership and elites is related to the extraordinary reliance of the Russian regime upon lies and disinformation as primary tools of politics and policy-making in various areas, both domestically and internationally. This widespread Kremlin practice, dubbed "informational autocracy" or "spin dictatorship" by Sergei Guriev and Daniel Treisman, can have a devastating effect in terms of misperceptions by the Russian elites and leadership in two differing though interrelated ways.[20] First, the Russian political class may become victims of their own propaganda, which tends to reinforce already strong confirmation biases. Data from the Survey of Russian Elites, a longitudinal study of Russian foreign policy elites based on surveys conducted from 1993 to 2020, seem to support this argument.[21] According to this data, many misperceptions by Russian elites have tended to intensify over time against the backdrop of increasingly powerful propaganda and disinformation via the mechanism of "the Kremlin's cues."[22] In addition, the in-depth analysis of the political views of key Russian national security policymakers conducted by Martin Kragh and Andreas Umland convincingly demonstrated that their perceptions were increasingly affected by conspiratorial ideas over time, very much along the lines of the increasing role of conspiracy theories in Russian propagandist narratives and public discourses.[23] Second, and probably, more important, is the fact that under conditions of "informational autocracy," Russian elites and leaders are not always able to realize which pieces of information are true and which ones are deliberately false.[24] During Soviet times, Communist leaders attempted to resolve this problem via secret circulation of information about the real state of affairs (addressed to a narrow circle of users and allegedly free from propagandist biases).[25] However, this solution was imperfect, as the secretly circulated information often was also incorrect; post-Soviet rulers have inherited this practice of secret information exchange without reality checks. Moreover, according to some journalists' accounts, certain secret reports addressed to the Russian top leadership were intentionally distorted and presented in a less negative light for delivery to Putin in order "not to upset him"[26] (a problem typical for a number of authoritarian regimes but particularly acute for "informational autocracies").

Although explanation of misperceptions by the Russian leadership and elites through the possible effects of "informational autocracy" may be plausible, the problem is that Russia is not the only autocracy of this kind, as "spin dictatorships" have become widespread over last two decades in various parts of the globe, ranging from China to Hungary and Turkey. Yet Turkish and Chinese political leaders and elites are not as deeply affected by their misperceptions as their Russian counterparts. Although some of their policies have been rather poorly chosen (such as Erdoğan's macroeconomic policy or the zero-tolerance approach to the COVID-19 pandemic in China), they were largely rationally driven by leaders' political and policy priorities rather than by their misperceptions. This is why one should not attribute causes of misperceptions solely to the effects of "informational autocracy." Instead, one might argue that the atmosphere of lies and disinformation in "informational autocracies" may reinforce existing misperceptions rather than causing them.

To summarize, these guesses and interpretations, while useful and popular among scholars, do not provide a consistent explanation for the self-deceptive misperceptions of the Russian elites and leadership about international politics in general and about Ukraine in particular. My own approach, although it utilizes some elements of both the "degeneration" and the "informational autocracy" theories, is somewhat different from existing frameworks for analysis. It pays more attention to the effects of the organizational and ideational legacies of Russian elites and the uses of these legacies for the construction of normative ideals on the one hand, and for responses to ongoing challenges amid high uncertainty before and after the Russian assault on Ukraine on the other.

Security Elites and Legacies: Organizational Culture, Generational Trajectory, and Groupthink

The group of top Russian officials in charge of security issues during the period from the early 2000s to the assault on Ukraine was relatively homogeneous. This group, which included Putin, Patrushev, Bortnikov, Naryshkin, Chemezov, and a number of others, comprised men mostly born in the first half of the 1950s who had initially built their careers in the Soviet KGB or related establishments, and whose background greatly contributed to their numerous misperceptions.[27] One might argue that the organizational and ideational legacies of these security elites' late-Soviet experience did not just outlive their initial conditions by decades; they also had negative effects in terms of these officials' organizational culture and generational trajectory, and played an important role in the formation of their groupthink over time.[28] The narrow recruitment pool of Russian security elites, their reliance on personal networks in their career paths, and the stability of their composition over time only aggravated these problems.

According to the data from the Survey of Russian Elites, security elites tend to be the most isolationist, militant, and anti-democratic segment of the Russian political class. As Sharon Werning Rivera and David Rivera demonstrated, in this respect they are rather different from the Russian military elites, whose views are closer to those of their civilian counterparts.[29] Their views were shaped both by the logic of career trajectories in the Soviet and post-Soviet periods and by the collective experience of the "seventies" generation. It would not be a wild exaggeration to link these attitudes and perceptions to career experience in the late-Soviet security apparatus, which was hardly conducive to the formation of healthy worldviews. Contrary to the romantic image of spy novels, late-Soviet second-tier security officials were largely involved in routine paperwork that had little to do with security as such. As Mark Harrison showed in his analysis of Soviet economic history, most activities of provincial branches of the KGB in late-Soviet decades involved monitoring of excessive secrecy regulations and maintenance of largely useless networks of informers.[30] Even Putin himself, during his service in East Germany (a highly prestigious job at that time), performed nearly the same routines, as his horizon of thinking in that period was limited to career promotion and drinking beer.[31]

Furthermore, the educational background of those in the Soviet security apparatus (except for intelligence officers) was rather poor even amid the overall highly problematic social science training in Soviet higher education. At best, during their training future security elites gained some practical skills at the expense of getting in-depth knowledge. As for ideological indoctrination in Soviet higher education in general and in security schools and academies in particular, at that time it was rather formal and unconvincing. In particular, obedience, diligence, and unconditional loyalty were extensively cultivated at the expense of critical thinking (which was not welcomed at all).[32] It is no wonder that the background of second-tier Soviet security officers was marked by severe narrow-mindedness. At the same time, the late-Soviet security apparatus exploited the combination of the top priority of their activities for the Soviet political leadership with high secrecy, which also served as a good excuse for bloating the KGB and increasing its budget. The keyword of the late-Soviet security apparatus was "special," which meant not only secrecy but also exclusivity (and later on, this notion was reflected in the very term "special military operation"). While the formal and informal status of the KGB and other security agencies in this period was rather high, many of the rules and regulations of their activities were based on a top-down hierarchy of "power verticals" within these agencies, and the local state and Communist Party apparatus had a limited impact on their officers. Exclusivity offered the security apparatus a certain bubble, protected from encroachment from outside by relevant state agencies. In practical terms, this exclusivity also meant more professional and personal autonomy for second-tier security officers compared to their civilian counterparts, and also provided for a better state-directed supply of goods and services amid increasing economic problems in the Soviet Union. Being largely insulated from outside influence, the late-Soviet security apparatus not only inherited but also even further developed the conspiratorial practices of its predecessors from Stalin's decades.[33]

Meanwhile, Soviet top-level security officials, including the long-standing chief of the KGB Yuri Andropov, invested a great deal of effort into building an image of the highly professional, non-corrupt, and patriotic milieu of its servants, which was far from reality, to put it mildly.[34] To summarize, the organizational culture of the late-Soviet security apparatus provided fertile ground for the future rise of misperceptions among the post-Soviet security elites, although it did not predetermine these features.

The other factor, which contributed to the rise of misperceptions among post-Soviet elites in general and security elites in particular was their generational trajectory. The late-Soviet generation, the so-called "seventiers," who reached adolescence during the period of the "long 1970s" (between the end of Khrushchev's Thaw and the beginning of Gorbachev's perestroika), developed an attitude of non-adherence to any ideals, and pragmatism if not cynicism.[35] Before perestroika, they expected that the status quo would not change at all, and planned their life course and careers accordingly.[36] However, the turbulent changes during the late 1980s and early 1990s became an exogenous shock for many representatives of this generation, who were not ready for sudden changes in the midst of their lives. Their previous frame of reference became irrelevant, and a new political and economic order was perceived as highly unattractive even by those "seventiers" who became winners rather than losers in the post-Soviet changes. The post-Soviet trauma from the collapse gave birth to a great deal of resentment among both elites and the general public and remained very powerful for several decades after the Soviet collapse. Most probably, Putin was sincere when he claimed that the Soviet collapse was the greatest geopolitical catastrophe of the twentieth century, despite the fact that Putin himself, as well as his entourage, were among the major beneficiaries of this catastrophe. Without these events, Putin would probably have retired as a second-tier KGB official without serious chances of ascension to elite status.

While for ordinary "seventiers" the Soviet collapse and subsequent deep and protracted transformation recession meant a difficult adjustment to new conditions amid a decline in living standards, the elites faced different problems. They suddenly realized that the status of their country had dramatically declined after the end of the Soviet Union, that Russia was no longer a superpower, and that their status-seeking efforts were not much appreciated by their American and European counterparts. Even the members of the first post-Communist Russian government who greatly hoped for support for their market reforms were disappointed by Western politicians' cold reception of their requests for foreign aid.[37] It is no wonder that with this profound disillusionment, Russian elites changed their views starting from the late 1990s. According to the Survey of Russian Elites, in the early and mid-1990s the "seventiers" represented the most pro-Western segment of the Russian elites, but by the late 2000s, representatives of this generation had turned in an anti-Western direction.[38] They were deeply afflicted by severe post-Soviet resentment, and over time, these attitudes and multiple grievances were only aggravated further.

As one can see, the background and life trajectories of the Russian security elites were very homogeneous. They largely shared a common professional and personal experience with similar worldviews: pragmatic and cynical on the one hand, and driven by disillusionment and grievances on the other. This fact streamlined internal communications among security elites, who were able not only to act cohesively but also to expand their influence beyond security-related policy areas. However, such homogeneity and cohesiveness made security elites vulnerable to groupthink,[39] which also developed within the context of a personalist authoritarian regime. In a way, the meeting of the Security Council of Russia before the assault on Ukraine on February 21, 2022 (described in chapter 2) was a clear manifestation of this negative tendency. The Russian security elites not only avoided searching for any alternative solutions for Russian–Ukrainian relations since the overthrow of Yanukovych in 2014, but also abandoned any independent thought in favor of loyalty and conformity. As a result, the dynamics of this "in-group" of Russian elites in general and of security elites in particular produced an increasing illusion of invulnerability and impunity (see chapter 5). In other words, the Russian elites developed a highly exaggerated perception that the Kremlin was always making the right decisions in regard to Ukraine and other foreign nations, irrespective of what those decisions actually were. This was the case for the Russian annexation of Crimea in 2014 (which was perceived by the elites as a "success story"),[40] and once again in February 2022.

As a result, the Russian security and foreign policy elites greatly overrated their own decision-making abilities and greatly underrated those of their opponents, including foreign governments. To put it simply, they reinforced the perceptions of their own high competence in foreign affairs and security issues, even though some of these perceptions, as I will demonstrate below, were ultimately wrong. Furthermore, groupthink is considered by many experts to be detrimental to companies and organizations and in all work situations, and the planning of the assault on Ukraine was not an exception. One must admit, however, that Putin and his entourage from among the security elites were well aware of the limits of their knowledge and expertise when it came to socio-economic affairs, and did not greatly encroach into these policy areas. They outsourced policy-making to professional technocrats like Elvira Nabiullina, which is why socio-economic policies were not so badly affected by the groupthink among security elites and instead are driven by professional discussions and policy expertise.[41] However, with regard to the planning of the assault on Ukraine, the situation was completely different. The Russian security elites, driven by Putin, were excessively self-confident; they believed too strongly in their own expertise and in the omnipotence of the leadership, and were too homogeneous in terms of their background and trajectories: they shared the same experience, assessments, and grievances. This is why the individual confirmation biases of the representatives of the Russian security elites became a collective confirmation bias, and collective deliberations in the Kremlin only reinforced their previous misperceptions.

What went wrong with the Russian security elites' perceptions, and why did they so heavily contribute to the undesired outcomes of the Russian policy towards Ukraine? The answer is that they were based not only on imperfect and biased knowledge about the contemporary world and about Russia itself, these misperceptions were also driven by overly high and poorly substantiated claims of Russia's status as a global veto player, by unreasonable desires for the partial restoration of the late-Soviet political order both domestically and internationally, and by the vulnerability of the thinking of the Russian elites and leadership to numerous conspiracy theories. These factors contributed to the transformation of Russian misperceptions into a great self-deception during the assault on Ukraine.

Claims, Desires, and Conspiracies

What is Russia's place among other countries? Looking at alphabetical order, one might correctly locate Russia's place between Romania and Rwanda. Looking at the degree of socio-economic development (according to one's indicators of choice), one might place Russia in the category of upper-middle-income countries alongside Brazil and Turkey. Although many observers would argue that Russia is an exceptional country not only because of its possession of nuclear weapons but also because of its size, nature, history, culture, etc., in fact this is just an ordinary country, one of more than 200 states across the globe – nothing more and nothing less. Many discussions about Russia's place tend to emphasize its similarities and differences to global leaders such as the US or China.[42] However, speaking in positive (rather than normative) terms, many statements about Russia's uniqueness in the twenty-first century are in one way or another related to somewhat unsubstantiated claims that it merits some sort of special treatment and exclusive conditions, for whatever reasons.

The Soviet Union was known as a country with excessively long queues, and many Soviet citizens spent long hours waiting to buy food, clothes, theater tickets, and the like. However, numerous categories of Soviet people were able to purchase these goods while bypassing the queues. Most were able to do so either by virtue of belonging to certain segments of Soviet elites or through informal connections within the Soviet system of distribution.[43] Those who had no such preferential access to goods and services considered these practices unjust but also wished they could bypass the long queues themselves. In a way, post-Soviet Russia tends to behave somewhat similarly to the Soviet consumers who felt themselves underprivileged within the Soviet system and wished to bypass queues. Unlike these consumers, who sought foreign shoes or toilet paper rolls, Russian elites aim for the benefits of high status for their country and themselves, and/or for exchanging these benefits for other bonuses.

In reality, Russia inherited its high status in the international arena as the legal successor of the Soviet Union, similarly to heirs of long-established aristocratic families. Apart from nuclear weapons, which are still considered its most powerful global assets, it also received a seat as a permanent member of the UN Security Council and some other forms of official and unofficial recognition. However, this formal status during the post-Soviet period did not bring major benefits to the country, as Russia was no longer a first-rate superpower in terms of its global influence. Even bonuses such as Russia's membership in the G8 club of leading developed democracies in

1996–2014 did not change the situation much, as Russia's elites felt deprived in the same way as the Soviet consumers who attempted to bypass long queues. This deprivation became clear in 2015, when after Russia's intervention in the civil war in Syria, Barack Obama openly and loudly stated that Russia was a "regional power" and had no reason to be involved in a bloody conflict in the Middle East.[44] Such a statement was perceived by Russia's leadership as heavily offensive and humiliating; Putin even accused the US of claiming that Russia deserved a place "near the latrine."[45] In fact, Russia was (and remains) a regional power, and its role in the Syrian civil war was hardly justified (in a way, Russia only aggravated the conflict). Meanwhile, the goal of restoring the status of global superpower was irresistible for Russian elites.[46]

Officially, the goal of elevating Russia's status to that of global veto player was summarized in the doctrine of multi-polarity first promoted by the former Russian Prime Minister Yevgeny Primakov.[47] The idea behind this doctrine is that the international arena is essentially an oligarchy, and the world should be de facto divided between several superpowers controlling their respective spheres of influence (see chapter 1). All other countries are considered to be client states of superpowers at best. In practical terms, this doctrine implies that the three major superpowers, namely, the US, China, and Russia, will achieve an agreement at a certain point, a new equivalent of the post-1945 Yalta system, and the international order will be stabilized for decades. Apparently, Russia considered post-Soviet Eurasia its exclusive sphere of influence, but its appetite went much further, and it perceived Europe as part of its sphere of influence as well. As early as November 1999, during his meeting with Bill Clinton, Yeltsin said, "I ask you one thing. Just give Europe to Russia" and disregarded Clinton's response "Give Europe to Europe itself."[48]

During Putin's reign, attempts to bring Europe under Russian control turned from pure wishful thinking into a foreign policy agenda. The Kremlin put serious efforts into building solid support for Russia in various European states, supported pro-Russian parties and candidates in elections, promoted Brexit, and also coopted European politicians and business people into its networks.[49] As the Kremlin perceived the European Union as a weak actor, it attempted to engage EU member states and their elites individually, offering them certain perks in exchange for loyalty. However, these efforts, even if they were not wholly in vain, saw limited success. In a broader sense,

Russia's claims of multi-polarity were not supported by its economic capabilities, and so the gap between Russia's overly high expectations and relatively modest opportunities has tended to increase over time. This major misperception prompted the Kremlin to raise the stakes vis-à-vis the US and the "collective West."[50] The Russian ultimatum issued to NATO in December 2021, with its demand to withdraw alliance troops from Eastern Europe and undo all decisions regarding post-1997 NATO expansion, was a prime example of this approach. It is no wonder that both the US and the NATO leadership unequivocally rejected these demands, considering them unreasonable and unacceptable proposals, if not blatant bluffing.

The other issue, which greatly affected misperceptions by Russian elites, was their construction of a new normative ideal for post-Soviet Russia, which I call elsewhere the "Good Soviet Union" (see chapter 2).[51] This ideal emerged as a response to the irrelevance of the Communist model and the unacceptability of Western models as normative ideals for post-Soviet personalist authoritarianism in Russia.

The use of the Soviet experience as a set of building blocks for post-Soviet institution building and practices of governing the state resulted in the translation of this social construct into major choices and solutions. Examples include the transformation of the structure of government after the Soviet collapse with regard to the state apparatus, as well as practices of control and accountability in law enforcement agencies, both of which extended the outdated practices of Soviet-era institutions and organizations, thus contributing to the ineffectiveness of government.[52] This approach influences policy-making with regard to the organization of the state bureaucracy and its motivations.[53] Over time, the Russian ruling elites used these selectively chosen elements of the late-Soviet experience, and their patchwork-like adjustment to present-day Russia lies at the heart of many policy ideas and their conversion into state programs and projects. For instance, the creation of huge state-owned industrial conglomerates in many ways looks like an intentional elite-driven replica of the very powerful Soviet ministries with an outstandingly large volume of assets, which dominated the defense industry during the Cold War.[54] These ministries made a major contribution to the economic burdens of the over-militarized Soviet Union. Still, they are considered role models in spite of an isolationist state-led approach to post-Soviet economic policy and the Kremlin's drive towards technological modernization of the Russian military. In a way, Soviet foreign policy also serves as a role model for post-Soviet Russia, and has offered a number of ready-made templates for continuity of old practices.[55] Moreover, some of the policy proposals within the framework of the "Good Soviet Union" model, which referred to the Soviet experience, largely covered the vested interests of numerous rent-seekers, who gained preferential access to resources amid poor institutionalization of policy-making in Russia. However, to put it simply, major obstacles faced the full-scale implementation of the Soviet model of policy-making: the lack of a centralized planned economy, of comprehensive top-down control of the Communist Party, and of coercive mechanisms like the Gulag. As a result, the "Good Soviet Union" as a normative ideal has not produced incentives for Russia's development, overcome the trap of bad governance in Russia, or improved government effectiveness – even should these be declared policy goals. To a major degree, the use of this model for military and security policy has been faced with major gaps between the Kremlin's high expectations and mediocre realities. The Russian elites perceived themselves as successors of their Soviet predecessors, but did not have enough resources and capabilities to turn their constructed, outdated normative ideal into a driver of successful policy-making.

While the Kremlin successfully sold the propagandist narrative of a "Good Soviet Union" to its domestic audience, this approach worked very poorly for export to post-Soviet Eurasia and beyond. The elites of Eurasian countries, ranging from Moldova to Kyrgyzstan, highly valued their own sovereignty, invested a great deal of effort into nation- and state-building, and had little incentive to sacrifice these benefits for the sake of a real or imagined restoration of the "Good Soviet Union" under Russia's auspices. Even though some of these countries, such as Belarus under Lukashenko's leadership, attempted to employ homemade versions of the "Good Soviet Union" model or selectively borrow practices from their Russian neighbors, their elites and leaders were rather suspicious of the unconstrained import of Russian practices aggressively promoted by the Kremlin.[56] This is why some of the Kremlin-driven projects of international integration of Eurasian countries around Russia's leadership (such as the Eurasian Economic Union vigorously advocated by the Kremlin) were essentially limited to subsidizing the economies of Belarus and/or Kazakhstan from Russia's side, but did not result in major policy advancements for Russia. Moreover, the Russian pressure on the Ukrainian President Yanukovych not to sign an association agreement with the EU in 2013, together with offering Ukraine membership in the Eurasian Economic Union (alongside $15 billion credit to Yanukovych, widely considered a bribe), became the trigger event for the overthrow of Yanukovych's regime in February 2014.[57] The fact that these efforts were in vain, and the Ukrainian "Revolution of Dignity" ruined Russia's plans, has been easily explained by the Kremlin solely as an effect of the US-driven conspiracy against Russia.[58] The use of the "Good Soviet Union" model for foreign policy beyond Eurasia was even more problematic, as numerous legacies of the Soviet Union were perceived in a rather negative light in various parts of the world, from Eastern Europe to Africa. In other words, the Kremlin's desire for a "Good Soviet Union" on the international arena was not convertible into desirable policy outcomes and remains more or less wishful thinking.

The third and probably the most problematic component of the misperceptions by Russian security elites was their vulnerability to conspiracy theories of various sorts.[59] On the one hand, the security apparatus had been a major provider of numerous conspiracy narratives since Soviet times (such as the myth that the spread of HIV/AIDS in the 1980s was a product of the efforts of US security services, which was used as a tool for anti-American propaganda during the Cold War).[60] These practices multiplied during the post-Soviet period – for example, Russian propaganda invented a fake statement, attributed to the former US Secretary of State Madeleine Albright that Russian control over the natural resources of Siberia was unjust and should be revised in favor of international control.[61] These narratives affected not only the Russian general public (indeed, conspiracy theories are quite widespread among the Russian and post-Soviet public), but also the Russian elites. Under conditions of "informational autocracy," it is possible for elites to lose touch with reality and not always make a distinction between true and intentionally false information produced by state officials, agencies, and media. To summarize, the Russian elites gradually became victims of their own propaganda, which intentionally, blatantly, and shamelessly used various conspiracy narratives. At the same time, the negative selection into the security elites (based upon loyalty and informal ties rather than on merit-based criteria), their rather imperfect education and knowledge, deeply embedded stereotypes from the Cold War, and the cohesiveness of this group amid their groupthink made them a likely target for any conspiracy theories, irrespective of their origins and the mechanisms of transmission and persuasion. The media and bloggers have reported numerous examples of superstitions among Russian elites, episodes of their participation in various occult practices, such as Putin and Shoigu visiting Siberian shamans. Even though these reports may not be true, the spread of such rumors is symptomatic. These kinds of elite habits form a social environment, which is highly vulnerable to various conspiracy theories. These factors in the development of conspiracy thinking may mutually reinforce each other and contribute to the penetration of such worldviews among elites and society-at-large. In essence, over time, against the background of ongoing "degeneration,"[62] conspiracy theories have come to be a prevalent mode of thinking in Russia. In other words, state officials tend to believe that ongoing political and socio-economic changes across the globe result from the implementation of secret plans of powerful enemies, aimed at major harm to Russia and imposition of their will onto it and the entire world. Leading Russian security officials such as Nikolai Patrushev and Sergey Naryshkin serve as prime examples of the prevalence of these conspiracy theories among Russian elites.[63]

Beliefs in conspiracy theories contribute to misperceptions by elites both directly and indirectly. In the most pragmatic sense, such beliefs tend to perform protective functions, filtering out bad news and denying the painful and inconvenient truth regarding the existence of spontaneous developments and/or of structural constraints on any actions, but rather tending to describe any undesirable developments exclusively as by-products of enemy efforts. For example, soon after the assault on Ukraine, the Russian elites generated a new (though short-lived) conspiracy theory, which stated that US bio-laboratories in Eastern Ukraine had developed new coronaviruses and intended to spread a new epidemic by using birds to infect Russians.[64] Moreover, these labs also conducted secret experiments, which transformed Ukrainian soldiers into horrible monsters, and this was why the Russian army demonstrated poor progress in the wake of the launching of the "special military operation." Yet another version of this conspiracy theory accused the US and NATO of breeding and spreading "combat mosquitoes" in Ukraine for use against Russian troops.[65] Such an approach was also aimed at protection of the general public and the elites themselves from the painful truth. However, in a broader sense, reliance upon conspiracy theories in Russia may perform not only protective but also substitutive functions. They can provide Russian elites and masses with a replacement for evidence-based knowledge, especially in foreign and security policy areas, in the form of various myths and misinformation, offering ready-made if ultimately wrong answers to many difficult questions.

The spread of conspiracy theories has greatly contributed to misperceptions by Russian security elites in two different ways. First, these theories tend to multiply confirmation biases in their worldviews and reinforce initially incorrect assumptions and expectations – the narratives about US bio-labs and "combat mosquitoes" serve as prime examples. Second, they lead to elites ignoring or even denying certain information that does not fit these theories. Such information may simply be filtered out as irrelevant, irrespective of its content or truthfulness. For example, the Russian security elites' mistrust of data obtained via open-source intelligence techniques (also known as OSINT analytics)[66] and their preference for relying on numerous conspiracy narratives had a visibly negative impact on policy performance in the process of preparing for invasion (see chapter 3). However, the Kremlin preferred to deny objective and unbiased sources of knowledge available to it.

The awkward combination of unreasonable claims of global status and power, outdated ideals, and desires for a "good Soviet Union," and unreasonable conspiracy theories greatly increased misperceptions among Russian security elites, distorting their performance both domestically and internationally. In particular, these misperceptions seriously affected preparations for the Russian "special military operation" and its conduct.

Russian Misperceptions, Ukraine, and Beyond: What Went Wrong?

The entire set of perceptions and expectations held by the Kremlin with regard to Ukraine and its Western allies before the assault in February 2022 was based upon three major pillars:

(1) Ukraine is a natural part of Russia, which was separated from it only due to some accidents of history and the efforts of Russia's enemies, and this is why Ukraine will be easily taken over by Russia soon after the assault;

(2) Ukraine is a weak state, governed by weak and inexperienced leaders and elites, and this is why this country cannot resist Russia and will not be able to do so for a long period of time; and
(3) Ukraine's Western allies have limited resources and incentives for supporting Ukraine on a long-term basis, and this is why they will concede and accept Russia's conquest of Ukraine after facing Russia's assault.

None of these perceptions and expectations proved to be correct, but they played an important role in the planning of Russia's assault on Ukraine. Why did Russia's misperceptions on Ukraine and beyond emerge and how did they lead to negative consequences?

Although the second president of Ukraine, Leonid Kuchma, entitled his 2003 book *Ukraina – ne Rossiya* (*Ukraine is not Russia*),[67] and a significant part of the Russian elite gradually accepted Ukrainian independence from Russia,[68] Putin understood Ukraine in quite the opposite way. In his long article about Ukraine entitled "On the historical unity of Russians and Ukrainians," published in July 2021, Putin further elaborated an extensive narrative account of the Ukrainian past. According to him, Ukraine was always included in a tripartite Slavic cultural and spiritual unity (which also included Russia and Belarus). It reunited with Russia as a part of the Russian state in the mid-seventeenth century, and remained part of the Soviet Union (implicitly considered to be an extended Russia) until the Soviet collapse (which was, as Putin had claimed earlier, "the greatest geopolitical catastrophe of the twentieth century"), and this was why Ukrainians and Russians were "the same people" (*odin narod*). As to the very idea of Ukrainian independence from Russia, Putin attributed it to the errors of his predecessors and the influence of Russia's enemies. He mentioned Austro-Hungarian intrigues against the Russian Empire in the late nineteenth and early twentieth centuries, the policy choice of Soviet ethnic federalism made by Vladimir Lenin during the early years of Communist rule, and the actions of Ukrainian radical ethnic nationalists endorsed by Western patrons. This was why, according to Putin, Ukraine had recently turned into an "anti-Russia," and should be liberated from these influences and reintegrated with Russia.[69]

Such a narrative was misleading, both factually and substantively, contradicting scholarly knowledge about the past of Ukraine and Russia.[70] It presented not only a very selective and biased interpretation of the past (used instrumentally, only as a tool for justification of future actions), but also rejected any deviation from the perceived mainstream of history. If something had happened in the past in Russia's favor (such as the Russian absorption of Ukraine in the mid-seventeenth century), then it should remain so forever, and any undesired changes (such as Ukrainian independence after the Soviet collapse) were perceived as an error to be corrected thereafter. In addition, Putin's primordial understanding of nations (based on the belief that national or ethnic identities are fixed, natural, and ancient) denied the very idea of a Ukrainian nation being constructed other than as an "anti-Russian" scheme, and excluded the possibility of the evolution of nations over time.[71] Judging from this perspective, one may consider, for example, the British and Americans to be "the same people" not only before but also after American independence and use this argument as a justification for the War of 1812. However, one must admit that Putin quite correctly identified an independent Ukraine as "anti-Russia." In a way, it was an accurate definition, not in terms of Ukraine's hostility towards Russia but in terms of the difference between the political trajectories of the two countries after the Soviet collapse. While Russia embraced personalist authoritarianism and attempted to restore a centralized imperial state, Ukraine built a relatively stable (if imperfect) electoral democracy[72] and decentralized nation-state.[73]

This narrative was not only a propagandist instrument of the Kremlin, but also reflected the Russian elites' vision of Russo–Ukrainian relations and their expectations of the possible effects of the assault. In practical terms, these misperceptions implied that Ukraine and its people had been hijacked by radical nationalists and would easily switch sides when Russia liberated them from the "Banderovites." In a way, these misperceptions were also driven by the very fact that some of the people responsible for the Kremlin's policy towards Ukraine were natives of Ukraine themselves. They felt alienated from Ukraine after the Soviet collapse, and had personal reasons to aim at the reunification of Ukraine with Russia in one way or another. This is true for the Kremlin's (in)famous spin doctor Gleb Pavlovsky – a native of Odessa who orchestrated Yanukovich's election campaign in 2004, which led to the Orange Revolution. Sergey Glaziev, Putin's statist economic advisor, a native of Zaporizhzhia who served as the major driving force behind pulling Yanukovych out of signing an association agreement with the EU in November 2013 (a trigger event for the Revolution of Dignity), may be listed in the same category. So may Putin's aide in charge of relations with the post-Soviet area Dmitry Kozak, a native of the Kirovohrad region (now Kropyvnytskyi), as well as Vladimir Medinsky, another aide who was supposedly the ghostwriter of Putin's aforementioned article, a native of the Cherkassy region.[74]

Before the Russian assault on Ukraine, these misperceptions were fueled by an over-supply of inaccurate information from the Kremlin's loyalists in Ukraine (those close to former president Yanukovych and/or "the Kremlin's man" in Kyiv, Viktor Medvedchuk).[75] But the problem was that this inaccurate information was laid down on a fertile ground of misperceptions formed many years before the assault. In fact, pro-Russian sentiments virtually disappeared in Ukraine after the Russian assault, while support for Russia remained low even in the territories of Ukraine taken over during the first days of the assault.[76] In other words, Kuchma was right and Putin was wrong.

The narrative about Ukraine belonging to Russia and its non-existence as an independent entity promoted by Putin was, in all likelihood, much too radical even in the eyes of the Russian elites. However, a more moderate version of this narrative had emerged some decades before Putin and was considered by the Russian elites to be well-grounded. The author of this narrative was Samuel P. Huntington, a famous Harvard political scientist, who in 1993 published his essay, "The Clash of Civilizations?" in the *Foreign Affairs* magazine and in 1996 extended it into a book.[77] Among other things, he considered Russia the core of an Orthodox civilization distinct from and incompatible with Western civilization, and argued that Ukraine could become a battlefield between the two conflicting civilizations. According to Huntington's vision, Ukraine could (but not necessarily should) be divided between the eastern and western parts of the country, oriented towards Russia and the West respectively. Huntington did not base his civilizational analysis in general and his comments about Russia and Ukraine in particular on any evidence-based empirical research. However, despite this rather unsubstantiated claim (or probably precisely because of it), Huntington's civilizational approach became incredibly popular in Russia not only among elites but also within academia. According to the survey of Russian political scientists conducted in 2021, they perceived *The Clash of Civilizations* as the most important piece of political science ever, much more important than the texts by Machiavelli, Aristotle, Plato, and Weber taken together.[78] In a way, in intellectual terms, in twenty-first-century Russia, Huntington took on the role played by Marx and Lenin in the twentieth century.

In many ways, Huntington's vision of Russia and Ukraine and his prediction of a possible clash between Russia and the West over Ukraine fit the actual experience of post-Soviet Ukrainian politics. The electoral map of Ukraine during the presidential elections of 1994–2010 largely reflected a deep division between Eastern and Western Ukraine, and conflict between pro-Russian and pro-Western candidates (Kuchma in 1994 and Yanukovych in 2004 and 2010 were pro-Russian, while Kravchuk in 1994, Kuchma in 1999, Yushchenko in 2004, and Timoshenko in 2010 were pro-Western).[79] However, this division reflected not so much a societal cleavage among Ukrainian voters but rather a structure of bi-polar political competition. When this structure dramatically changed during the 2014 presidential elections, and Yanukovych infamously left the political scene, electoral conflict between Eastern and Western candidates almost disappeared, and by the 2019 presidential elections it had completely lost its relevance.[80] Moreover, neither Eastern nor Western Ukraine were politically homogeneous units; rather, their composition reflected a mix of regional-based politico-economic conglomerates. In particular, the conflict between regional oligarchic groups based in Dnipropetrovsk (now Dnipro) and Donetsk was protracted and notorious, even though both areas are considered parts of Eastern Ukraine.[81]

The irrelevance of the Huntington-inspired vision of Ukraine already became apparent in 2014, when the Kremlin attempted to organize a separation of certain regions of Eastern Ukraine and to create a new political entity, Novorossiya (New Russia). While some segments of elites in the Donetsk and Luhansk regions closely linked with the ousted president Yanukovych initially endorsed the Kremlin-backed separatist claims, in other regions of Eastern Ukraine this plan failed due to the reluctance of regional elites (Kharkiv, Odessa) or their open resistance (Dnipropetrovsk).[82] In 2022, the situation looked even more problematic, as it was the regions of Eastern rather than Western Ukraine that became primary victims of the Russian assault and there was no evidence of their endorsement of Russia's actions at the levels of elites or masses. In fact, over the period since 1991, the Ukrainization of Eastern regions of Ukraine gradually developed in terms of the use of Ukrainian language and other features, and in a sense, the process of nation-building had weakened the East–West divide by the time of the Russian assault.[83] To summarize, even if one might argue that before the Soviet collapse, Ukraine and Russia could be somehow understood as "the same people" (or at least the Eastern part of Ukraine could be considered through that lens), by the time of the Russian assault in February 2022 these perceptions were outdated and completely wrong.

The notion of Ukraine as a weak state had remained the mantra of all observers of Ukrainian politics and governance since the Soviet collapse. Ukraine not only demonstrated a poor quality of governance through the entire post-Soviet period (in this respect, it performed no better than Russia, and sometimes even worse), but also a limited coercive capacity immediately after the deposal of Yanukovych in February 2014. Due to this state weakness, the Russian annexation of Crimea and separatist takeover of Donetsk and Luhansk met almost no resistance, as no one was able and willing to protect the state. Moreover, many oligarchic wars and political conflicts in the Ukrainian parliament so vividly resembled certain Russian practices of the "roaring" 1990s that the Russian elites easily recognized their own past experience in Ukraine (which they preferred to forget). In this respect, even the deposal of Yanukovych initially changed little in Ukraine – the president of the country was the opportunistic oligarch Poroshenko, the government remained highly corrupt and ineffective, many state officials kept their posts (especially in courts and law enforcement agencies),[84] and many old vices of bad governance just reproduced themselves.

However, things begin to change in 2019, when 41-year-old Volodymyr Zelensky, surprisingly for many observers, was elected as President of Ukraine.[85] His ascent to power was not taken seriously in the Kremlin – the former comedian without serious political experience was perceived as an amateur who could be easily deceived both domestically and internationally. However, Zelensky's political and personal potential was wildly underestimated. His presidency gave birth to major generational changes among Ukrainian elites. Many key positions became occupied by the people who grew up and socialized after the Soviet collapse, lacked the organizational and ideational legacies of the Soviet Union, and overall were better educated and more Westernized and modernized than the representatives of the "seventiers" who formed the core of the Russian elites.[86]

In addition, Zelensky's profound break with old elites damaged the established corrupt networks of Ukrainian officials that had survived both the Orange Revolution of 2004 and the Revolution of Dignity of 2014 (although some new corrupt networks did emerge instead of or in addition to old ones). Of course, not all of Zelensky's nominees performed their duties successfully, either before or after the Russian assault. In particular, Ivan Bakanov, a long-standing friend of Zelensky, who was appointed as the new head of Ukraine's national security service, the SBU, remained passive during the beginning of the assault, and was replaced after several months.[87] However, overall, the major cadre revolution initiated by Zelensky (which aimed at a degree of renewal of the Ukrainian state) was a correct move. Furthermore, elite reshufflings diminished potential support for the Kremlin among Ukrainian elites (a tendency, which became visible after early 2021, when Zelensky initiated a ban on TV channels controlled by Medvedchuk, and later, criminal charges against him).[88] In this respect, a lack of previous experience in politics became an asset rather than a liability for Zelensky and his team.

Aside from political changes, institutional changes were also important for rebuilding the Ukrainian state. The program of decentralization initiated during the period of Poroshenko's presidency, and fully implemented under Zelensky's leadership, included not only a major empowerment of local communities (*hromada*) but also new local elections and a partial replacement of local elites. While Russia's elites and leadership saw the top-down "power vertical" as the only plausible mechanism of control of subordinates, despite the aggravation of principal-agent problems, Ukrainian politicians took a different path. They opted for major fiscal, administrative, and political decentralization, and greatly improved the effectiveness of local governments in Ukraine. The advantages of this reform became especially important after February 2022, in the wake of the Russian assault, when Ukrainian local communities played an important role in the coordination of many activities related to resistance against the assault.[89]

Finally, the previously inexperienced Zelensky proved to be a cunning and consistent negotiator on the diplomatic front, both before and after the Russian assault. Despite initial expectations that the status of separatist Donbas would be renegotiated in order to appease Russia, Zelensky effectively pursued Ukrainian interests during these negotiations. In December 2019, when Putin and Zelensky met in

THE GREAT SELF-DECEPTION

Paris for a top-level discussion on the implementation of the Minsk agreement regarding the future fate of Donbas, Zelensky openly and unequivocally denied the idea of having elections in these separatist areas before taking the Russian–Ukrainian border under Ukrainian control. As this issue was vague in the text of the Minsk agreement, Russia attempted to retain its control over the borders with separatist areas. Putin failed to impose his interpretation of the Minsk agreement on Zelensky, and, according to some observers, was left severely offended by the meeting.[90] Later on, during the first weeks after the Russian assault, Zelensky not only demonstrated personal courage, refusing to leave Kyiv despite personal danger and high risk of assassination, but also demonstrated outstandingly successful diplomatic skills, quickly establishing a major pro-Ukrainian coalition of Western countries which played an important role in the Ukrainian resistance. To summarize, the notorious weakness of the Ukrainian state and of Ukrainian elites was greatly overestimated by the Kremlin. In particular, its assessments ignored and/or misinterpreted changes in Ukraine after 2014, and the reasons for these misperceptions strongly reflected the Kremlin's worldviews. Most probably, the political and institutional changes in Ukraine were considered symptoms of its weakness, while the preservation of the political status quo in Russia was seen as a sign of its strength. Again, the reality was the opposite of the Kremlin's expectations.

The most far-fetched misperceptions by the Kremlin were related not to Ukraine as such but rather to support for Ukraine in the West, which was greatly underestimated. Russian elites do not believe in any values-based actions at all, either domestically or internationally, and tend to see only the pragmatic short-term interests of cynical politicians – in a sense, they see their own mirror image in their adversaries. The very idea of international democratic solidarity was considered in the Kremlin to be naïve at best. Rather, the Kremlin's policymakers considered American- and European-driven democracy promotion to merely be cover for imposing American and/or European control over other countries (especially with regard to Ukraine, where Western support for both the Orange Revolution and the Revolution of Dignity proved to be an important, though not decisive, factor in their successes and the Kremlin's defeats).

At the same time, the Russian elites very cynically expected that any form of support for allies abroad was more or less a bargaining chip between pivotal actors of global politics, and could be easily sold for material or other benefits during top-level negotiations. In fact, Russia behaved more or less in this way during the new round of military conflict between Armenia and Azerbaijan over Nagorno-Karabakh, which began in 2020 as a follow-up to the 1990s war. Instead of serving as a guarantor of the preservation of the previous status quo both politically and militarily, Russian authorities abstained from any actions and closed their eyes to Azerbaijani attacks on Nagorno-Karabakh (populated by Armenians), and the subsequent conquest of its territory in 2023.[91] Despite the fact that Armenia was a member of the Russia-led Collective Security Treaty Organization, aimed at protecting the security of its respective member states, Russia blatantly ignored Armenian requests for assistance. The reasons for this included the fact that Russia was heavily dependent on Turkey's support, especially in the wake of Western sanctions imposed after February 2022. As Turkey was (and is) a major patron of Azerbaijan, Russia simply betrayed its junior ally in the South Caucasus for the sake of certain benefits from cooperation with Turkey, an increasingly powerful actor (or, more importantly, for the sake of avoiding potential conflict with Turkey amid ongoing US and EU sanctions).[92] In other words, Russia's hopes and fears with regard to Turkey outweighed its obligations to its Armenian allies.

Such behavior is viewed in the Kremlin as a role model for dealing with any other countries, even with regard to their security obligations within the NATO framework. For example, the idea of military conquest of the Baltic States was more or less acceptable among Russian observers, as it was expected that the US and European NATO members would not shed the blood of their soldiers for the freedom of Estonians, Latvians, and Lithuanians.[93] Moreover, the major Russian expert on international relations Sergey Karaganov even argued in June 2023 that Russia could drop a nuclear bomb on the Polish city of Poznan with impunity, as Russia's military might and its retaliatory nuclear strike capability would prevent any NATO military response.[94] In other words, the Kremlin expected that the Russian military assault on Ukraine would not provoke any serious reaction from Ukraine's American and European allies. Even if they did not completely withdraw from Ukraine similarly to the US fleeing from Afghanistan, they would probably limit themselves to symbolic gestures and not provide meaningful military assistance. However, Russia heavily overestimated not only its own military capability but also the pragmatic cynicism of the Western elites and leadership.

THE GREAT SELF-DECEPTION

The Kremlin misunderstood the fact that, unlike the relatively minor burden of the failure in Afghanistan, the Russian assault on Ukraine was perceived by the "collective West" as a major challenge to its ontological security, if not to its survival.

The other manifestation of the Kremlin's pragmatic cynicism was its extraordinarily strong belief not only in its military might but also in its major economic weapon vis-à-vis Europe, namely, Russian gas. Since the 2000s, Russian state officials had openly positioned Russia as an "energy superpower"[95] and proudly argued that European reliance upon Russian gas supply would be a major tool of Russian political dominance in Europe, as Russia would be able to dictate its terms to European consumers not only economically but also politically.[96] Gazprom, the Russian state gas monopoly, imposed its conditions on prices and terms of supply on foreign consumers, using both the carrot of attractive conditions of long-term contracts and the stick of the threat of cutting off the supply of gas, especially during cold winter seasons. These threats took the form of not only words but deeds, as Russia actually cut the gas supply to Ukraine several times in the period of the "gas wars" in the 2000s, during Victor Yushchenko's presidency, as a major tool of political pressure against Ukraine.[97] It is no wonder that the Kremlin expected that heavy EU dependence on the supply of gas from Russia (about 45% of total gas imports in 2021) would make many European countries (including Germany, Austria, Hungary, and Finland) very vulnerable to Russia and less active in supporting Ukraine and imposing sanctions on Russia. The Kremlin openly threatened European consumers with their gas supply being cut during the winter of 2022–3. But in fact, as chapter 5 demonstrates, the effects of the Russian gas attack on the EU were quite the opposite of its initial expectations.[98]

In fact, the Kremlin greatly overestimated the market strength of its monopoly, both in economic and in technical terms. In 2022–3, European consumers were able to substitute the Gazprom supply with various alternatives, including (but not limited to) increasing imports of liquid natural gas up to 60% of volume compared to the pre-2022 period. This liquid gas was imported to Europe from elsewhere, including Russia (at least, until 2024).[99] To some extent, European consumers used major reserves of gas bought by Germans, as well as other consumers, before the Russian assault on Ukraine and accumulated in storage. Gas import via pipelines to the EU from other suppliers, such as Norway and Azerbaijan, also increased. In this respect, Russia's threats of major crises in Europe due to cutting off its gas supply were unreasonable and not evidence-based. In turn, Russia suffered much more than European consumers in economic terms: its major losses in the European markets could not be compensated by any prospective consumers (including Chinese ones).[100] Apart from incredibly inaccurate calculations of the costs and benefits of the Russian gas offensive, misperceptions by the Kremlin played another important role in this failure. The Russian elites overly believed in the short-term pragmatic cynicism of Europeans and their fear of immediate losses, and overly expected that they would quickly surrender rather than search for long-term alternatives to Russia's pressure.

Finally, the Russian elites perceived the Western countries not only as internally weak and incapable adversaries but also as actors poorly prepared for collective action. For a long time, the Kremlin and its experts considered any multilateral organizations, especially the European Union, to be inefficient entities[101] known for long discussions and internal contradictions, and vulnerable to Russia's divide-and-rule attacks.[102] In particular, the pro-Russian lobby in the EU (led by Hungary) was perceived as a potentially strong veto player which could inhibit, if not prevent, support for Ukraine.[103] The Kremlin also expected that pro-Russian parties and politicians in individual European countries (ranging from AfD and Die Linke in Germany to the Five Stars, League and Forza Italia in Italy) could perform similar functions on the national level of other EU member states.[104] Misperceptions about the internal weakness and lack of cohesiveness of elites in European countries and their inefficiency at the EU level resulted, to a great degree, from the major disdain of Russian elites toward the political and institutional constraints on arbitrary actions typical for many democracies as well as for international organizations. But this vision was very much fueled by the unreasonable claims and outdated desires of the Russian elites, who considered their own country and themselves to be superior to any other country and any international organization, being more decisive, active, and aggressive than their rivals.

As with many other Kremlin perceptions, this vision proved to be wrong. Contrary to the expectations of weakness of European countries and of the EU, they swiftly and consistently responded to the Russian assault on Ukraine, both individually and collectively. European soft-liners like Germany (which were previously more oriented toward compromise with Russia) joined their efforts with hard-liner critics of Russia like Poland and Estonia, and the EU acted quite decisively[105] despite visible (but not veto-level) resistance from Hungary. Furthermore, pro-Russian parties and politicians had limited impact in individual European states (with some notable exceptions, such as in Bulgaria).[106] In particular, Finland became a major source of disillusionment for Russia. A previous client state of the Soviet Union, which had remained relatively loyal to Russia before February 2022 and had no previous intentions of joining NATO, it quickly changed its positioning vis-à-vis Russia soon after the assault on Ukraine.[107] A new consensus of the Finnish elites emerged, and the country soon applied for NATO membership;[108] moreover, the Finnish elites persuaded their Swedish neighbors to join NATO as well. Even though Turkey and Hungary attempted to block NATO accession for a while, these barriers were overcome by 2023. As a result, the Kremlin, which had requested a major retreat of NATO from Russia's borders some months before the assault, found its greatest enemies just next door, and was unable to resist the new NATO expansion. Although the pro-Ukrainian coalition in the EU and NATO did not always work smoothly, and tensions between hawkish and dovish states and their governments sometimes became apparent, the solid international support for Ukraine stabilized and Russia's actions were not able to undermine it.[109]

Conclusion

Looking at this long list of misperceptions by Russia's elites, one can see how they had a devastating impact on the very idea of the Russian assault on Ukraine and on its implementation. The vision of Russia's elites was greatly undermined by various prejudices, feelings of disdain, and wrong estimations that laid down the foundations of their worldviews. The numerous flaws of this vision resulted from unreasonable status-seeking claims and outdated normative ideals of Russia's elites, whose worldviews failed to change over time due to the organizational and ideational legacies of the Soviet security apparatus and the generational trajectories of the aging "seventiers." They had remained in power for too long and were not able to resist the process of "degeneration" of Russia's regime. Their vulnerability to conspiracy theories amid conditions of "informational autocracy" further aggravated these vices.

Misperceptions as such are hardly unique to contemporary Russian elites. Moreover, misperceptions have been a norm rather than an exception in world politics in various historical periods. In many states, in the past and today, politicians and policymakers demonstrate a long history of misperceptions about their adversaries and themselves, and these misperceptions often have a negative impact on their foreign policy choices.[110] Among many other examples, the Western approaches to the Soviet Union as well as to post-Soviet Russia are not much different in this respect.[111] The difference is that various Western politicians and policymakers often (but not always) were able to adjust their perceptions (including perceptions of Russia), correcting errors if and when they realized that their previous visions were wrong. However, in Russia's case, acceptance of harsh realities and open recognition of previous misperceptions may be very costly for Russian leaders and elites. This is why this issue may become of crucial importance for the future. Even if they realize that their frame of reference before February 2022 was misleading and contributed to numerous errors, the correction of these errors is considered a dangerous choice for the rulers of the country. Judging from this perspective, the continuity of misperceptions despite understanding of their negative consequences is not just a side effect of self-deceptive wrongdoings, but rather a conscious choice made by Russian leadership and elites. This is why, after the failure of the initial plans to take over Ukraine, instead of adjusting its perceptions, the Kremlin refused to recognize that its well-developed vision of Ukraine, of the West, and of Russia itself was a great self-deception, which contributed to far-reaching negative policy consequences. Russian elites persisted in their misperceptions over time, and their self-deception remained largely unchanged despite the fact that it was only aggravating these negative consequences further. Deeply rooted misperceptions prevented Russian elites from accepting the harsh reality, and Russia continued to act according to the principle of "in for a penny, in for a pound."

Chapter 5

THE VICTIMS OF PREVIOUS SUCCESSES

The Russian assault on Ukraine in February 2022 did not come out of the blue just because of a one-off decision by Putin and his entourage. This assault was the culmination of a long preparation, which involved more than purely military activities. The preparation for the Ukrainian "special military operation" to a large degree involved a process of diminishing both domestic and international constraints on the military conflict. This process took a relatively long time and was fairly successful until the military assault. Over the course of these preparations, the Kremlin was able to weaken all potential sources of anti-military resistance domestically (political parties, civil society NGOs, and independent media)[1] and met little resistance to growing militarism internationally. The Russian five-day war in Georgia in 2008, the annexation of Crimea in 2014, the war in Donbas in 2014–15, and the military intervention in Syria (with its most active phase in 2015–17) could not be punished by the targets of these attacks, while Western states responded to these actions sluggishly and inconsistently. They did not use political and military instruments to contain Russia until February 2022. This experience told the Russian strategists who planned the assault on Ukraine that this time everything would be the same: despite a great deal of noise in the media, numerous protests by activists and celebrities, and much official concern from major international organizations, there would be no meaningful resistance to Russia. The Kremlin could reasonably expect that powerful global political and economic actors would prefer to continue "business as usual" in terms of relations with Russia and close their eyes to the expansion of Russia's sphere of influence to cover Ukraine.[2] Furthermore, perceptions that Russian military might was so strong that the Kremlin could easily swallow Ukraine in a matter of weeks, if not days, dominated the minds of most domestic and international observers.[3] The widespread (although not the only) narrative before the assault was that any resistance against Russian military action was a completely useless enterprise and only a waste of time and resources, that appeasement of an aggressive Russia was the only solution for the West, and that Ukrainians had no choice other than to surrender to Russia.[4] One might argue that the use of force as the Kremlin's tool covered the weakness of any other tools, but after the tool of coercion was applied successfully previously, why were any other tools necessary at all? In a way, the spirit of the time in Europe some months before the Russian assault closely resembled the spirit of Munich in September 1938, when the British and French leadership were so afraid of Hitler that they allowed him to do whatever he wanted.[5]

These perceptions and expectations proved to be wrong. However, the problem was not only that they were based upon wild overestimation of Russia's military might and its overall capabilities. The increasing fear of the Kremlin's aggression in the West greatly contributed to the increasing appetites of Russia's leadership. In judging by the previous experience of successful use of fear and blackmail as major tools of Russian aggressive dominance, alongside the threat of use of nuclear weapons as its instrument of foreign policy, the Kremlin developed and solidified a feeling of impunity due to Russia's invincibility.[6] This impunity increased with every unpunished expression of the Kremlin's drive toward international aggressiveness and domestic repressiveness. Russia's rulers believed that they would never be punished, either legally or politically.[7] Similarly to a street hooligan who may impose his control over the entire neighborhood because of the fear of local residents and the absence or inaction of the police, the Kremlin believed that there was no way to resist its actions, and therefore it could do whatever it wanted. From this perspective, Russia's December 2021 ultimatum to the US and NATO about unconditional acceptance of Russia's demands in Europe and elsewhere was not merely Kremlin bravado but rather a logical extension of previous achievements of its assertive and ruthless foreign policy. If Western objections to the assault on Georgia or the annexation of Crimea were so inconsequential,[8] then why not go further and raise the stakes? Why not try to redesign the global order, given the fact that your counterpart previously behaved like a scared, passive, and indecisive weakling? This is why the Russian leadership could expect that potential Western sanctions due to the "special military operation" in Ukraine would remain largely personal, symbolic, and easy to bypass (as they were after the annexation of Crimea in 2014), and would not harm key sectors of the Russian economy. The fact that before the assault on Ukraine, a significant portion of Russian currency reserves were still routinely kept in US dollars and euros accumulated in the West, was very telling in this respect. Yet in 2022, everything was different. Instead of humiliating its adversaries, Russia faced strong resistance from Ukraine and its supporters in the "collective West," and Russia's reliance on threats of coercion was firmly countered for the first time since the end of the Cold War. However, this counter came too late, as the elaborated practice of assertive and aggressive behavior by the Kremlin, both domestically and internationally, had already become a kind of spiral. This spiral meant that the Kremlin's invincibility bred its impunity, while impunity paved the way to its further invincibility, and the expansion of this spiral was perceived as seemingly endless. In a way, the Kremlin became a victim of its previous successes, as its impunity was expected to continue virtually forever.

This is why the Kremlin was unwilling and, in all likelihood, unable to limit itself. Quite the opposite, given all of the vices analyzed in the previous chapters of this book – the regime's personalism, bad governance, and major misperceptions – the Kremlin had no serious incentives to stop further expansion of the spiral of its ambitions before the assault on Ukraine. Since the very idea of containing Russia was taboo for many American and European politicians, the Kremlin perceived the sluggish Western response as evidence of its invulnerability and further increased its appetite. The trap of impunity contributed to a firm expectation that Russia would never be punished by any adversary, irrespective of Russia's actions. In other words, Russia would never face any major constraints or effective resistance. Thus, the Kremlin expected to have free rein to do whatever it wanted both domestically and internationally. After the assault on Ukraine, the critical (although not decisive) blow to these aims came as an unpleasant surprise to the Kremlin.

The trap of impunity may have become a certain consequence of the vices of the regime's personalism, bad governance, and major misperceptions. Still, its emergence and development over time followed its own distinctive logic. This logic was driven by the previous trajectories of Russia's domestic politics and its foreign policy after the Soviet collapse. Although the Kremlin faced several major setbacks in the 1990s, after these bumps on the road, successful use of coercion met with limited resistance both domestically and internationally, which paved the way to further expansion of the spiral of impunity. The further advancement of unpunished use of violent and aggressive tools in domestic politics and foreign policy in post-Soviet Russia was primarily related to the rise of the coercive apparatus, of *siloviki*, who became key players in politics and policy-making. They achieved major successes through various means of coercion at home (ranging from imprisonment to attempted killings) and abroad (ranging from conquest of foreign territories to attempted coups), and until February 2022 were able to reach their goals without serious risks of failure. Constraints on this behavior weakened over time, and the Kremlin intended to go further and further after every success of its aggressive approach.

Even though these expectations of impunity were largely socially constructed and promoted by the Kremlin, they were based on lessons learned by the Russian leadership during the post-Soviet decades. The main lessons were related to the fact that once successful coercion was justified domestically and met little resistance internationally, the extensive use of this instrument became the default option for Russian politics and policy-making, while compromise solutions were pushed off the agenda. This chapter will concentrate on analysis of the development of post-Soviet Russian impunity and on its effects on the assault on Ukraine. With regard to the domestic arena, the development of impunity was mostly driven by the rise of *siloviki* and the increasing impact of coercion as a major tool of politics. As to the international arena, the development of impunity resulted from a complex combination of post-Cold War miscalculations by the US and its European allies, their inconsistent policies toward Russia, and the sluggish and cowardly response to early Russian offenses. In addition, the use of nuclear threats against Russia's rivals has remained the Kremlin's last resort since Soviet times, and the frequency of the threats of use of this tool increased some months before and especially after the assault on Ukraine. These two interconnected approaches by the Kremlin greatly influenced the construction of the trap of impunity and its persistence after the Russian assault on Ukraine and its initial failure in the first stage of the "special military operation."

Domestic Politics: from Offense to Offense

The entire post-Soviet history of Russia is largely a history of the rise of its *siloviki*.[9] This segment of the state, which was previously tightly controlled by the Communist Party, and suffered heavily from the Soviet collapse and turbulent economic transformation, became the main beneficiary of the construction of the post-Soviet political and institutional order. This process is often attributed to the dominance of Vladimir Putin and his entourage, but the roots of the unconstrained and unpunished use of violence and coercion run much deeper. In essence, civilian segments of the Russian elites relied heavily upon *siloviki* during the conflicts of the 1990s, built tacit alliances with these actors in the 2000s, and then surrendered and submissively accepted their unconditional dominance in the 2010s, if not earlier.[10] The *siloviki*, in turn, faced fewer and fewer constraints over time. Over the three post-Soviet decades, they became free from political and institutional control, seized a monopoly on legitimate use of violence on behalf of the state, and embraced voracious rent-seeking at all levels of Russian governance. Meanwhile, *siloviki*, known for their militarist, anti-Western, and non-democratic political preferences,[11] gradually imposed their firm control over all segments of the Russian polity, economy, and society, with the intention of keeping this control in their hands for long decades, if not centuries. By the 2020s, they felt themselves invincible in the domestic arena and also expanded their influence internationally.

One might imagine that the Russian *siloviki* were omnipotent and super-talented actors that resembled characters from spy movies and crime novels. In fact, they were more or less standard post-Soviet state bureaucrats, who were not particularly educated or intellectually sophisticated, albeit able to establish dense patronage networks since late-Soviet times. After the Soviet collapse, the state security apparatus was not seriously reformed, and largely preserved its previous structure despite attempts at its fragmentation and decentralization in the 1990s.[12] Although the institutional regeneration of old state security agencies and proliferation of new ones in the 2000s contributed to further empowerment of *siloviki*, the major source of their strength was different. In fact, *siloviki* became strong not so much because of their outstanding excellence in security and law and order but rather because of the poor performance of other actors, who were forced to rely upon their resources and capabilities, and over time degenerated into hostages of *siloviki* in various ways. In other words, the rise of *siloviki* to some extent resulted from a lucky combination of favorable circumstances, and perceptions of impunity spiraled out as a side effect of repeated victories over time. Certainly, the multiple grievances of the Russian elites regarding the decline of Russia's global status after the Soviet collapse and their revanchist stance greatly fueled a security-dominated approach to politics and policy-making.

The first step toward the rise of *siloviki* was the 1993 conflict between President Yeltsin and the Russian parliament. This conflict initially emerged as a policy disagreement between market reformers in the government and a loose informal coalition of their parliamentary critics, but soon developed into a zero-sum game. Instead of seeking compromise and a peaceful resolution to the conflict, both sides attempted to use the coercive apparatus as an instrument in their power struggle. Yeltsin disbanded the parliament and insisted on its further disempowerment within the framework of the new constitution. The parliament, in turn, impeached Yeltsin, thus turning the conflict into a deadlock. As negotiations between sides failed, and supporters of the parliament launched riots in the center of Moscow, Yeltsin used the military against the parliament, and coerced his political opponents into giving in after shelling the parliamentary building.[13] As a result, not only did the top military and security officials greatly increase their influence, but also Yeltsin himself demonstrated his vulnerability. It made his potential exit from the political arena highly problematic. After using force against the parliament, he faced a real threat of criminal prosecution in case of electoral defeat. This is why during the 1996 presidential elections, Yeltsin could not allow himself to lose and leave the Kremlin, as he did not intend to bear responsibility for the 1993 conflict. In essence, the actual political choice at that time was between Yeltsin's victory in an unfair electoral contest and the abolition of elections as such (with the latter option advocated by *siloviki*).[14]

The major problem for *siloviki* in the 1990s was their poor performance and loose control over the use of violence. The increase in crime amid the decline of state capacity and protracted transformation recession contributed to the rise of "violent entrepreneurship" by criminal gangs, which was absorbed by the state agencies only in the 2000s.[15] The greatest failure of *siloviki* related to the First Chechen

War of 1994–6.[16] The idea of a "small victorious war" against the separatist region of Chechnya, which declared its independence in 1991, and was out of the Kremlin's control, was considered an attractive option for increasing Yeltsin's approval ratings before the 1996 presidential election. However, the "special military operation" in Chechnya completely failed from the very beginning, and became a protracted local war with thousands of Russian soldiers killed (and the number of victims among residents of Chechnya was outstandingly high). The First Chechen War had been poorly prepared and became very unpopular. In the end, *siloviki* were discredited and faced personnel reshuffling, and thus their influence decreased for a while. During Yeltsin's reelection campaign in 1996, their plan to disband parliament and postpone elections failed, and in the end, they were nearly expelled from the informal ruling coalition.

However, the economic crisis of 1998 clearly demonstrated Yeltsin's weakness and his need to rely on *siloviki* for his political or even physical survival. Yeltsin was incredibly unpopular, was attacked by the Communist majority in the State Duma with the threat of impeachment (an attempt to do so failed in May 1999), and many representatives of the elites openly blamed Yeltsin and his entourage for multiple political and policy failures. The prospect of bearing responsibility for these failures at the end of Yeltsin's rule was certainly unacceptable for the Kremlin. This issue was resolved by Yeltsin's choice of a loyal successor, Vladimir Putin, who made *siloviki* the center of his new ruling coalition and used this milieu as the main recruitment pool for new elites.[17] The most important turning point was the launching of the Second Chechen War (1999–2002), which was perceived by the Russian general public as a response to terrorist attacks in Moscow and other Russian cities, attributed to Chechen separatists. The new war, unlike its 1994–6 predecessor, was largely perceived by the Russian elites as righteous and a legitimate use of state violence in domestic politics. As the Kremlin was much better prepared in military terms and endorsed by the public, the war resulted in the seizure of Chechnya's territory.[18] The subsequent outsourcing of violence within this territory to local cadres loyal to the Kremlin – first, to Akhmad Kadyrov, and after his assassination in 2004, to his son Ramzan (the ruler of Chechnya at the time of writing) – was considered by the Russian elites to be a desirable outcome.[19] Russia's successful revenge, which was able to restore the coercive capacity of the state and achieved the conquest of Chechnya, contributed to the further rise of militarism among elites, both domestically and internationally. This success dramatically changed the Russian elites' perceptions, as they were persuaded that use of force was the most efficient and powerful instrument of politics. In a way, this is true: as Mao Zedong noted, "political power grows out of the barrel of a gun" in various countries, including post-Communist Russia. However, the problem is that in contrast to Communist regimes, with their high institutionalization and firm party-based control over the coercive apparatus of the state, no such mechanisms were built under personalist authoritarianism.[20] As these mechanisms of control were almost exclusively linked to personal ties between top military and security officials and the political leadership, it is no wonder that in the wake of the consolidation of the personalist regime in Russia, the influence of *siloviki* greatly increased.

The further rise of *siloviki* was marked by the "Yukos Affair" in 2003,[21] which contributed to the launching of large-scale nationalization of economic assets and made *siloviki* veto players in Russian domestic politics and policy-making, placing technocratic state bureaucrats and business actors into a subordinated role.[22] During the wave of "color revolutions" and especially the Arab Spring, the Russian political leadership realized the high risk of losing political power, and by that time *siloviki* were considered the only domestic actors able to prevent such a scenario. After the series of mass protests in 2011–12, the use of violence (or threat thereof) as a mechanism for maintenance of the political status quo became the Kremlin's main approach. The shift towards repression launched by Putin in 2012 made *siloviki* pivotal players in Russian politics; civilian state bureaucrats and business actors, as well as the media and civil society, became subordinate to them. The increasing use of state repression in various forms, ranging from imprisonment of ministers, regional governors, city mayors, and entrepreneurs to contract killing of major opposition figures, such as the assassination of the former deputy prime minister Boris Nemtsov in 2015 and the poisoning of the opposition leader Alexei Navalny in 2020 (who died in prison in 2024), dramatically transformed Russia's public landscape.[23] The state-sponsored "politics of fear"[24] made Russia's elites hostages of *siloviki* well before the Russian assault on Ukraine, despite visible opposition activism in various forms. One might argue that by the early 2020s, *siloviki*, who had received carte blanche to do virtually anything they wanted, had achieved almost everything they could in Russian domestic politics and policy-making and might have felt themselves invincible. Given the well-established connections between leading *siloviki* and Vladimir Putin, they were able to retain their impunity, once acquired, irrespective of their performance, being rewarded with an increasing share of rents and power.

It is no wonder that the *siloviki* not only retained but also increased their control over domestic issues after launching the assault on Ukraine. Due to the previous successful "politics of fear" and toughening of state repression in February 2022, the "special military operation" faced weak open opposition domestically. Civil resistance in Russia was subjected to coercion in one way or another: opposition-leaning media outlets and independent NGOs were closed or silenced, many activists were jailed or forced to emigrate, social media sites were banned or accepted self-censorship, and the like. In a way, *siloviki* were able to celebrate their full victory from the beginning of the assault. They could behave offensively without any risk of punishment for poor performance, and expansion of their domestic offenses abroad after February 2022 was a logical extension of what they had achieved so far. At that time, the perceptions of their impunity skyrocketed, and have remained very high to date despite the fact that the goals of the Russian assault on Ukraine have not been achieved: as long as the domestic political status quo persists, *siloviki* can feel themselves invincible. However, as the case of Prigozhin's failed mutiny, described in chapter 3, demonstrated, the impunity of *siloviki* amid a lack of political and institutional control has made the political order itself rather vulnerable and fragile, while the performance of the Russian state apparatus in general, and of *siloviki* in particular, remains highly imperfect, to put it mildly.

In essence, following the weakness and fragmentation of the Russian elites and their poor performance in the 1990s, *siloviki* were able to seize the moment of Russia's recovery in the 2000s and maximize their control and rents without any meaningful resistance. This lack of resistance resulted from major miscalculations, illusions, and short-term preferences of the Russian elites. Being frightened and/or coopted by *siloviki*, they rather timorously, reluctantly, and unequivocally surrendered before the coercive apparatus of the Russian state, even though they had had enough resources and capacities to prevent the rise of *siloviki* before it occurred. Curiously, in addition to the weak resistance of domestic actors,[25] the weak resistance of international actors to Russia's attitude of impunity followed the same pattern of passivity and obedience to some extent, albeit for different reasons.

The International Arena: How Russia Became Unconstrained

In a way, the United States and their allies (the "collective West") also became victims of their previous success, achieved at the end of the Cold War when Communism in Europe suddenly and unexpectedly collapsed. Although the debate on what caused this collapse, and to what extent the West contributed to it, seems endless, it is important to reconsider not the causes of the West's sudden victory over its Soviet rival, but rather its consequences. The fall of the Berlin Wall and the end of Soviet Communism were not only perceived as "the end of history,"[26] but also had numerous policy implications.[27] The victory of the West did not result in any official recognition, which would imply the losing side's acceptance and its recognition of its own defeat (as happened at the end of World War II), and was therefore perceived as a victory almost by default.[28] Such an outcome meant a big question mark over its irreversibility, as the possible revision of the events of 1989–91 was a matter of the losers' good or ill will and capabilities. The West was so euphoric on the one hand, and so naïve and shortsighted on the other, that it did not invest any serious effort into containment of Russia, the main loser at the end of the Cold War, from revanchist foreign policy in the future. At minimum, major Russia-related risks were widely misunderstood by the American and European establishments, and addressed more retrospectively (such as the possible restoration of Communist rule in the 1990s) rather than prospectively. Except for control over the potential spread of nuclear arms beyond Russia after the Soviet collapse, there was no clear and consistent strategy for dealing with these issues, and the measures taken by the Western governments were largely ad hoc. As a result, Russia's revanchist potential was greatly underestimated in the 1990s, when Russia was not able or willing to transform itself into a major revisionist power.[29] In fact, not many observers expected such a U-turn to come.

This is not to say that the question "what to do with Russia?" was totally off the agenda of Western policymakers in the 1990s. However, the proposed answers addressed only current affairs and rarely concerned long-term perspectives beyond these needs. In essence, strategic directions for dealing with an ex-enemy who was suddenly defeated may be considered along the lines of "good cop" or "bad cop" approaches. A "good cop" approach implies integration of the ex-enemy into the Western world as a junior partner, based on its acceptance of a subordinate role and readiness to obey, driven mostly by positive incentives. The East European integration into the EU in the 1990s and the 2000s, or West German integration into the "collective West" in the 1950s, may be prime examples of this. The "bad cop" approach implies further toughening of policy towards the ex-enemy, destruction and/or elimination of its potential for aggression, and direct and/or indirect control over its policies, based on enforcement of new rules of the game and driven mostly by negative incentives. The actions of the Allies against the Central Powers after World War I may be a prime example. However, in the case of Russia after the Soviet collapse, the "collective West" was unwilling to pursue either of these options.[30]

The "bad cop" approach was not considered a plausible solution after decades of a difficult and costly Cold War, which had consumed so much effort and so many resources of Western policymakers. They were sick and tired of aggressive Soviet foreign policy, happily welcomed Gorbachev's perestroika and its numerous effects, and had no intention of continuing the previous confrontation after victory in the Cold War. The very idea that Russia's retreat from the Soviet-style approach was just a temporary and short-term phenomenon, and that Russia would dream of restoring its stance of the early years of the Cold War as a "golden age,"[31] was unthinkable in the early 1990s. This is why the use of the moment to further weaken Russia could hardly have made it onto the policy agenda, even though retrospectively from a post-2022 perspective, it may seem a missed opportunity. As to the "good cop" approach, matters were even more complicated. On the one hand, the efforts of Western policymakers to integrate Russia were half-hearted at best: the amount of Western aid to Russia was fairly limited, while the many warm words about friendly relationships with Russia (in particular, offered by the Clinton administration) were scarcely converted into deeds. The approach of US policymakers to Russia in the 1990s vacillated between attempts to outmaneuver Russia's leaders (as in the case of NATO expansion into Eastern Europe with only moderate objections from Yeltsin) and their selective appeasement (as in the case of Russia's acceptance into the prestigious G7 group, a club of leading democracies, which later transformed into the G8). These tactical successes, however, did not resolve problems but rather postponed them. On the other hand, Russian politicians and policymakers after the Soviet collapse were not ready to accept that their country was just an ordinary second-order state rather than a global leader, and were strongly dissatisfied with the major decline in Russia's status compared to the Soviet Union, perceiving it with a great sense of grievance. The feeling of disillusionment among elites became particularly strong during the 1999 war in Yugoslavia, when the Russian Prime Minister Primakov cancelled his official visit to Washington, DC, protesting against the NATO bombing of Belgrade. This demonstrative move, however, did not bring Russia success in the Balkans.[32] At the same time, in the 1990s, Russia's state officials behaved not so differently from their counterparts in numerous Third World countries toward the West. They begged the IMF and the World Bank for aid and cheated donors in one way or another, offered them unfulfilled promises, and frightened Western politicians with claims that without their unconditional support for the political status quo, the coming of Communists to power would send Russia into a hell of turmoil, if not outright civil war.[33] Such tactics yielded some fruit, as Western politicians easily bought the Kremlin's narratives during the political crisis of October 1993 and during Yeltsin's reelection bid in June–July 1996, afraid of possible Communist revenge more than anything else. However, their conspicuous, yet mostly rhetorical, support did not affect Russia's domestic developments in a serious way. Moreover, justly or not, Russian elites believed that they deserved more serious concessions and better treatment from the West and were not ready to serve as rank-and-file officers under the court of the "collective West."

The post-Soviet Russian elites faced a fundamental problem in their status-seeking. The Soviet Union had claimed to have the highest possible status, that of global superpower, and these claims were justified in various ways; for post-Soviet Russia, which inherited many attributes of highest status (such as permanent membership in the UN Security Council), this was in fact an overstatement. In other words, Russia's claim of highest status poorly fit its material capabilities, economic conditions (especially in the 1990s) and the like. Such a disjuncture became a major source of strain between Russia and the "collective West," which only increased over time. The statement by Barack Obama, who labeled Russia a "regional power" and nothing more in the 2010s, correctly reflected the real state of affairs. However, during Russia's turbulent transformation in the 1990s, the preservation of its highest status and even its expansion to greater heights became an *idée fixe* for Russian elites. Indeed, Yeltsin's 1999 demand to Clinton, "just give Europe to Russia" (see chapter 4), was quite telling in this respect. Even at that time, Russian elites refused to be integrated into the post-Cold War world under Western conditions, and demanded equal status with the United States. As no acceptable substitution for the lost great power status was proposed either by the "collective West" or by the Russian elites themselves, the sense of injustice paved the way for numerous grievances and revanchist feelings. If the transformation recession of the 1990s had continued for a longer period of time, then most probably, Russian elites would sooner or later have been forced to accept Russia's status as an ordinary country (or, as Andrei Shleifer and Daniel Treisman labeled it, "a normal country"),[34] which could not claim more than the role of "regional power." This would also mean that over time they could accept previous losses as an undesirable yet inevitable outcome of Russia's developmental trajectory, and be ready for gradual integration into the "collective West" as its more or less loyal semi-periphery. But quite the opposite, in the 2000s, Russia rebounded too rapidly in its post-transition economic recovery, and this sudden turn from bust to boom (unexpected by the Russian elites themselves) dramatically changed Russia's international positioning in the direction of major revisionism.

The economic boom of the 2000s in Russia not only helped Putin to consolidate his authoritarian regime domestically but also paved the way to more assertive positioning of Russia in the international arena. Initially, Putin attempted to flirt with Western leaders, sincerely supported the United States after the terrorist attacks in September 2001, and even discussed the idea of Russia's membership in NATO. However, these steps did not bring immediate benefits to the Russian leadership, as the US and its European allies were not ready to treat Russia as a global superpower, a major international veto player, and Russian leaders, in turn, were not ready to accept their second-order global status, even though it probably corresponded with the country's capabilities. Moreover, the wave of "color revolutions" which struck Serbia, Georgia, Ukraine, and Kyrgyzstan in the first half of the 2000s, together with US intervention in Iraq within the context of "democracy promotion" (or, rather, of overthrow of autocracies), was perceived in the Kremlin as a dangerous challenge to Russia both domestically and internationally.[35] These fears further multiplied in the early 2010s, when the deposal of authoritarian regimes in Tunisia, Egypt, and Libya during the Arab Spring was largely perceived in the Kremlin as a Western-driven conspiracy amid the 2011–12 wave of mass protests in Russia.[36] This combination of fears, disillusionments, and grievances, alongside the desire for further restoration of Russia's role as a global superpower, paved the way to more assertive and unconstrained international positioning by Russia. The turning point was marked by Putin's speech at the Munich Security Conference in February 2007, in which he lambasted the US-led international order, accusing the "collective West" of deceiving Russia in advance of NATO's eastward expansion. He also warned that further steps in this direction would become a major threat to Russia's national security, and announced a decisive response based on the use of force (or threats thereof).

Judging from a post-2022 perspective, Putin's Munich speech may be regarded as revelatory of his later intentions of Russia's international assertiveness, if not an open declaration of future military conflict against the West. However, at that time, the Western response was rather cowardly and sluggish, despite certain warning calls from various experts.[37] On the contrary, a turn to a policy of containing Russia was not on the agenda of the US and NATO not only in 2007, but also later, up until February 2022. On the one hand, policy toward Russia continued to follow the path of business as usual, which had developed amid the rapid economic growth in Russia in the 2000s. On the other hand, the idea of further expanding NATO and offering membership to Ukraine and Georgia, initially proposed by the US in 2008, was postponed until better times because of Russia's loud objections.[38] In a sense, Putin's Munich speech successfully achieved its immediate goals of intimidating Western policymakers, while Russia sought to use its increasing capabilities to raise its international assertiveness further and restore its status as a major international veto player. High oil prices and a significant increase in Russia's oil-related revenues greatly fueled these ambitions, while the promotion of the unconstrained domestic and international "sovereignty" of Russia (understood as the ability to do whatever the Kremlin wanted) became a primary goal of the Russian authorities.[39] The very claim by Russian leaders of Russia's new global role as a major "energy superpower" clearly demonstrated their status-seeking intentions. Meanwhile, the "collective West" seemingly lost interest in relations with Russia, especially in the wake of the 2008–9 global economic crisis, and neglected the risks relating to its rising revisionism and assertiveness. Thus, Russian elites felt themselves more and more unconstrained and began preparations for further revanchist actions based on the Kremlin's use of force and violence.

Expanding the Spiral of Invincibility

The first testing ground of new Russian revisionism occurred in August 2008 in Georgia. At that time, the Georgian president Mikheil Saakashvili, who came to power after the Rose Revolution of 2003, had moved the country in a pro-Western direction, initiated numerous policy reforms, and aimed to take Georgia out of the Russian "sphere of influence." In addition, Saakashvili had a very tense relationship with Putin and had been involved in several personal clashes with the Russian leader. In 2008 Saakashvili initiated a poorly prepared attack on the breakaway republic of South Ossetia (which had claimed its independence since the early 1990s), which, in turn, provoked the use of Russia's military against Georgians. When the Georgian military first attacked South Ossetia's capital Tskhinvali, Russian peacekeepers (who had been deployed in the region after the first wave of conflict in the 1990s) were also targeted, intentionally or unintentionally. After that, the Russian authorities accused Georgia of aggression against South Ossetia and launched a full-scale military operation in Georgia. Having an overwhelming advantage over Georgians in terms of military might, the Russians heavily attacked Georgians not only in South Ossetia but also in other territories of Georgia. Finally, Georgia, facing a risk of major military defeat, if not occupation, was forced to initiate a ceasefire, which was achieved under the mediation of the French president Nicolas Sarkozy five days after the start of the military campaign. Georgian troops withdrew from South Ossetia and no longer attempted to regain control, while Russia officially recognized the independence of South Ossetia (which was de facto controlled by Russia long before the 2008 conflict), and clearly demonstrated its dominant role in the region.[40]

The Russo–Georgian War of 2008 can be considered a minor episode compared to the later battles in Ukraine, but it was quite indicative that Russia acted unilaterally with full-scale use of military force, and the "collective West" accepted and recognized Russia's moves as legitimate, as Russia was acting within its "sphere of influence." This episode also greatly contributed to Saakashvili's subsequent downfall (his party lost the 2012 parliamentary elections to the opposition party Georgian Dream, which took a softer if not directly pro-Russian position later on)[41] and also to the subsequent launching of the military reform in Russia under Serdyukov. But most importantly, it was a clear sign of Russia's impunity and demonstrated that its assertiveness, supported by the use of military force, would most likely not meet with meaningful resistance. This lesson was learned for the future in the Kremlin, especially with regard to Ukraine.

On February 21, 2014, Ukrainian President Viktor Yanukovych fled Kyiv, leaving his post after three months of large-scale street protests in the center of the Ukrainian capital. These protests began when Yanukovych, under strong pressure from Russia, refused to sign an association agreement with the European Union.[42] The government used various means to counter these protests, including shooting some of the regime's rivals, but in the end the result was the de facto ousting of Yanukovych: the day after his escape, the Ukrainian parliament voted for his removal from the position and called for new presidential elections.[43] As the Kremlin condemned this regime change in Ukraine as a coup d'état plotted by American and European backers (who openly expressed their support for protesters), the Russian authorities also considered these developments a major challenge to their own regime. These risk perceptions contributed to the Kremlin's domestically driven politics of pre-emptive counterrevolution,[44] and the reaction from the Kremlin was disproportionate and far-reaching. Immediately after the regime change in Ukraine, Putin initiated annexation of the Crimean Peninsula (a region that had belonged to Ukraine since 1954 and in 2014 was used as a naval base for the Russian Black Sea fleet). The region, known for the pro-Russian stance of local elites and population at large, was easily conquered by Russian special task forces in a handful of days without any meaningful resistance. Some days later, the Crimean parliament, taken over by pro-Russian forces, announced the Crimean status referendum on the rejoining of this region to Russia as two federal units (the Republic of Crimea and the federal city of Sevastopol). This referendum, held on March 16, 2014, was allegedly fraudulent (officially, 97% of participants voted for the integration of both areas into the Russian Federation with a turnout of 83%), although a large portion of Crimean voters sincerely endorsed such a move.[45] After that, the Russian annexation of Crimea was complete: Russia quickly achieved its goals without major bloodshed[46] and without any serious resistance from the Ukrainian authorities (which was very natural, given the turmoil in the country after Yanukovych's deposal).[47]

Although, predictably, the annexation of Crimea provoked a furious reaction both from Ukraine and from Western countries, which placed personal sanctions on the top Russian and Crimean officials involved in this process, overall these developments were considered in the Kremlin to be Russia's greatest achievement since the Soviet collapse. First, domestically this annexation was enthusiastically endorsed by the Russian public, and Putin's approval rating skyrocketed.[48] Second, the personal sanctions were very targeted, and had only a minor impact on Russia's international behavior. Not only were the personal losses of some Kremlin cronies compensated for by lavish state contracts, but certain sectors of the Russian economy (such as agriculture) also benefited from protectionist state policies (such as a partial ban on food imports from the EU and the US).[49] Third, the successful annexation of Crimea served as evidence of the effectiveness of the Russian personalist regime and its practices of decision-making. According to some statements (including Putin's own words), the decision on the annexation of Crimea was made by Putin unilaterally, only upon some consultation with a handful of his closest advisors.[50] Fourth, the sluggish international response to Russia's actions was limited to words rather than deeds, and even sanctions imposed on Russia were rather minor at that time. The "collective West," after some months of verbal condemnation of Russia and certain demonstrative moves (such as the expulsion of Russia from the G8 group, now once again the G7), returned to "business as usual" practices of dealing with Russia.[51] In fact, by 2014, the "collective West" had very limited (if any) levers of influence on Russia, and its reluctant acceptance of the annexation of Crimea to some extent was a recognition of this fact. Furthermore, there was no will to launch a major confrontation with Russia with regard to this relatively minor issue among Western politicians (by and large, they perceived Ukraine in general and Crimea in particular as parts of Russia's "sphere of influence"). However, such a response was recognized by the Kremlin as a sign of the lack of international constraints on its behavior and as a predictor of future impunity. Thus, the annexation of Crimea provided the Kremlin with a major signal that this step was a correct one, the punishment for it was mostly symbolic and negligible, and that such actions would not face more serious resistance. In a sense, the Kremlin's impunity after the annexation of Crimea lit a green light for further steps toward international aggression.

Subsequently, the Kremlin did not stop at Crimea, and extended its appetite to the entire area of Southern and Eastern Ukraine, which was considered "Novorossiya," heavily populated by Russian-speaking residents and presumably loyal to the Russian rather than to the post-Yanukovych Ukrainian leadership.[52] The attempts by pro-Kremlin proxies to seize power largely failed in many regions of Ukraine. However, in Donbas, the industrial hub of Eastern Ukraine, which had previously served as a local power base for Yanukovych for decades, the situation was different. Amidst major turmoil, Russia-sponsored troops led by the Russian security services veteran Igor Girkin (also known as Strelkov) seized certain areas of Donbas and proclaimed the emergence of the separatist Donetsk and Luhansk "people's republics" (DNR and LNR, respectively). They de facto usurped power, thus launching a full-scale war with Ukraine.[53] The Ukrainian army, unprepared for full-scale war, and the National Guard (formed from volunteers) engaged in ground operations against rebels armed and backed by the Russian military; these attempts met with little success. In July 2014, a Malaysian Airlines Boeing-777 flying from Amsterdam to Kuala Lumpur was shot down over the separatist controlled zone, presumably by a Russian surface-to-air missile, and almost 300 people were killed.[54] The Russian authorities denied accusations and shifted blame to the Ukrainian military. Meanwhile, a new round of Western sanctions (this time affecting not only individuals but also certain Russian businesses, including the energy and financial sectors) became inevitable. Still, this response was not strong enough. The Kremlin, in turn, only extended the confrontation with the West and Ukraine. Furthermore, in August 2014, when Ukrainian troops nearly defeated the separatist rebels, Russian military forces encroached into the territory of Donbas and, using heavy arms, pushed the Ukrainian military out of the separatist-controlled area.[55]

The Minsk ceasefire agreement of September 2014, achieved under the mediation of France and Germany, stopped casualties for a while but did not bring peace and stability to these regions of Ukraine. Instead, the war in Donbas continued, and DNR forces, backed by the Russian military, launched a new offensive against the Ukrainian military and pushed it into a major retreat. Thus, the new Minsk II agreement was proposed by the French and German leadership in February 2015. The protocol, officially signed by representatives of Russia and Ukraine as well as by representatives of the DNR and LNR, called for a ceasefire as the first step toward resolution of the conflict, but its political consequences were rather vague.[56] The Russian interpretation of the agreement implied that Ukraine would observe the special status of separatist-controlled Donbas areas and only upon local elections held in these areas (and organized by DNR and LNR separatists) could Ukrainian control over the border with Russia be restored. The idea behind this Kremlin plan was that Donbas would become a veto player in Ukrainian politics, and the DNR and LNR would dictate Russian-imposed rules of the game to Kyiv. The Ukrainian interpretation of the agreement was completely different, as it implied restoring Ukrainian control over the border with Russia first, and conduct of local elections in Donbas only after that. These two interpretations were incompatible with each other, and this was why the military conflict in Donbas over time turned into a steady deadlock, or into a "frozen" stage, which continued in more or less the same way until the beginning of the Russian assault in February 2022.[57]

Although Russia could not achieve its initial goals of de facto partitioning Ukraine and taking control of its major southern and eastern regions, even relatively minor spoils such as the DNR and LNR, which became Russia-controlled areas, were considered successes by the Kremlin. Russia positioned itself as a major veto player in the Minsk agreements, and did not allow Ukraine to preserve its territorial integrity in Donbas. From this perspective, the DNR and LNR were perceived in the Kremlin as springboards for a future full-scale takeover of Ukraine (which is how the Kremlin has been attempting to use them since February 2022). Meanwhile, the Russian military and its separatist proxies demonstrated their clear superiority over Ukrainian forces in 2014–15, thus further expanding the spiral of Russian invincibility. During the process of the Minsk negotiations and the subsequent discussions on the implementation of the Minsk agreements, also known as the Normandy talks, Western mediators were unable to resist Russian demands, while their opportunities to impose any constraints on Russia's international behavior remained very limited, if not purely symbolic. In essence, the Russian proxy war in Donbas further increased the perceptions of impunity among Russian elites and provided them with expectations of an easy victory over Ukraine.

The next episode of expanding the spiral of Russian invincibility was the Russian intervention in the Syrian civil war, launched in September 2015. Before the intervention, the Kremlin officially provided the Assad government in Syria with money and weapons. However, the Assad government faced significant losses of control over Syrian territory amid a major offensive from Islamic State and opposition militants, and, according to some statements, the regime was on the verge of collapse. Upon Assad's request to Russia for major military aid, Russian forces as well as private military contractors (such as the Wagner Group) entered the war. Although Russia initially portrayed its intervention as a "war against terrorism" solely focused on targeting Islamic State, in fact, Russian airstrikes almost exclusively focused on targeting the anti-Assad opposition militants, which were also involved in fighting against Islamic State. Putin openly stated that Russia's main objective was to maintain the allied Assad government and recapturing Syrian territories from US-backed militants, with a broader goal of rolling back US influence in Syria and in the Middle East in general. Although during the first year of the Russian intervention no major gains were achieved by the Assad government, by early 2017 massive Russian airstrikes had major effects. With Russian military involvement, which was accompanied by very harsh attacks on opposition-controlled areas, the Assad government was able to restore its control over major Syrian cities such as Aleppo, Palmyra, and Deir ez-Zor, and finally to defeat both the Islamic State and opposition troops. In December 2017, the Kremlin announced that Russia's troops would be deployed to Syria on a permanent basis, thus acquiring an important military base in the Middle East.[58]

For the Kremlin, the military intervention in Syria was considered a great success well beyond the area, which it already considered its "sphere of influence" in post-Soviet Eurasia. Russia not only presented itself as a major kingmaker in the region, but also greatly enhanced its position in the global competition with the US, guaranteed the Russian navy access to Eastern Mediterranean ports, and increased its capacity to conduct military operations across the wider region, ranging from the Red Sea to Libya. To some extent, Russia had recaptured Soviet military might and powerful presence in the region, and nobody there or beyond was able to resist the expansion. This is why the Kremlin considered Obama's claim that Russia, as a "regional power," should not be involved in military conflicts in the Middle East to be a sign of lack of respect for its military omnipotence and its new global role in general (see chapter 4). Once more, there was no way to place any serious constraints on Russian assertive foreign policy, while the military success in Syria elevated Russia's status beyond its capabilities, expanding the spiral of Russian invincibility to a scope which had been unthinkable just a few years before. This was exactly what the Kremlin wanted: the conspicuous demonstration of Russian military might in Syria aggravated and strengthened the feeling of impunity more than ever, not only among the Russian elites but also among international observers.[59] After victory in Syria, Russia increased the scope of its global ambitions and encroached into Africa, using somewhat similar templates of aiding dictatorships of various colors (ranging from the Central African Republic to Burkina Faso) and/or powerful military rebels, such as Khalifa Haftar in Libya. These practices of covert Russian influence, often outsourced to the Wagner Group, continued over time,[60] including developments after the beginning of the Russian assault on Ukraine in 2022.

The spiral of Russian invincibility unwound against the background of increasing problems in the "collective West" on various fronts. Major signs that Russia's Western rivals were growing weaker, ranging from Brexit to the US withdrawal from Afghanistan, were welcomed enthusiastically in the Kremlin as indicators of irreversible decline of the West. Russia also greatly contributed to the rise of turmoil in the West by employing a counter-offensive in the form of hybrid warfare.[61] Although whether Russian meddling in the US presidential elections of 2016 played an important role in Donald Trump's victory is unclear, perceptions of its impact were exceptionally strong. In Russia, Trump's electoral victory met with enthusiastic applause in a State Duma session, and was widely considered a success for Russian trolls and disinformation campaigns. Despite the fact that Trump's presidency did not meet the Kremlin's high expectations, his poor performance increased the feeling of impunity among Russian elites, as such a rival was not perceived as particularly dangerous.[62] At the same time, the "collective West" regarded the seeming rise of Russian invincibility with a combination of fear and doom. The cry of the irreversible decline, if not collapse, of the liberal world order and the coming triumph of a China-led world, and the like, which dominated the public mood by the early 2020s, formed an atmosphere of inevitable failure of any attempts to resist Russian assertiveness.[63] It is no wonder that various experts, ranging from the leading scholar of international relations John Mearsheimer[64] to the left-wing historian Stephen Cohen,[65] argued that the "collective West" should unilaterally and unequivocally accept the global demands of a rising Russia.

Expanding the spiral of Russian invincibility both in Russia and in the "collective West" brought a significant shift from great underestimation of Russia in the 1990s to its great overestimation in the 2010s and early 2020s. Retrospectively, one might argue that although both views on Russia were rather superficial and somewhat far-fetched, they had major policy implications as they were based on incorrect assumptions, which led to incorrect solutions. In the early 1990s, with the end of Communism, the US and its allies appeared to have fallen into the deadly sin of pride because of their misperceptions of irreversible triumph. At the same time, for a while Russia fell into the deadly sin of sloth. However, by the early 2020s everything changed in the opposite direction. By that time, Russia, trapped by its feeling of impunity, fell into the deadly sin of pride, while the frightened US and its allies appeared to have fallen into the deadly sin of sloth.

Illusory Invincibility

The illusory Russian invincibility in Russia and in the West and the feeling of impunity among the Russian elites contributed to the failure of the Russian assault on Ukraine in two different, albeit interrelated, ways. First, the great overestimation of Russian military and economic capabilities (both in Russia and in the West) greatly inflated expectations of Russia's quick achievement of its goals in the assault on Ukraine and weak resistance to its actions, both in Ukraine and in the West.[66] Second, these expectations, together with previous experience of successful assault (especially in the case of the annexation of Crimea), stimulated the Kremlin to further unhesitating risk-taking. In other words, the "special military operation" against Ukraine was initially considered just an extension of the previous successful annexation of Crimea, with a strong expectation that both Ukrainian and Western responses would be similarly weak and sluggish because of their lack of both capability and will to resist Russia's assertive actions. These expectations proved to be incorrect, and Russia became a victim of the previous successes of its foreign policy.

Before February 2022, both Russian and Western experts and commentators wildly overestimated Russia's military might.[67] As Bettina Renz correctly pointed out, these overestimations were often based on numerical projections of Russia's manpower, weapons, and technologies, without taking into account numerous other factors such as quality of personnel, quality of governance, and the like.[68] This was why predictions about Russia's conquest of Kyiv in 72 or 96 hours after the launch of the "special military operation" were widespread among Western observers just before and immediately after the beginning of the Russian assault. However, more importantly, Russian planners were also affected by similar illusions. In a way, they followed the same template as the previous successful "special military operation" back in August 1968.[69] The Russian military attempted to take over the Hostomel airfield near Kyiv very similarly to the capture of Ruzine International Airport in Czechoslovakia during the suppression of the Prague Spring. Implicitly, Russia's planners expected that Ukrainians would be passive and inept in Kyiv similarly to their previous behavior in Crimea in 2014 or to that of the Czechoslovakians in 1968, but the reality was very different. The failure of initial expectations was more than surprising for the Kremlin. No kind of Plan B had been prepared and developed before the assault because of over-confidence in the inevitability of Russia's coming success. The illusion of Russian invincibility played an important role in the resulting backlash. Over time, both Western observers and the Russian military learned some lessons from this failure and no longer relied on mechanical projections of the past Russian experience onto the future. However, the fallacy of retrospective assessments of potential played an important role in policy planning and conduct. Moreover, Russia's failure in the initial stage of the "special military operation" later contributed to the opposite phenomenon, namely to both Western and Ukrainian underestimations of Russia's military potential and learning capabilities, like a swinging pendulum. This error, in turn, played an important role in the unsuccessful Ukrainian planning of a counter-offensive during the summer of 2023.[70]

THE VICTIMS OF PREVIOUS SUCCESSES

The illusion of Russian invincibility in the energy arena developed in a somewhat similar way, driven by the Kremlin's misperceptions (outlined in chapter 4). Before February 2022, the Russian authorities portrayed their country as the "energy superpower," having in mind the increasing energy dependency of European countries on Russia.[71] This energy dependency dated back to Soviet times, when the Kremlin turned its oil and gas reserves in Western Siberia into a major economic weapon through the politics of pipelines, which came from the Soviet Union to Western Europe. After the skyrocketing of global oil prices in the 1970s, Soviet oil and gas came to West Germany and to other European countries, and for a long while the gas supply softened European stances toward the Soviet Union. Some attempts by the US to extend sanctions against the Soviet Union after the invasion of Afghanistan met with a cool response from their European counterparts, who at that time were not ready to sacrifice the regular supply of Soviet energy for the sake of the unity of the "collective West."[72] Likewise, the high oil prices in the early twenty-first century served as a key driver of aggressive Russian foreign policy.[73] In the 2000s and 2010s, the Kremlin and its major energy arm, Gazprom, continued nearly the same policy of buying the political loyalty of foreign customers with the supply of gas.[74] The use of gas prices as a bargaining chip in negotiations with governments in post-Soviet Eurasia, as well as blackmailing them with threats of cutting the gas supply during long, cold winters, became routine for the Kremlin. Due to the use of long-term contracts, this tool was unavailable for the Kremlin in relationships with European customers. However, in the wake of global liberalization of the gas market and the increase in supply of liquefied natural gas, the Kremlin attempted to strengthen its monopoly in the European markets and invested a great deal of money and effort into building an expensive pipeline network, Nord Stream. In economic terms, Nord Stream was probably not particularly necessary due to its excessive construction costs and there being no shortage of gas supply. However, politically it was considered a highly effective instrument for the Kremlin's pressure on European governments, allowing it to further increase energy dependency on Russia and thus maintain its dominant position in the European market forever as it intended. This perceived effectiveness was why the Kremlin expected to be able to use divide-and-rule tactics vis-à-vis the "collective West" as the Soviet Union had in the early 1980s.

THE VICTIMS OF PREVIOUS SUCCESSES

These expectations, based on the previous successful experience of using gas pipelines as a major political and economic weapon, increased the feeling of impunity among Russian elites, but after the assault on Ukraine, they proved to be wrong. In March 2022, amidst the widening scope of international sanctions against Russia, Russian banks were cut off from SWIFT, and the assets of the Central Bank of Russia held abroad, as well as Gazprom accounts in Western banks, were frozen. In turn, the Kremlin announced that the "unfriendly countries" of the European Union were to pay for gas in Russian rubles (this option ran counter to the rationale of EU financial sanctions imposed on Russia). After the European Union countries (first and foremost Germany, the largest customer for Russian gas) rejected this demand, Russia demonstratively and completely cut off its gas supply to Germany via the land pipeline. Although payment for Russian gas in US dollars and euros was later restored through the special mechanism of currency exchange by the Gazprom subsidiary Gazprombank, Russia opted to cut off gas supply to Poland, Bulgaria, and Finland, and later on halted gas supply via Nord Stream. As gas prices in Europe increased by up to 30%, the Kremlin expected that its European customers would be suffering greatly and that Russia would be able to use the gas supply as a weapon of pressure on European governments. Moreover, in September 2022, the Nord Stream network ceased to operate after the sudden and nearly simultaneous underwater implosions of three out of four pipes in the Baltic Sea (at the time of writing, the causes of these implosions remain unknown).[75] The Kremlin-sponsored media expected mass freezing of Europeans during the winter period; however, the outcome of this major gas conflict was completely different. In fact, European governments were able to find substitutes for Gazprom in various countries, ranging from Norway to Qatar, filled their gas stores in advance of the winter of 2022–3, and sharply reduced their consumption of Russian gas. By October 2022, the share of Russian gas supply decreased to 7.5% of all gas imports in the European Union, and a plan to end gas imports from Russia to the European Union by 2027 was soon announced in Brussels.[76] As a result of these political adventures, Gazprom lost the European market after 40 years of Soviet and Russian dominance mostly because of the Kremlin's political ambitions and the unreasonable feeling of impunity in its blackmailing of Europeans.[77] Furthermore, the loss of the European market will be barely compensated for even after the ongoing reorientation of Gazprom to Chinese and other Asian markets is complete, so now Russia's positioning of itself as a "global energy superpower" (at least in terms of gas supply) is coming under serious question, to put it mildly.

Finally, the illusory Russian invincibility had a strong effect on risk perceptions among the Russian elites before the beginning of the assault on Ukraine. As experts in behavioral economics argue, most people (including elites) tend to be risk-averse, and rarely prefer risk-taking behavior.[78] Even though the media often portrayed Putin as a risk-taker well before the assault on Ukraine, he has been rather cautious and risk-averse during the entire period of his rule with regard to many domestic issues (such as economic policy). However, with the feeling of impunity, especially after the annexation of Crimea in 2014, which had been proposed by Putin almost unilaterally and greatly endorsed by the Russian elites, the arrangement of preferences in decision-making under conditions of uncertainty shifted toward risk-taking. This shift not only contributed to the expectation that next time everything would be the same and that the Russian invincibility of the past would continue indefinitely into the future. More importantly, it reduced the doubts of Russian elites about their fundamental political and policy choices nearly to zero.

In Dostoevsky's *Crime and Punishment*, as the main character, Raskolnikov, ponders the option of killing an old woman, he seeks to convince himself that certain crimes are justifiable if they are committed in order to remove obstacles to the higher goals of "extraordinary" men like Napoleon. Then he asks himself "whether I am a trembling creature [in Russian, *tvar' drozhashchaya*] or whether I have the right [to kill],"[79] and in the end, decides to murder the woman. The problem with the Russian elites was that they did even not consider such questions, especially after the successful annexation of Crimea in 2014. The feeling of impunity provided them with ex ante expectations that they "had the right" to kill whomever they wanted, once and forever, and did not have to bother themselves with existential Dostoevsky-type questions as they were protected from any real or potential ex post punishments. In reality, every person (including members of the elites) is nothing but a "trembling creature" and has no right to kill. However, as the economist and Nobel Prize winner Gary Becker convincingly argued in his oft-cited article (which was named after Dostoevsky's novel), when the risk of punishment is low, individuals tend to commit crimes both more frequently and of worse nature.[80] The major decline in perception of risks among the Russian elites, which was a side effect of their previous successful systematic breaking of formal and informal rules of the international order, further lowered the psychological barriers to launching the "special military operation," which soon developed into a full-scale war. And similarly to Raskolnikov, who after murdering the old woman was unable to stop and also killed her sister (otherwise, his crime could be easily discovered and punished), the Kremlin intended to continue the ongoing military conflict virtually forever for similar reasons to Raskolnikov's after the initial failure of the "special military operation." Although the illusion of Russian invincibility disappeared soon after the failure of the initial plan to quickly take Kyiv, with the endless continuation of the Russian military assault, the path out of the trap of impunity has become increasingly difficult and problematic over time.

Chapter 6

LOST ILLUSIONS, DASHED HOPES, AND UNLEARNED LESSONS

By the time of completion of this manuscript in summer 2024, the Russian assault in Ukraine has reached a point of standoff. Although the initial goals of the "special military operation" launched more than two years earlier went unfulfilled and hopes of successful swift conquest of Ukraine were dashed on the battlefield, Russia's rulers followed the path of further escalation of the conflict with no intention of stopping the military assault (rather, they pursued further attacks and established Russia's control over some new areas in Donbas). In essence, the Kremlin continued the chain of previous errors without making major corrections, and further compounded them, increasing Russia's problems in the international arena. However, in the domestic arena, the military assault greatly contributed to empowerment of the Kremlin to the highest degree seen in the post-Soviet period. As Russian elites and masses alike have been unable and/or unwilling to resist the further rise of the regime's personalism, the overwhelming dominance of *siloviki*, the increasing scope of repressions, and the ubiquity of fear and propaganda, the Kremlin's powerful position appears unchallenged despite the existence of domestic threats such as Prigozhin's mutiny. Moreover, in February 2024 the Kremlin celebrated the death of its domestic enemy No. 1, the leader of the Russian opposition Alexei Navalny, incarcerated in a special prison in the far north of Russia.[1] Even though concerns regarding spiraling military-related state expenditures and other warning signs for the Russian economy have been quite serious,[2] state bureaucrats and economic agents were moderately optimistic about its prospects amid international sanctions and increasing technological lag. Moreover, after two years of the "special military operation," its continuity has paved the way to the strengthening of powerful interest groups of beneficiaries of militarism not only among top *siloviki* and managers of the military-industrial complex and related sectors of economy. The well-being among certain groups of ordinary people such as employees of military-industrial enterprises and even families of mobilized soldiers, also improved due to war-driven state expenditures.[3] Moreover, by the summer of 2024, observers noted an unprecedented consumer boom in Russia, caused by economic growth and rising incomes of many Russians.[4]

It is no wonder that elite-level beneficiaries intend to make the "special military operation" endless – much like the decades of the Cold War in the Soviet Union. Meanwhile, Putin is perceived even by critics of the "special military operation" as the only domestic political actor who could stop the military conflict and restore peace to the country.[5] These expectations only intensified by the time of the new presidential elections, held in March 2024. These elections were conducted in an atmosphere of unprecedented pressure from the Kremlin via all levers of the "power vertical," ranging from denying registration to independent candidates to widespread use of non-transparent practices of electronic voting in many of Russia's regions. In the end, the combination of administrative pressure, mobilization of voters and, last but not least, blatant electoral fraud allowed the Kremlin to achieve the desired numbers and demonstrate a landslide victory by Putin, who was triumphantly reelected for the next six-year term in office until 2030. Against this background, Russia has aggravated the negative consequences of its previous actions against Ukraine and, most probably, will continue to do so at least until the very end of Putin's rule.

This chapter reviews the lessons of the Russian experience of the failed military assault on Ukraine, both for a study of Russian politics and for analysis of its prospects for the future, as well as for an understanding of the international behavior of states and nations and of the nature of war and peace in theoretical and comparative perspectives. It also addresses lessons from Russia's military assault for understanding the global agenda and for the study of domestic and international politics in the twenty-first century. I will begin with an overview of major domestic and international issues for Russia that emerged as side effects of the military assault on Ukraine. Then, I will consider the short- and long-term consequences of the military assault on Ukraine for Russia's political, economic, and international trajectory and major causes of Russia's turn against the grain of global change. Some implications of Russia's post-Communist experience for this country, for the region, and for international politics across the globe will be discussed in the conclusion.

The Deadlock: No Way Out?

By summer 2024, the deadlock became a feature not only of the state of affairs on the battlefield, where rather limited Russian advancements at the frontline became possible only after large-scale casualties among Russian and Ukrainian soldiers, but also of the overall domestic and international positioning of Russia. Although Russia is very far from major defeat in military, economic, and other terms, it was not able to achieve major decisive victory on the frontline, while the claims of Ukrainian politicians about pushing Russian troops back to the 1991 boundary between Russia and Ukraine were unrealistic, to say the least.[6] Attempts by the Russian leadership to reach a tacit agreement with the US about a ceasefire and de facto acceptance of the Russian takeover of Ukrainian territories up to the existing frontline have been unsuccessful, at least as of yet,[7] and the Russian confrontation with the "collective West" was only aggravated further in a very conspicuous manner. In fact, Russia did not even attempt to offer any new chips at the bargaining table. Rather, it continued to insist on unconditional acceptance of the Kremlin's claims in the West, similarly to its December 2021 ultimatum, and multiplied its subversive activities in various European countries and elsewhere. No wonder that a potential ceasefire or any other form of agreement over Ukraine was widely perceived, both in Russia and in the West, as just a temporary pause before a new Russian military assault on other targets, be they in the Baltic states, in Kazakhstan, or elsewhere.[8] Meanwhile, the Russian attempt to position itself as the vanguard of collective resistance by non-Western countries vis-à-vis the US-led world brought no meaningful results,[9] as Russia had neither material resources nor attractive ideas for such a collective resistance. Instead, Russia became increasingly dependent on the supply of arms and military equipment by Iran, which, in turn, pushed Russia into the position of full-scale support of the Hamas terrorist network after its bloody assault on Israel in October 2023 and the subsequent Israeli counter-offensive.[10]

Domestically, the Kremlin not only tightened the screws and insisted on conspicuous absolute loyalty from virtually all segments of society, conducting numerous public campaigns aimed at justification of its actions and the silencing of any dissenting voices. It also completely buried any plans for socio-economic development of the country for the sake of militarism. While any political liberalization had become a taboo long before February 2022, economic liberalization was also tabooed on the path of increasing military expenditures and further centralization of governance. The revision of the privatization deals of the 1990s launched in February 2024, officially for reasons of national security, was indicative in this respect,[11] as was the rise of economic statism, which fits both the ideational visions of *siloviki* and their vested interests. Moreover, the Russian leadership increasingly aimed to build a resistance economic model similar to that of Iran, which may become a new role model for the Kremlin. Although this economic policy approach presumed that the economy could survive and, indeed, flourish despite international sanctions, in fact post-1979 Iran sacrificed long-term economic growth for the sake of continuity of its regime for many decades.[12] Russia's rulers perceived such an approach as imperfect but still the second-best option to resolve the dilemma of "development versus preservation of the status quo" and, in the process of endless war, became increasingly approving of similar recipes.

In essence, the hope of the Russian elites for a decisive victory over Ukraine and subsequent restoration of Russia's status as a key global veto player alongside the US and China was illusory, to say the least. At the same time, admission of the wrong path taken by the Russian leadership in February 2022 was unacceptable for the Kremlin and its subordinates, as such an admission was considered risky in terms of disequilibrium of the political status quo. This was why the Kremlin had no choice other than to persist along the wrong paths despite their negative consequences. Such an approach was considered the second-best choice for the Russian elites and society at large. Despite the gloomy prospects of continuation of ongoing military conflict and related setbacks both domestically and internationally, it was perceived as a lesser evil relative to major changes aimed at revisions of the strategic choice made in February 2022. Such changes were considered very dangerous and unacceptable for the Russian elites, who became hostages of the Kremlin's previous political moves. In other words, Russia's deadlock in the domestic and international

LOST ILLUSIONS, DASHED HOPES, AND UNLEARNED LESSONS

arenas, visible by summer 2024, became an instance of negative equilibrium, in which the status quo brings little payoff, but changes may become a source of great losses. A negative equilibrium could promote the continuity of the status quo for a long time, until incentives for major changes emerge and real losses from the status quo for elites and society-at-large prevail over potential losses caused by these changes. However, no such incentives are available or even imaginable in Russia in 2024, while the Kremlin invests tremendous efforts into maintaining this negative equilibrium as long as possible. In practical terms, this maintenance is based on very severe sanctions for disloyalty to the Kremlin, which makes domestic challenges to the status quo prohibitively dangerous if not completely unthinkable.

This is why Russia's elites, despite worsening conditions of the status quo for the country and for themselves, are faced with a lack of alternatives and see no way out of the deadlock, which emerged soon after February 2022 due to the initial failure of the "special military operation," and are allowing it to persist indefinitely. Although certain exogenous shocks, ranging from heavy military losses to major economic hardships, may potentially shake the negative equilibrium in Russia or even completely overthrow it, at least in the foreseeable future these shocks are perceived as highly unlikely by the Kremlin. Meanwhile, in the absence of viable alternatives, over time Russia may experience significant degradation and decay in political, economic, and societal terms without meaningful resistance from elites and society-at-large to these trends. Such a possibility becomes more and more likely as long as the negative equilibrium in Russia persists. In this respect, the four traps presented and analyzed in the previous chapters of this book have further aggravated Russia's increasing problems.

The trap of personalist authoritarianism, with its low level of institutionalization, reduces the chances of correction of errors made by the political leadership. In highly institutionalized party-based autocracies, the collective leadership is more flexible and can find a way to achieve major revisions of previous political and policy decisions, sometimes shifting the blame to certain segments of the elites or even political leaders (as in the case of the ousting of Nikita Khrushchev under the one-party regime in the Soviet Union in 1964).[13] In personalist autocracies, where political leaders equate themselves with the regime and with the state, meaningful corrections of errors (especially in cases of military assault) are, largely, possible only upon replacement of these leaders due to their deaths and/or due to their (often violent) deposal. In practical terms, this means that the deadlock of the Russian assault on Ukraine will be likely to continue at least as long as Vladimir Putin is still in power. Moreover, the refusal of long-standing personalist political leaders to recognize their major errors (let alone correct them) increases the likelihood that these leaders will make new, probably even more grave errors in the future.

The trap of bad governance works in a somewhat similar way to the trap of personalist authoritarianism but also greatly expands the pool of beneficiaries of the persistent status quo. Not only top elites (including, but not limited to *siloviki*), but also rank-and-file state officials and civil servants are strongly motivated to avoid potential major changes in Russia, which may be unacceptable for them because of the risks of losing wealth, status, or even their freedom if not their lives. Unlike the proletarians described by Marx and Engels in the *Communist Manifesto*,[14] they have something to lose and feel that the chains of supporting the status quo of bad governance are not so heavy and unbearable. As there is, by default, no way to revise practices of bad governance, while the chances of top-down policy reforms aimed at improving quality of governance are close to zero under the current regime, the further expansion of these practices in the face of a potentially shrinking pie of rents is highly likely over time.

The trap of misperceptions also reduces the chances of correction of errors, albeit in a different way. For many individuals, especially those who belong to the elites, the acceptance of inconvenient truths and the open recognition of their previous wrong visions and worldviews, which were elaborated over a long period of time, is an exceedingly difficult issue. Among other effects, it places the status and credentials of elites into question and contributes to loss of face in one way or another. This is why even deep disillusionment and hopelessness may only pave the way for a replacement of one set of misperceptions by another. Instead of reliance upon belief in Putin's outstanding leadership and his imagined genius, Russia's elites may shift their hopes and expectations to potential miracles of support for Russia from Trump, Xi Jinping, or Khamenei, or to other sources of the expected collapse of the "collective West." The spread of conspiracy theories among Russian elites has made this trap of misperceptions even more persistent, while the low level of elite rotation in Russia within the echo chamber of continuing Kremlin-driven misinformation has made overcoming this trap even more difficult over time.

Finally, the trap of impunity is probably the most complicated one in terms of potential correction of errors. Everything that happened to Russia after February 2022 (ranging from international sanctions to attacks by Ukrainian drones against the Russian Black Sea fleet ships)[15] placed the previous feelings of eternal Russian impunity among elites under a large question mark. However, these setbacks were far from the decisive and irreparable defeats that could have made Russia's confrontation with the "collective West" no longer possible. As a result, instead of providing incentives for major revisions of the wrong strategic choices made in February 2022, Russia's multiple misfortunes have only contributed to persistence of these feelings, and to the search for compensation for the loss of previous impunity and, furthermore, for decisive revenge against its enemies. As Russia has limited opportunities for such revenge, the importance of nuclear weapons as a powerful tool of Russian influence, became more and more visible. These incentives for an adverse response to the loss of Russia's impunity in a manner of *ultima ratio* may become irresistible over time.

Pernicious Consequences

Although numerous short-term pernicious effects of continuing Russia's military assault on Ukraine for Russia's politics, economy, demographics, culture, and education, are highly visible and widely discussed in numerous publications, these effects, with all their importance, can be considered just the tip of the iceberg. Russia's assault on Ukraine may be perceived as a tipping point for long-term developmental failure, which may result in the irreversible decay of the country. Even though such trends were observed long before February 2022, they were largely considered temporary deviations driven by the personalities of Putin and his entourage.[16] Judging from this perspective, one may believe that potential liberalization and democratization of Russia, which first stopped in the 1990s and then was reversed in the 2000s and 2010s, are just a matter of time with the process of generational change and elite turnover in the country. Although these changes are probably still a matter of time, after February 2022 the time horizon for such changes certainly expanded a great deal, and Russia's movement in this direction is not guaranteed (although neither is it completely precluded).

In a way, long-term developmental failure in twentieth-century Russia was a side effect of the Russian Revolution of 1917 and the emergence of the long-standing revolutionary regime after a violent civil war. Although before the revolution Russia was a European laggard in terms of socio-economic modernization and political liberalization, it attempted to catch up its European neighbors after the Great Reforms of the 1860s and made significant progress in the early twentieth century. The seizure of power by the Bolsheviks and their subsequent drive for the world Communist revolution and the USSR's global leadership were not predetermined. However, this outcome of revolutionary dictatorship[17] cost tens of millions of human lives during violent repressions, and an increasing lagging of the country behind the socio-economic and political developmental trends in advanced countries of Europe and North America despite major achievements in industrialization and urbanization. In the end, the degradation and decay of Communism paved the way to the collapse of the regime and of the Soviet state in 1991.[18] After decades of Communism, the lagging of Russia and other post-Soviet states behind Western counterparts only increased, and became insurmountable. The problem is that although this long-term developmental failure was recognized by post-Soviet elites, they still considered the drive for Russia's global leadership to be an ultimate goal for the country. In a way, this drive was considered as a means of compensating for such a failure.

Certainly, it is too early to judge to what extent the Russian military assault on Ukraine in 2022 could become a trigger for similar long-term developmental failure for Russia. In the most general sense, the turn to such a trajectory heavily depends on the longevity of the current deadlock. To be sure, a certain portion of the Russian elites (especially among *siloviki*) would greatly appreciate it if they were able to transform Russia into a long-standing besieged fortress like that of Russian writer Vladimir Sorokin's dystopian novel *Day of the Oprichnik*.[19] According to the plot of this novel, in 2028 the equivalent of sixteenth-century monarchy is restored and Russia is isolated from the rest of the world by a "Great Wall of Russia." A heavily repressive, anti-modern, traditionalist, and ideologically rigid new Tsarist regime imposes xenophobia and ethnic nationalism on

Russia, while its economy is based upon sales of natural gas and transit of goods from China to Europe. The novel, published in 2006, in a sense resembles Russian realities, but the practical implementation of such a scenario, as well as potential transformation of Russia into an equivalent of Iran with its resistance economy, would face several major obstacles. In a way, these obstacles also result from Russia's four traps outlined above.

The trap of personalist authoritarianism poses major obstacles to long-term regime continuity beyond the life cycle of the personalist leader. The chances of dynastic succession look dubious in Russia's case. Conversely, the transformation of personalist regimes into other types of autocracies such as military or one-party regimes (let alone monarchies) is nearly impossible.[20] Although some personalist autocrats (such as the leader of Cameroon Paul Biya, who has remained president of this country since 1982), have kept power in their hands for a long while,[21] their days are numbered nonetheless, especially as they age. Against the background of low institutionalization of Russia's personalist regime, its problems and expectations of major changes are likely to increase over time. For similar reasons, numerous attempts to construct a new state ideology in Russia and impose it on the country as a mandatory set of beliefs, which intensified after February 2022,[22] may not prove very successful under the conditions of a personalist regime.

The trap of bad governance has not only drastically inhibited Russia's socio-economic performance, but also provided poor incentives for its improvement in the long term for the reasons stated above. Even though the rise of *siloviki*-led statist economic policy may result in the reshuffling of elites in the government, it is difficult to expect that this approach will be productive for the quality of governance. The persistence of bad governance has also made the state machinery itself vulnerable to potential political instability (as in the case of Prigozhin's mutiny) or other exogenous shocks. The fragility of the negative equilibrium may not necessarily lead to collapse, though.

The trap of misperceptions has not only contributed to an increase in the vulnerability of the state machinery to exogenous shocks (similarly to the trap of bad governance) but has also provided incentives for making new errors instead of correcting previous ones. The poor state of policy expertise in post-2022 Russia and the Kremlin's prioritizing responses to immediate threats and challenges at the expense of long-term planning are also hardly conducive to maintaining a long-term continuity of negative equilibrium and preservation of the status quo, despite the interests of Russia's elites and leadership.

Finally, the trap of impunity has produced incentives for the Kremlin to continue its previous risky games domestically and internationally and repeatedly raise the stakes. Instead of investing in endless continuity of the status quo, it may launch new risky enterprises (in addition to the risks from previous ones), ranging from increasing the scope of domestic repressions against real or imagined enemies of the Kremlin to new international assaults using both military and non-military means. This approach is not only counter-productive for long-term preservation of the status quo and for its further consolidation. Indeed, such actions may contribute to the negative equilibrium being undermined from within, by Russia's rulers themselves, because of unintended and/or undesired consequences.

Some observers discuss the potential effects of Russia's disequilibrium in terms of state breakdown along the lines of ethno-territorial disintegration, similarly to the Soviet Union in 1989–91.[23] Although one should not completely rule out such an outcome, it is highly unlikely in present-day Russia due to weak incentives for ethnic and regional separatism and the lack of interest in such scenarios among Russia's nationwide elites and society at large.[24] Contrary to these expectations, some optimistic observers consider disequilibrium as a path to Russia's gradual recovery after the failure of Russian militarism and a period of major turbulence, somewhat similarly to West Germany after World War II. Without completely rejecting this possibility either, one should take into account not only that Russian failure under whatever circumstances will not be even slightly comparable with that of Germany in 1945 but that even West German post-1945 recovery became possible only due to the major post-war economic boom and gradual generational changes.[25] At least as of yet, neither of these conditions is on the agenda for Russia.

Apart from these fears and hopes, disequilibrium in Russia may result in degradation and decay of the country in a different manner, which may be compared to the consequences of protracted chronic illness. In the world of medicine, a patient who behaves irresponsibly regarding his or her disease, that is, ignores professional recommendations, refuses medical treatments, and worsens his or her health using alcohol and smoking, usually dies prematurely. However, in the world of present-day politics, states and societies, unlike individuals, are immortal – for good or ill, they do not die at all, neither disappearing from the global map by themselves nor being conquered by other powers. Rather, those miserable countries which are afflicted with the chronic disease of sacrificing development for the sake of greatness may endlessly continue their mediocre, hopeless, and meaningless existence under worsening conditions, and over time be left with fewer and fewer chances of recovery. This is the real threat for Russia after its protracted military assault on Ukraine and it is a threat that tends to become more and more acute over time. After a certain stage of decay, the degradation of the country may reach a point of no return irrespective of major changes in domestic politics and governance.[26] If so, then it will not be possible to improve the Russian state and political regime by any available means. Rather, the question for politicians, policymakers, scholars, and experts may be how to make the very existence of Russia least harmful to the human beings in the country and across the globe. To what extent such a question may become a major item on Russia's agenda in the foreseeable future is not so clear, however.

Concluding Remarks: Lessons from Russia

During the three decades since the Soviet collapse, Russia followed a thorny path, from a would-be beacon of democratization in post-Soviet Eurasia under the slogan of returning to Europe, to a revisionist power and aggressive state, which launched a major military assault against its close neighbor, Ukraine, and placed itself in opposition to the rule-based international order. Such a turn from great expectations to great disasters is uncommon by any standards of the contemporary world and merits further in-depth examination.

Although the current state of Russia and its prospects after its military assault on Ukraine appear very gloomy, for political scientists there should be no grounds for sloth in terms of a scholarly agenda. On the contrary, present-day Russia can be perceived as a kind of El Dorado for experts in the study of the failure of great expectations and the rise of revanchist tendencies in domestic and international politics. From this perspective, the Russian experience offers evidence that can be used to test existing theories and develop new approaches. Instead of condemning post-Soviet Russia as an example of unfulfilled promises, with its failed democratization and subsequent turn to militarism and assault on Ukraine, we have to answer the central scholarly question of "why?" from the viewpoint of lessons that might be learned from Russia's experience of post-Soviet changes.

The core argument of this book is based upon the statement that Russia's turn to military assault is a textbook example of the behavior of politicians who face few domestic and international constraints to achieving their assertive global aspirations. These constraints were not built properly in the 1990s, systematically weakened in the 2000s and 2010s, and were finally eliminated by the 2020s. This statement, however, covers only part of the story. While a complete answer to this question would require an entire additional book, one might argue that the fact that these constraints on the unchecked behavior of Russia's elites and leaders did not emerge in a way reflected the failure of democratization in the country, as well as their response to the relative decline of the country within the global landscape. Indeed, many electoral authoritarian regimes across the globe appeared as by-products of failed democracies,[27] although not all of them are inclined towards international assaults.

Some scholars have discussed whether the shock of the Soviet collapse in Russia was excessively strong, and whether the country successfully coped with it, but in either case, this shock presented a variety of problems for the further trajectory of domestic and international changes in Russia over several decades. It caused a political hangover, which produced a number of false signals for Russia's political elites and contributed to the country's authoritarian drift and revanchist foreign policy. The anti-democratic domestic and international trajectory became path-dependent over time, such that the menu of choices for political actors was limited by what they had chosen during previous events. In a sense, Russia was somewhat similar to a hard drinker who cannot (and/or does not wish to) change his or her self-destructive behavior, and with each shot of vodka gradually becomes an alcoholic who cannot stop him- or herself and tends to behave more and more aggressively over time. Russia's actors after the Soviet collapse had insufficient incentives for different behavior, thus turning the trajectory of authoritarian regime-building and aggressive foreign policy in Russia into a dead end, if not a vicious circle.

The first false signal, which can be considered both a product and a cause of Russia's political hangover, was related to the dilemma of simultaneity during the "triple transition" of the 1990s, which in Russia's case was resolved in favor of economic reforms over democratization and state-building.[28] This choice, made by Russia's self-interested rulers, greatly favored Yeltsin and his winning coalition. However, at the moment of the Soviet collapse it was also welcomed by some domestic and international observers and by Russian society at large. It provided the Russian elites with the perception that the agenda of democratization could be sacrificed for the sake of economic change. However, market reforms in Russia took place amid a deep and protracted transformation recession that was overcome only after a decade of major hardships. It is no wonder that in the 2000s, when Russia experienced economic growth without democratization, this agenda was abandoned completely.[29] Meanwhile, even though the recession of the 1990s was very painful, Russia's swift and successful economic recovery during the 2000s fueled revanchist feelings on the part of the elite.[30] Most probably, if the Russian economy in the 1990s had suffered in a more severe way and its rebound had taken long decades, it would have lost any potential for revenge and its elites would never have dreamt of restoring greatness.

The second false signal resulting from the political hangover after the Soviet collapse is related to the role of the legacy of the past in terms of political changes and institution-building.[31] The Soviet political, economic, and foreign policy model was initially heavily discredited after the Soviet collapse, and in the 1990s no one seriously proposed going "back to the USSR": all political and policy discussions revolved around various approaches to inevitable changes, but not the adaptation, let alone restoration, of the Soviet political and institutional legacy. However, over time the Soviet legacy was increasingly perceived by elites as a role model for Russia and used as a set of building blocks for the country. When it came to rebuilding the Russian state agencies, this approach played a major role in their post-Soviet remaking, at least since the 2000s: it is from the Soviet past that they inherited their centralized hierarchy, lack of political and societal accountability, supremacy of secret services, and arbitrary use of coercion for protecting the state against its citizens.[32] The same logic might be applied to Russia's foreign policy, with its overall rejection of the Western-dominated rule-based international order. In a sense, it was also a Soviet-style response to post-Soviet changes. The reliance upon late-Soviet practices of domestic politics and foreign policy was a by-product of the rejection of the democratization agenda: in the absence of viable alternatives, it was the only role model readily available to Russia's elites.[33]

The third false signal from the experience of the Soviet collapse and early post-Soviet developments related to the "collective West." Since the Soviet Union had ceased to exist and Russia was no longer perceived as a source of major potential threat, the victors of the Cold War considered their goal achieved and paid little attention to political developments in Russia thereafter. There were no incentives to offer Russia comprehensive economic aid during the transformation recession in the 1990s, let alone to take advantage of the opening window of opportunity for full-scale use of pro-democratic leverages.[34] As international influence is complementary rather than substitutive for domestic actors, no one believes that even immediately after the Soviet collapse the West would have been able to impose its set of political institutions on domestic actors in Russia. Indeed, its impact was negligible after the Soviet collapse, and declined over time even before the Kremlin's efforts to counter Western influence on Russia and beyond. American and European actors made few rhetorical concessions to Russia, and, to put it bluntly, simply did not consider the advancement of democratization in Russia and/or placing constraints on its international assertiveness a priority. The irreversibility of the changes in the domestic politics and foreign policy of Russia after the Soviet collapse was greatly overestimated in the West, while the risks of the rise of new authoritarianism were not taken seriously enough by Western actors. Excessively triumphant after the end of the Cold War, they did not recognize rising challenges, underestimated the increasing threat from Russia, closed their eyes to the assault on Georgia and the annexation of Crimea, and responded cautiously and sluggishly overall.[35] This was why the post-2022 Western response came too late, when Russia had already crossed all red lines.

The fourth false signal of the political hangover was related to the major decline in Russia's international status, which was unacceptable for post-Soviet Russian elites. They failed to recognize the fact that Russia's past greatness, cultivated domestically and internationally since pre-Communist times due to its military might, vast territory, rich natural resources, and high culture, had ended after

1991. Indeed, Russia had seemingly become "a normal country" of secondary global importance,[36] just an ordinary item in a list of countries, alphabetically located in between Romania and Rwanda. Russia's changing place in the world after the end of the Soviet Union appeared to be a humiliation and insult in the eyes of the Russian elites, and was considered by Putin and his entourage to be "the place near the latrine,"[37] imposed on the country by the "collective West." Despite the fact that such a place merely reflected changing global realities, Russia's elites were not willing to accept these losses and objected to Russia's subordination to the West in various ways.

These four false signals that resulted from the post-Soviet political hangover in Russia – (1) a replacement of the democratization agenda with authoritarian drift; (2) a search for Soviet-style solutions for post-Soviet problems as building blocks in domestic politics and foreign policy; (3) a lack of Western agenda of promoting democracy in Russia and of constraining its aggressive foreign policy; and (4) a major dissatisfaction with decline in Russia's international status – made building barriers to the unconstrained domestic and international behavior of Russia's rulers impossible. From this viewpoint, one might expect that if these effects continue and deepen in coming decades, it will make Russia's potential return to the trajectory of domestic democratization and peaceful foreign policy even more difficult and complex, if not impossible.

The political hangover in Russia, which began with the Soviet collapse, has continued until now, and will likely continue into the future, caused the Russian assault on Ukraine in February 2022. But it was not only a mutiny of the Russian elites, led by Putin, against the dominance of the "collective West" elsewhere, including post-Soviet Eurasia. In a broader perspective, it was and remains a mutiny against global modernity[38] – the trends of modernization, socio-economic development, and cultural change[39] which not only could reinforce Russia's place at the global semi-periphery but also could result in Russia's shift onto a path of change which followed the trajectories of countries of Western and Eastern Europe with a certain time lag.[40] Russia's elites launched this mutiny against the grain of global trends, based upon the assumption that Russia is a major international outlier rather than laggard and upon their sense of mission of reversing the tide of international history after the "end" that had been declared during the times of Soviet collapse.[41] Such a reversal, however, was in all likelihood beyond the reach of Russia's

LOST ILLUSIONS, DASHED HOPES, AND UNLEARNED LESSONS

elites and leaders, as they wildly overestimated their capabilities and learned the wrong lessons from international history, which they largely misunderstood. Russia's elites expected that their ambitions and desires were fated to be unconstrained. However, as has been known since early Christian times, "whoever exalts himself will be humbled."[42] Exactly when and how this humbling may happen in Russia, and what will be its price as well as its possible consequences for Russia and for the entire world, remain to be seen.

NOTES

Preface

1 Among the voluminous literature on the Soviet collapse see, in particular, Stephen Kotkin, *Armageddon Averted: The Soviet Collapse, 1970–2000* (Oxford: Oxford University Press, 2001); Yegor Gaidar, *Collapse of an Empire: Lessons for Modern Russia* (Washington, DC: Brookings Institution Press, 2007); Vladislav Zubok, *Collapse: The Fall of the Soviet Union* (New Haven, CT: Yale University Press, 2021).
2 See Vladimir Gel'man, "Exogenous Shock and Russian Studies," *Post-Soviet Affairs*, 39, nos. 1–2 (2023), 1–9.
3 See George Kennan (X), "The Sources of Soviet Conduct," *Foreign Affairs*, 25, no. 4 (1947), 566–82.

Chapter 1. February 2022: Why Russia Fails

1 Hereafter, the term "Kremlin" is used synonymously with the top Russian state officialdom (unless otherwise stated).
2 See "How Putin's War in Ukraine Became a Catastrophe for Russia," *New York Times*, December 16, 2022, https://www.nytimes.com/interactive/2022/12/16/world/europe/russia-putin-war-failures-ukraine.html.
3 See Paul Sonne, Ellen Nakashima, Shane Harris and John Hadson, "Hubris and Isolation Led Vladimir Putin to Misjudge Ukraine," *Washington Post*, April 11, 2022, https://www.washingtonpost.com/national-security/2022/04/11/putin-misjudged-ukraine-hubris-isolation/.
4 See Dara Massicot, "What Russia Got Wrong: Can Moscow Learn

NOTES TO PP. 3–5

from Its Failures in Ukraine?" *Foreign Affairs*, February 8, 2023, https://www.foreignaffairs.com/ukraine/what-russia-got-wrong-moscow-failures-in-ukraine-dara-massicot; David V. Gioe and Marina Miron, "Putin Should Have Known His Invasion Would Fail," *Foreign Policy*, February 24, 2023, https://foreignpolicy.com/2023/02/24/ukraine-russia-putin-war-invasion-military-failure/.

5 See Evan Gershkovich, Thomas Grove, Drew Hinshaw and Joe Parkinson, "Putin, Isolated and Distrustful, Leans on Handful of Hard-Line Advisers," *The Wall Street Journal*, December 23, 2022, https://www.wsj.com/articles/putin-russia-ukraine-war-advisers-11671815184.

6 See, for example, Adam N. Stulberg, *Well-Oiled Diplomacy: Strategic Manipulation and Russia's Energy Statecraft in Eurasia* (Albany, NY: State University of New York Press, 2007); Marshall I. Goldman, *Petrostate: Putin, Power, and the New Russia* (Oxford: Oxford University Press, 2010).

7 For a very detailed account of Russia's interference in the 2016 presidential elections in the United States, see Robert S. Mueller III, *Report on the Investigation into Russian Interference in the 2016 Presidential Election*, Vol. I (Washington, DC: US Department of Justice, 2019), https://copblaster.com/uploads/files/mueller-report_compressed.pdf.

8 For an overview, see Anton Shekhvostov, *Russia and the Western Far Right: A Tango Noir* (Abingdon: Routledge, 2018); for a quantitative analysis, see Grigorii V. Golosov, "Useful, but Not Necessarily Idiots: The Ideological Linkages among the Putin-Sympathizer Parties in the European Parliament," *Problems of Post-Communism*, 67, no. 1 (2020), 53–63.

9 See Daron Acemoglu and James A. Robinson, *Why Nations Fail: The Origins of Power, Prosperity, and Poverty* (New York: Crown, 2012).

10 As there is no way to provide a comprehensive bibliography, for interested readers, I would particularly recommend: Paul D'Anieri, *Ukraine and Russia: From Civilized Divorce to Uncivil War*, 2nd edn (Cambridge: Cambridge University Press, 2023); Olga Onuch and Henry Hale, *The Zelensky Effect* (Oxford: Oxford University Press, 2023); Serhii Plokhy, *The Russo-Ukrainian War* (London: Allen Lane, 2023); Maria Popova and Oxana Shevel, *Russia and Ukraine: Entangled History, Diverging States* (Cambridge: Polity Press, 2024).

11 See, for example, Tuomas Forsberg and Heikki Patomäki, *Debating War in Ukraine: Counterfactual Histories and Future Possibilities* (Abingdon: Routledge, 2023); Aderito Vicente, Polina Sinovets and Julien Theron (eds.), *Russia's War on Ukraine: The Implications for the Global Order* (Cham: Springer, 2023).

12 See, for example, Bettina Renz, "Western Estimates of Russian Military Capabilities and the Invasion of Ukraine," *Problems of Post-Communism*, 71, no. 3 (2024), 219–31; Jonas J. Driedger and Mikhail Polianskii, "Utility-based Predictions of Military Escalation: Why Experts Forecasted Russia Would Not Invade Ukraine," *Contemporary Security Policy*, 44, no. 4 (2023), 544–60.

13 For a methodological discussion, see Bryn Rosenfeld, "Survey Research in Russia in the Shadow of War," *Post-Soviet Affairs*, 39, nos. 1–2 (2023), 38–48; Jeremy Morris, "Political Ethnography and Russian Studies in a Time of Conflict," *Post-Soviet Affairs*, 39, nos. 1–2 (2023), 92–100.

14 For a detailed account of these regimes, see Sergei Guriev and Daniel Treisman, *Spin Dictators: The Changing Face of Tyranny in the 21st Century* (Princeton, NJ: Princeton University Press, 2022).

15 See Barbara Geddes and John Zaller, "Sources of Popular Support for Authoritarian Regimes," *American Journal of Political Science*, 33, no. 2 (1989), 319–47. See also Johan Gerschewski, *Two Logics of Autocratic Rule* (Cambridge: Cambridge University Press, 2023), especially chapters 1 and 2.

16 On repressions in Russia under Putin's rule, see Vladimir Gel'man, "The Politics of Fear: How Russia's Rulers Counter their Rivals," *Russian Politics*, 1 no. 1 (2016), 27–45; Kirill Rogov, "The Art of Coercion: Repressions and Repressiveness in Putin's Russia," *Russian Politics*, 3, no. 2 (2018), 151–74. See also Olga Nadskakula-Kaczmarczyk, "Repression in Russia: The Evolution of the Political System," *Central European Journal of Politics*, 9, no. 1 (2023), 1–16.

17 For an analysis of the effects on pre-emptive repression on public opinion in Russia, see Katerina Tertytchnaya, "'The Rally is Not Authorized': Preventive Repression and Public Opinion in Electoral Autocracies," *World Politics*, 75, no. 3 (2023), 482–522.

18 See Vladimir Gel'man, *Authoritarian Russia: Analyzing Post-Soviet Regime Changes* (Pittsburgh, PA: University of Pittsburgh Press, 2015), especially chapters 1 and 2.

19 See Bruce Hecht, Sam Greene and Graeme Robertson, "Yes In My Name? The Problem of Agency in Russians' Response to the War," *Russia.Post*, June 7, 2024, https://russiapost.info/society/response_war.

20 On causes and effects of status-seeking politics in international relations, see Rohan Mukherjee, *Ascending Order: Rising Powers and the Politics of Status in International Relations* (Cambridge: Cambridge University Press, 2022).

21 See George F. Kennan (X), "The Sources of Soviet Conduct," *Foreign Affairs*, 25, no. 4 (1947), 566–82. This article was based upon Kennan's famous "long telegram," addressed to the US state leadership

in February 1946, which formed a basis for the politics of containment, pursued by the United States during the Cold War to prevent the spread of Communism. See https://nsarchive2.gwu.edu/coldwar/documents/episode-1/kennan.htm.

22 For a detailed elaboration of this argument, see Vladimir Ryzhkov, *Dlinnaya ten' SSSR: Ocherk istokov vneshnepoliticheskogo povedeniya sovremennoi Rossii* (Riga: Shkola grazhdanskogo prosveshcheniya, 2023), especially chapters 3 and 4.

23 For further elaboration of this argument, see Maxim Samorukov, "Why Putin Will Never Agree to De-escalate," *Foreign Policy*, June 13, 2023, https://foreignpolicy.com/2023/06/13/ukraine-counteroffensive-russia-putin-war-negotiation-ceasefire-successor/.

24 See William McNeill, *The Pursuit of Power: Technology, Armed Force and Society since A.D. 1000* (Chicago, IL: University of Chicago Press, 1982).

25 See Charles Tilly, *Capital, Coercion, and European States, AD 990–1992* (Oxford: Basil Blackwell, 1992).

26 See Bruce Bueno de Mesquita, Alastair Smith, Randolf M. Silverson and James D. Morrow, *The Logic of Political Survival* (Cambridge, MA: MIT Press, 2003), especially chapter 1.

27 For a comprehensive account, see Mark Kramer, "The Kremlin, the Prague Spring, and the Brezhnev Doctrine," in Vladimir Tismaneanu (ed.), *Promises of 1968: Crisis, Illusion, Utopia* (Budapest: Central European University Press, 2010), 285–370.

28 See John Higley and Michael Burton, *Elite Foundations of Liberal Democracy* (Lanham, MD: Rowman and Littlefield, 2006), 9.

29 For a thoughtful analysis of the transformation of Russian elites from the 1990s to the 2020s, see Andrei Yakovlev, "Composition of the Ruling Elite, Incentives for Productive Use of Rents, and Prospects for Russia's Limited Access Order," *Post-Soviet Affairs*, 37, no. 5 (2021), 417–34.

30 For similar arguments, see Stephen E. Hanson and Jeffrey S. Kopstein, "The Weimar/Russia Comparison," *Post-Soviet Affairs*, 13, no. 3 (1997), 252–83; Stephen E. Hanson and Jeffrey S. Kopstein, "The Weimar/Russia Comparison Revisited," *Russian Politics*, 8, no. 4 (2023), 419–39.

31 See Sharon Werning Rivera (ed.), *Survey of Russian Elites 2020: New Perspectives on Domestic and Foreign Policy* (Clinton, NY: Hamilton College, 2020), https://hamilton.edu/documents/SRE2020ReportFINAL.pdf.

32 See Sharon Werning Rivera, "The Views of Russian Elites on Military Intervention Abroad," *Russian Analytical Digest*, 299 (2023), 2–7.

33 This list of principles of Russian foreign policy is based upon the

author's interpretation of mainstream sources of contemporary Russian thought on international relations, including the publications of scholars and experts from organizations such as the Council of Foreign and Defense Policy, the Moscow State Institute of International Relations (MGIMO), the Russian Council of International Affairs, journals such as *Russia in Global Affairs*, and the like. Although these principles do not directly correspond with official Russian state documents such as the Concept of the Foreign Policy of the Russian Federation, in many ways they reflected the visions, perceptions, and preferences of certain segments of the Russian elites before February 2022. See Rivera, *Survey of Russian Elites 2020*.

34 For various typologies of authoritarian regimes, see Milan Svolik, *The Politics of Authoritarian Rule* (Cambridge: Cambridge University Press, 2012); Michael Wahman, Jan Teorell and Axel Hadenius, "Authoritarian Regime Types Revisited: Updated Data in Comparative Perspective," *Contemporary Politics*, 19, no. 1 (2013), 19–34; Barbara Geddes, Joseph Wright and Erica Frantz, *How Dictatorships Work: Power, Personalization, and Collapse* (Cambridge: Cambridge University Press, 2018).

35 See Sergey Radchenko, *To Run the World: The Kremlin's Cold War Bid for Global Power* (Cambridge: Cambridge University Press, 2024).

36 See Kennan (X), "The Sources of Soviet Conduct."

37 See Jim Garamone, "Russian Forces in Initial Phase of Invasion of Ukraine, Official Says," *US Department of Defense*, February 24, 2022, https://www.defense.gov/News/News-Stories/Article/Article/2945254/russian-forces-in-initial-phase-of-invasion-of-ukraine-official-says/; Maria Tsvetkova, "Fighting Reaches the Outskirts of Kyiv," *Reuters*, February 26, 2022, https://www.reuters.com/world/europe/ukraines-president-stays-put-russian-invaders-advance-2022-02-25/.

38 For some documents and analysis, see Anton Troianovski, Adam Entous and Michael Schwirtz, "Ukraine–Russia Peace Is as Elusive as Ever: But in 2022 They Were Talking," *New York Times*, June 15, 2024, https://www.nytimes.com/interactive/2024/06/15/world/europe/ukraine-russia-ceasefire-deal.html.

39 For an in-depth analysis, see Kimberly Marten, "Russia's Use of Semi-State Security Forces: The Case of the Wagner Group," *Post-Soviet Affairs*, 35, no. 3 (2019), 181–204.

40 See Natalia Drozdiak, Daryna Krasnolutska and Alberto Nardelli, "Ukraine's Struggle for Arms and Attention Gives Putin an Opening," *Bloomberg*, November 24, 2023, https://www.bloomberg.com/news/features/2023-11-24/ukraine-s-struggle-for-ammunition-gives-russia-opening.

41 See Pjotr Sauer and Andrew Roth, "Putin Prepares Russia for 'Forever

War' with West as Ukraine Invasion Stalls," *The Guardian*, March 28, 2023, https://www.theguardian.com/world/2023/mar/28/putin-prepares-russia-for-forever-war-with-west-as-ukraine-invasion-stalls.

42 For a detailed analysis of the performance of post-Communist central banks, see Juliet Johnson, *The Priests of Prosperity: How Central Bankers Transformed the Postcommunist World* (Ithaca, NY: Cornell University Press, 2016).

43 For an in-depth overview of Russia's post-Communist economic trajectory, see Marek Dabrowski, "Russia's Two Transitions (1992–2003 and 2003–2022)," in Marek Dabrowski (ed.), *The Contemporary Russian Economy: A Comprehensive Analysis* (Cham: Palgrave Macmillan, 2023), 383–98.

44 See Giovanni Capoccia and Daniel Kelemen, "The Study of Critical Junctures: Theory, Narrative, and Counterfactuals in Historical Institutionalism," *World Politics*, 59, no. 3 (2007), 341–69.

45 For a critical account, see Ilya Matveev, "From the Chicago Boys to Hjalmar Schacht: The Trajectory of the (Neo)liberal Economic Expertise in Russia," *Problems of Post-Communism*, 71, no. 6 (2024), 508–17.

46 See Graham Allison, *Essence of Decision: Explaining the Cuban Missile Crisis* (Boston, MA: Little, Brown, and Company, 1971).

47 See Graham Allison and Philip D. Zelikow, *Essence of Decision: Explaining the Cuban Missile Crisis*, 2nd edn (New York: Longman, 1999).

48 For an in-depth analysis of the personalization of Russian authoritarian regime, see Alexander Baturo and Jos Elknik, *The New Kremlinology: Understanding Regime Personalization in Russia* (Oxford: Oxford University Press, 2021).

49 For a comparative analysis of the variations in performance of authoritarian regimes, see Nicolas Charron and Victor Lapuente, "Which Dictators Produce Quality of Government?," *Studies in Comparative International Development*, 46, no. 4 (2011), 397–423.

50 For a game-theoretical elaboration of this argument, see Georgy Egorov and Konstantin Sonin, *Why Did Putin Invade Ukraine? A Theory of Degenerate Autocracy* (Chicago, IL: Becker Friedman Institute, University of Chicago, Working Paper no. 2023-52), https://bfi.uchicago.edu/wp-content/uploads/2023/04/BFI_WP_2023-52.pdf.

51 See Vladimir Gel'man, *The Politics of Bad Governance in Contemporary Russia* (Ann Arbor, MI: University of Michigan Press, 2022).

52 See Robert Jervis, *Perceptions and Misperceptions in International Politics* (Princeton, NJ: Princeton University Press, 1976).

53 See Max Seddon, Christopher Miller and Felicia Swartz, "How Putin Blundered into Ukraine – Then Doubled Down," *Financial Times*,

February 23, 2023, https://www.ft.com/content/80002564-33e8-48fb-b734-44810afb7a49.

54 On the spiral of gambling addiction, see Henry R. Lesieur, "The Compulsive Gambler's Spiral of Options and Involvement," *Psychiatry*, 42, no. 1 (1979), 79–87; Henry R. Lesieur and Robert L. Custer, "Pathological Gambling: Roots, Phases, and Treatment," *The Annals of the American Academy of Political and Social Science*, 474, no. 1 (1984), 146–56.

55 For Putin's biographies, see, in particular, Steven Lee Myers, *The New Tsar: The Rise and Reign of Vladimir Putin* (New York: Knopf Doubleday, 2015); Fiona Hill and Clifford Gaddy, *Mr. Putin: Operative in the Kremlin* (Washington, DC: Brookings Institution Press, 2015). For heavily critical accounts, see, in particular, Karen Dawisha, *Putin's Kleptocracy: Who Owns Russia?* (New York: Simon and Schuster, 2014); Anders Åslund, *Russia's Crony Capitalism: The Path from Market Economy to Kleptocracy* (New Haven, CT: Yale University Press, 2019). For a more balanced in-depth overview, see Brian Taylor, *The Code of Putinism* (Oxford: Oxford University Press, 2018).

56 See "Volodin: rossiyane vosprinimayut ataki na prezidenta RF kak ataki na svoyu stranu," *TASS*, October 22, 2014, https://tass.ru/politika/1525655.

57 For a critique of "Putinology," see Timothy Frye, *Weak Strongman: The Limits of Power in Putin's Russia* (Princeton, NJ: Princeton University Press, 2021).

58 See Rivera, *Survey of Russian Elites 2020*.

59 For some observations of elite and mass attitudes in the 1990s, see Judith S. Kullberg and William Zimmerman, "Liberal Elites, Socialist Masses, and Problems of Russian Democracy," *World Politics*, 51, no. 3 (1999), 323–58. For a longitudinal analysis of mass and elite survey data, see Boris Sokolov, Ronald F. Inglehart, Eduard Ponarin, Irina Vartanova and William Zimmerman, "Disillusionment and Anti-Americanism in Russia: From Pro-American to Anti-American Attitudes, 1993–2009," *International Studies Quarterly*, 62, no. 3 (2018), 534–47.

60 See Noah Buckley and Joshua A. Tucker, "Staring at the West through Kremlin-tinted Glasses: Russian Mass and Elite Divergence in Attitudes toward the United States, European Union, and Ukraine Before and After Crimea," *Post-Soviet Affairs*, 35, nos. 5–6 (2019), 365–75.

61 See, in particular, Samuel Greene and Graeme Robertson, "Explaining Putin's Popularity: Rally around the Russian Flag," *Washington Post*, September 9, 2014, http://www.washingtonpost.com/blogs/monkey-cage/wp/2014/09/09/explaining-putins-popularity-rallying-round-the-russian-flag/.

62 See Sharon Werning Rivera and James D. Bryan, "Understanding the Sources of Anti-Americanism in the Russian Elite," *Post-Soviet Affairs*, 35, nos. 5–6 (2019), 376–92; Kirill Zhirkov, "Militant Internationalism and Dogmatism among Foreign Policy Elites: Evidence from Russia, 1995–2016," *Post-Soviet Affairs*, 35, nos. 5–6 (2019), 422–32.

63 On the role of the general public in the "co-construction" of Putin's support in Russia, see Samuel Greene and Graeme Robertson, *Putin v. the People: Perilous Politics of a Divided Russia* (New Haven, CT: Yale University Press, 2019).

64 See Richard Pipes, *Russia under the Old Regime* (New York: Scribner, 1974).

65 See Stephen Hedlund, *Russian Path Dependence* (London: Routledge, 2005).

66 For an in-depth analysis of building foundations of democracy among the urban middle class in pre-revolutionary Russia, see Tomila Lankina, *The Estate Origins of Democracy in Russia: From Imperial Bourgeoisie to Post-Communist Middle Class* (Cambridge: Cambridge University Press, 2022).

67 See, for example, Timothy Snyder, "We Should Say It: Russia Is Fascist," *New York Times*, May 19, 2022, https://www.nytimes.com/2022/05/19/opinion/russia-fascism-ukraine-putin.html; Lev Gudkov, *Vozvratnyi totalitarism* (Moscow: Novoe literaturnoe obozrenie, 2022).

68 For a similar critique, see Marlene Laruelle, *Is Russia Fascist? Unraveling Propaganda East and West* (Ithaca, NY: Cornell University Press, 2021).

69 On these discussions, see, for example, Herbert Kitschelt, "Accounting for Postcommunist Regime Diversity: What Counts as a Good Cause," in Gregiorz Ekiert and Stephen Hanson (eds.), *Capitalism and Democracy in Central and Eastern Europe* (Cambridge: Cambridge University Press, 2003), 49–88; Vladimir Gel'man, "Bringing Actors Back In: Political Choices and Sources of Post-Soviet Regime Dynamics," *Post-Soviet Affairs*, 34, no. 5 (2018), 282–96.

70 See, in particular, John J. Mearsheimer, "Why the Ukraine Crisis is the West's Fault: the Liberal Delusions that Provoked Putin," *Foreign Affairs*, 93, no. 5 (2014), 77–89; John J. Mearsheimer, "The Causes and Consequences of the Ukraine War," *Horizons: Journal of International Relations and Sustainable Development*, 21 (2022), 12–27.

71 See John Mearsheimer, *The Tragedy of Great Power Politics* (New York: W.W. Norton, 2001).

72 See Carl von Clausewitz, *On War* (Princeton, NJ: Princeton University Press, 1984), 69.

73 See, in particular, James D. Fearon, "Rationalist Explanations for War," *International Organizations*, 49, no. 3 (1995), 379–414.

74 See Gel'man, *Authoritarian Russia*.
75 See Gel'man, *The Politics of Bad Governance in Contemporary Russia*, especially chapter 1.
76 See, in particular, Ronald Wintrobe, *The Political Economy of Dictatorship* (Cambridge: Cambridge University Press, 1998); Svolik, *The Politics of Authoritarian Rule*. On dealing with these issues in Communist regimes, see Martin K. Dimitrov, *Dictatorship and Political Information: Authoritarian Regime Resilience in Communist Europe and China* (Oxford: Oxford University Press, 2023).
77 See Sergei Guriev and Daniel Treisman, "Informational Autocrats," *Journal of Economic Perspectives*, 33, no. 4 (2019), 100–27. See also Guriev and Treisman, *Spin Dictators*, especially chapter 1.

Chapter 2. The Personalist Trap

1 For a detailed account of the role of the Security Council, see Ekaterina Shulmann and Mark Galeotti, "A Tale of Two Councils: the Changing Roles of the Security and State Councils during the Transformation Period of Modern Russian Politics," *Post-Soviet Affairs*, 37, no. 5 (2021), 453–69.
2 For a detailed account of the role of Patrushev and the evolution of his political ideas, see Martin Kragh and Andreas Umland, "Putinism beyond Putin: the Political Ideas of Nikolai Patrushev and Sergei Naryshkin in 2006–20," *Post-Soviet Affairs*, 39, no. 5 (2023), 366–89.
3 For a stenographic report and a video record of this meeting, see *Zasedanie Soveta Bezopasnosti*, February 21, 2022, http://kremlin.ru/events/president/news/67825.
4 For a detailed account of Russia's approach to the "people's republics" and their role in the conflict in 2014–2015, see, in particular, Andrew S. Bowen, "Coercive Diplomacy and the Donbas: Explaining Russian Strategy in Eastern Ukraine," *The Journal of Strategic Studies*, 42, nos. 3–4 (2019), 312–43. For more recent assessments, see Anna Matveeva, "Donbas: the Post-Soviet Conflict that Changed Europe," *European Politics and Society*, 22, no. 3 (2022), 410–41; Adam Potocnak and Miroslav Mares, "Donbas Conflict: How Russia's Trojan Horse Failed and Forced Moscow to Alter Its Strategy," *Problems of Post-Communism*, 70, no. 4 (2023), 341–51.
5 On the role of the "Normandy format," see Simond de Galbert, *The Impact of the Normandy Format on the Conflict in Ukraine: Four Leaders, Three Cease-fires, and Two Summits* (Washington, DC: Center for Strategic and International Studies, 2015), https://www.csis.org/analysis/impact-normandy-format-conflict-ukraine-four

-leaders-three-cease-fires-and-two-summits. On its failure in conflict management, see Andrew Lohsen and Pierre Morcos, *Understanding the Normandy Format and Its Relation to the Current Standoff with Russia* (Washington, DC: Center for Strategic and International Studies, 2022), https://www.csis.org/analysis/understanding-normandy-format-and-its-relation-current-standoff-russia.

6 For the programmatic statement by Russia's leadership about Ukraine as an artificial political construct, see Vladimir Putin, "Ob istoricheskom edinstve russkikh i ukraintsev," *Kremlin.ru*, July 12, 2021, http://kremlin.ru/events/president/news/66181.

7 See Emma Farge, "U.S. and Russia Still Far Apart on Ukraine after Geneva Talks," *Reuters*, January 11, 2022, https://www.reuters.com/world/europe/prospects-dim-us-russia-start-tense-talks-over-ukraine-crisis-2022-01-10/.

8 On discussions and expectations before the Russian assault on Ukraine, see, for example, Seth G. Jones and Philip G. Wasielewski, *Russia's Possible Invasion of Ukraine* (Washington, DC: Center for Strategic and International Studies, 2022), https://www.csis.org/analysis/russias-possible-invasion-ukraine; Mathieu Boulegue, *Is a Russia-Ukraine War Imminent?* (London: Chatham House, 2022), https://www.chathamhouse.org/2022/01/russia-ukraine-war-imminent.

9 For a selection of views from Russian and international observers before the assault, see Valentina Shwarzman and Dmitry Plotnikov, "Voina nachinaet upravlyat' sama soboi," *Lenta.ru*, January 25, 2022, https://lenta.ru/articles/2022/01/25/experts/.

10 For serious warnings by top Russian military officials, see, for example, Mikhail Khodarenok, "Prognozy krovozhadnykh politologov," *Nezavisimoe voennoe obozrenie*, February 3, 2022, https://nvo.ng.ru/realty/2022-02-03/3_1175_donbass.html; Olga Vandysheva and Valerii Bersenev, "Rossiya prekratit svoe sushchestvovanie: Leonid Ivashov o gotovyashcheisya voine," *Biznes-gazeta*, February 13, 2022, https://www.business-gazeta.ru/article/539470.

11 On Russian expectations of international sanctions before the assault, see, for example, Lidiya Misnik, "Evropa neodnorodna dazhe v voprose sanktsii," *Gazeta.ru*, December 17, 2021, https://www.gazeta.ru/politics/2021/12/17_a_14325835.shtml; Ivan Zhukovskii, "Rossiyu peredumali otklyuchat' ot SWIFT," *Gazeta.ru*, January 17, 2022, https://www.gazeta.ru/business/2022/01/17/14428843.shtml.

12 Kragh and Umland portray Naryshkin as a less hawkish politician than Patrushev. See Kragh and Umland, "Putinism beyond Putin."

13 For the TV series *Yes, Prime Minister*, see https://www.imdb.com/title/tt0086831/.

14 For a critical account of the Security Council meeting (including

discussion of its unofficial section, where some plans for the military assault were probably revealed to the participants), see the "Pertsev and Gaaze" podcast, February 26, 2022, https://podcasts.apple.com/us/podcast/перцев-и-гаазе/id1584842517.

15 See Max Seddon, Christopher Miller and Felicia Schwartz, "How Putin Blundered into Ukraine – Then Doubled Down," *Financial Times*, February 23, 2023, https://www.ft.com/content/80002564-33e8-48fb-b734-44810afb7a49.

16 On the role of acclamation as a major element in mass support for the political regime in Russia, see Greg Yudin, "Do Russians Support Putin?," *Journal of Democracy*, 33, no. 3 (2022), 31–7.

17 For an account of the evolution of Russian authoritarianism, see Vladimir Gel'man, *Authoritarian Russia: Analyzing Post-Soviet Regime Changes* (Pittsburgh, PA: University of Pittsburgh Press, 2015). For a theoretical and comparative analysis, see Grigorii V. Golosov, "The Place of Russia's Political Regime (2003–2023) on a Conceptual Map of the World's Autocracies," *Social Science Information*, 62, no. 3 (2023), 390–408.

18 On policy-making in personalist autocracies, see, for example, Brandon J. Kinne, "Decision Making in Autocratic Regimes: A Polihuristic Perspective," *International Studies Perspectives*, 6, no. 1 (2005), 114–28; Alexander Taaning Grundholm, "Taking It Personal? Investigating Regime Personalization as an Autocratic Survival Strategy," *Democratization*, 27, no. 5 (2020), 797–815.

19 For various accounts, see Georgy Egorov and Konstantin Sonin, "Dictators and Their Viziers: Endogenizing the Loyalty-Competence Trade-off," *Journal of European Economic Association*, 9, no. 5 (2011), 903–30; Alexei V. Zakharov, "The Loyalty-Competence Trade-Off in Dictatorships and Outside Options for Subordinates," *Journal of Politics*, 78, no. 2 (2016), 457–66.

20 For a detailed empirical account of the dynamics of the personalization of the political regime in contemporary Russia, see Alexander Baturo and Jos Elknik, *The New Kremlinology: Understanding Regime Personalization in Russia* (Oxford: Oxford University Press, 2021).

21 Dani Rodrik, "The Myth of Authoritarian Growth," *Project Syndicate*, August 9, 2010, http://www.project-syndicate.org/commentary/the-myth-of-authoritarian-growth.

22 For various typologies of authoritarian regimes, see Milan Svolik, *The Politics of Authoritarian Rule* (Cambridge: Cambridge University Press, 2012); Barbara Geddes, Joseph Wright and Erica Frantz, *How Dictatorships Work: Power, Personalization, and Collapse* (Cambridge: Cambridge University Press, 2018); Carsten Ancar and Cecilia

Fredriksson, "Classifying Political Regimes 1800–2016: A Typology and a New Dataset," *European Political Science*, 18, no. 1 (2019), 84–96.
23 On the persistence of monarchies in contemporary world, see Adria Lawrence, "Why Monarchies Still Reign," *Journal of Democracy*, 34, no. 2 (2023), 47–61.
24 For a comparative analysis, see Geddes, Wright and Frantz, *How Dictatorships Work*.
25 For a comparative analysis, see Nicolas Charron and Victor Lapuente, "Which Dictators Produce Quality of Government?," *Studies in Comparative International Development*, 46, no. 4 (2011), 397–423.
26 See Geddes, Wright and Frantz, *How Dictatorships Work*.
27 On institutional constraints in party-based authoritarian regimes, see Anne Meng, *Constraining Dictatorship: From Personalized Rule to Institutionalized Regimes* (Cambridge: Cambridge University Press, 2020). See also Qingjie Zeng, "All Power to the Party! The Sources of Ruling Party Strength in Authoritarian Regimes," *Canadian Review of Political Science*, 54, no. 1 (2021), 186–208.
28 On the evolution of collective leadership in the Soviet Union, see Graeme Gill, *Collective Leadership in Soviet Politics* (Cham: Palgrave Macmillan, 2018).
29 For an overview, see Barbara Geddes, Joseph Wright and Erica Frantz, "Military Rule," *Annual Review of Political Science*, 17 (2014), 147–62.
30 For a comparative analysis of dynastic leadership succession in party-based and personalist authoritarian regimes, see Jason Brownlee, "Hereditary Succession in Modern Autocracies," *World Politics*, 59, no. 4 (2007), 595–628. See also Anne Meng, "Winning the Game of Thrones: Leadership Succession in Modern Autocracies," *Journal of Conflict Resolution*, 65, no. 5 (2020), 950–81.
31 On the distinction between "roving" and "stationary" bandits, see Mancur Olson, "Dictatorship, Democracy, and Development," *American Political Science Review*, 87, no. 3 (1993), 567–76.
32 For a detailed account of electoral authoritarian regimes, see Andreas Schedler, *The Politics of Uncertainty: Sustaining and Subverting Electoral Authoritarianism* (Oxford: Oxford University Press, 2013). For a comprehensive account of the trajectory of electoral authoritarianism in Russia, see Golosov, "The Place of Russia's Political Regime (2003–2023) on a Conceptual Map of the World's Autocracies."
33 On political business cycles in autocracies, see Masaaki Higashijima, "Political Business Cycles in Dictatorship," *WIAS Discussion Papers*, no. 2016-002, https://www.waseda.jp/inst/wias/assets/uploads/2016/09/dp2016002.pdf; Kangwook Han, "Political Budgetary Cycles in

Autocratic Redistribution," *Comparative Political Studies*, 55, no. 5 (2022), 727–56. On the Russian experience in the 1990s, see Daniel Treisman and Vladimir Gimpelson, "Political Business Cycles and Russian Elections, or the Manipulations of 'Chudar,'" *British Journal of Political Science*, 31, no. 2 (2001), 225–46.

34 For the best description of this phenomenon in fiction, see Gabriel Garcia Marquez, *The Autumn of the Patriarch* (New York: Harper Modern Classics, 2006).
35 See Egorov and Sonin, "Dictators and Their Viziers."
36 For analyses of the declining performance of the Soviet regime from the perspective of economic history, see Philip Hanson, *The Rise and Fall of the Soviet Economy: an Economic History of the USSR from 1945* (London: Pearson Education, 2003); Yegor Gaidar, *Collapse of an Empire: Lessons for Modern Russia* (Washington, DC: Brookings Institution Press, 2007).
37 For a comparative analysis of China and Russia, see Alexander Libman and Michael Rochlitz, *Federalism in China and Russia: Story of Success and Story of Failure?* (Cheltenham: Edward Elgar, 2019).
38 For some accounts of practices of governance in the late-Soviet period, see Yoram Gorlizki and Oleg Khlevniuk, *Substate Dictatorship: Networks, Loyalty, and Institutional Change in the Soviet Union* (New Haven, CT: Yale University Press, 2020); Nikolay Mitrokhin, *Ocherki sovetskoi ekonomicheskoi politiki, 1965–1989*, 2 vols (Moscow: Novoe Literaturnoe Obozrenie, 2023).
39 On dealing with similar issues in Communist regimes, see Martin K. Dimitrov, *Dictatorship and Political Information: Authoritarian Regime Resilience in Communist Europe and China* (Oxford: Oxford University Press, 2023).
40 See Ilia Nadporozhskii, "Influence of Elite Rotation on Authoritarian Resilience," *Democratization*, 30, no. 5 (2023), 794–814.
41 See Charron and Lapuente, "Which Dictators Produce Quality of Government?"
42 See Gel'man, *Authoritarian Russia*, chapter 3.
43 See Boris Yeltsin, *Struggle for Russia* (New York: Times Books, 1994), 6.
44 For various accounts of Putin's personalist authoritarianism, see Brian D. Taylor, *The Code of Putinism* (Oxford: Oxford University Press, 2018); Timothy Frye, *The Weak Strongman: The Limits of Power in Putin's Russia* (Princeton, NJ: Princeton University Press, 2021).
45 See, in particular, Daniel Treisman, "Presidential Popularity in a Hybrid Regime: Russia under Yeltsin and Putin," *American Journal of Political Science*, 55, no. 3 (2011), 590–609.
46 See Gel'man, *Authoritarian Russia*, chapter 4.

47 On the "Yukos affair" and its effects, see Philip Hanson, "Observations on the Costs of the Yukos Affair to Russia," *Eurasian Geography and Economics*, 46, no. 7 (2005), 481–94; William Tompson, "Putting Yukos in Perspective," *Post-Soviet Affairs*, 21, no. 2 (2005), 159–81. See also Thane Gustafson, *Wheel of Fortune: The Battle for Oil and Power in Russia* (Cambridge, MA: Harvard University Press, 2012), chapter 7.
48 For an account of the stages of regime personalization in Russia, see Baturo and Elknik, *The New Kremlinology*, chapter 2.
49 See Gel'man, *Authoritarian Russia*, chapter 5.
50 Baturo and Elknik, *The New Kremlinology*, 43.
51 "Volodin: 'Est' Putin – est' Rossiya, net Putina – net Rossii'," *Moskovskii komsomolets*, October 23, 2014, https://www.mk.ru/politics/2014/10/23/volodin-est-putin-est-rossiya-net-putina-net-rossii.html.
52 For a detailed analysis, see Fabian Burkhardt, "Institutionalizing Personalism: The Russian Presidency after Constitutional Changes," *Russian Politics*, 6, no. 1 (2021), 50–70.
53 Baturo and Elknik, *The New Kremlinology*, 43–4.
54 Ibid., 80.
55 See Vladimir Gel'man, *The Politics of Bad Governance in Contemporary Russia* (Ann Arbor, MI: University of Michigan Press, 2022), chapter 5.
56 On the overcoming of the global economic crisis of 2008–9 in Russia, see Neil Robinson, "Russia's Response to Crisis: The Paradox of Success," *Europe-Asia Studies*, 65, no. 3 (2013), 450–72.
57 See Evgenia Pismennaya, Ilya Arkhipov and Brad Cook, "Putin's Secret Gamble on Reserves Backfires into Currency Crisis," *Bloomberg*, December 17, 2014, https://www.bloomberg.com/news/articles/2014-12-17/putin-s-secret-gamble-bet-on-ukraine-backfires-in-ruble-crisis.
58 For a systematic account, see Andrei Yakovlev, "Composition of the Ruling Elite, Incentives for Productive Use of Rents, and Prospects for Russia's Limited Access Order," *Post-Soviet Affairs*, 37, no. 5 (2021), 417–34.
59 See Gel'man, *The Politics of Bad Governance in Contemporary Russia*, chapter 5.
60 See Brian D. Taylor, *Politics and the Russian Army: Civil-Military Relations, 1689–2000* (Cambridge: Cambridge University Press, 2003), chapter 7; Zoltan Barany, *Democratic Breakdown and the Decline of the Russian Military* (Princeton, NJ: Princeton University Press, 2007), chapter 5.
61 See Vadim Volkov, *Violent Entrepreneurs: The Role of Force in the Making of Russian Capitalism* (Ithaca, NY: Cornell University Press, 2002); Brian D. Taylor, *State Building in Putin's Russia: Policing and*

Coercion After Communism (Cambridge: Cambridge University Press, 2011).

62 On the effects of the "Yukos affair" on the statist turn in the development of Russian capitalism in the 2000s, see Vadim Volkov, "Standard Oil and Yukos in the Context of Early Capitalism in the United States and Russia," *Demokratizatsiya: The Journal of Post-Soviet Democratization*, 16, no. 3 (2008), 240–64. See also Anders Åslund, *Russia's Crony Capitalism: The Path from Market Economy to Kleptocracy* (New Haven, CT: Yale University Press, 2019), chapter 4.

63 For some accounts, see Fiona Hill and Clifford G. Gaddy, *Mr. Putin: Operative in the Kremlin* (Washington, DC: Brookings Institution Press, 2013); Karen Dawisha, *Putin's Kleptocracy: Who Owns Russia?* (New York: Simon & Schuster, 2014).

64 See Sharon Werning Rivera (ed.), *Survey of Russian Elites 2020: New Perspectives on Domestic and Foreign Policy* (Clinton, NY: Hamilton College, 2020), https://hamilton.edu/documents/SRE2020ReportFINAL.pdf.

65 For a detailed account of military reforms in post-Soviet Russia and of the role of Serdyukov, see Alexander Golts, *Military Reform and Militarism in Russia* (Boulder, CO: Lynne Rienner, 2018), especially chapters 2 and 4.

66 See Gel'man, *The Politics of Bad Governance in Contemporary Russia*, chapter 1.

67 See Frye, *Weak Strongman*, especially chapter 9.

68 For an account of pension reform in Russia, see Linda Cook, Aadne Aasland and Daria Prisyazhnyuk, "Russian Pension Reform under Quadruple Influence," *Problems of Post-Communism*, 66, no. 2 (2019), 96–108; Elena Maltseva, "The Politics of Retirement Age Increase in Russia: Proposals, Protests, and Concessions," *Russian Politics*, 4, no. 3 (2019), 375–99.

69 On the impact of bad governance on high excess mortality in Russia during the COVID-19 pandemic, see Vladimir Gel'man, "Bad Governance in Times of Exogenous Shocks: The Case of the COVID-19 Pandemic in Russia," in Margarita Zavadskaya (ed.), *The Politics of the Pandemic in Eastern Europe and Eurasia: Blame Game and Governance* (Abingdon: Routledge, 2024), 80–94.

70 On the use of the "Good Soviet Union" by elites in contemporary Russia, see Vladimir Gel'man and Anastassia Obydenkova, "The Invention of Legacy: Strategic Uses of a 'Good Soviet Union' in Elite Policy Preferences and Filmmaking in Russia," *Communist and Post-Communist Studies*, 57, no. 1 (2024), 130–53.

71 On these matters, see Nicole Krome, "State Corporate Governance in Russia," *Europe-Asia Studies*, 74, no. 8 (2022), 1350–74.

72 For a report by the Russian Audit Chamber, see Iuliia Starostina, Egor Gubernatorov, Elizaveta Efimovich, Liudmila Podobedova and Svetlana Burmistrova, "Schetnaia palata ukazala nedostatki i riski natsproektov," *rbc.ru*, January 13, 2020, https://www.rbc.ru/economi cs/13/01/2020/5e184e2a9a79470bf49655c3.
73 For an overview, see John Willerton, *Patronage and Politics in the USSR* (Cambridge: Cambridge University Press, 1992).
74 For analyses, see Gordon H. Skilling, *Czechoslovakia's Interrupted Revolution* (Princeton, NJ: Princeton University Press, 1976); Jiri Valenta, *Soviet Intervention in Czechoslovakia, 1968: Anatomy of a Decision* (Baltimore, MD: Johns Hopkins University Press, 1979).
75 See Gill, *Collective Leadership in Soviet Politics*, especially chapter 6.
76 For a detailed and thoughtful account, see Mark Kramer, "The Kremlin, the Prague Spring, and the Brezhnev Doctrine," in Vladimir Tismaneanu (ed.), *Promises of 1968: Crisis, Illusion, Utopia* (Budapest: Central European University Press, 2010), 285–370.
77 Ibid., 304–10, 313–21, 329–34.
78 Ibid., 348.
79 On mechanisms of state secrecy in the Soviet Union, see Mark Harrison, *Secret Leviathan: Secrecy and State Capacity under Soviet Communism* (Stanford, CA: Stanford University Press, 2023); on practices of late-Soviet economic policy-making, see Mitrokhin, *Ocherki sovetskoi ekonomicheskoi politiki*.
80 See Kramer, "The Kremlin, the Prague Spring, and the Brezhnev Doctrine," 339.
81 Ibid., 351–4.
82 For various accounts, see Mark Galeotti, *Afghanistan: the Soviet Union's Last War* (London: Frank Cass, 1995); David N. Gibbs, "Reassessing Soviet Motives for Invading Afghanistan: A Declassified History," *Critical Asian Studies*, 38, no. 2 (2006), 239–63.
83 For an analysis in comparative perspective, see David C. Gompert, Hans Binnendijk and Bonny Lin, *Blinders, Blunders, and Wars: What America and China Can Learn* (Santa Monica, CA: Rand Corporation, 2014), chapter 11, https://www.rand.org/pubs/research_reports/RR768.html.
84 On Kovalchuk's role, see Betsy McKay, Thomas Grove and Rob Berry, "The Russian Billionaire Selling Putin's War to the Public," *The Wall Street Journal*, December 2, 2022, https://www.wsj.com/articles /russian-billionaire-selling-putins-war-ukraine-11669994410. See also Evan Gershkovich, Thomas Grove, Drew Hinshaw and Joe Parkinson, "Putin, Isolated and Distrustful, Leans on Handful of Hard-Line Advisers," *The Wall Street Journal*, December 23, 2022, https://www .wsj.com/articles/putin-russia-ukraine-war-advisers-11671815184.
85 On Shoigu's role, see Paul Sonne and Catherine Belton, "Russia's

NOTES TO PP. 55–60

Ultimate Political Survivor Faces a Wartime Reckoning," *Washington Post*, May 8, 2022, https://www.washingtonpost.com/national-security/2022/05/08/russia-ukraine-shoigu-putin/. See also Golts, *Military Reform and Militarism in Russia*, chapter 4.

86 On Medvedchuk's role, see Igor Burdyga, "The Rise and Fall of Putin's Man in Ukraine," *Open Democracy*, July 26, 2022, https://www.opendemocracy.net/en/odr/medvedchuk-putin-poroshenko-treason-ukraine-russia/.

87 See Paul Sonne, Ellen Nakashima, Shane Harris and John Hadson, "Hubris and Isolation Led Vladimir Putin to Misjudge Ukraine," *Washington Post*, April 11, 2022, https://www.washingtonpost.com/national-security/2022/04/11/putin-misjudged-ukraine-hubris-isolation/; David V. Gioe and Marina Miron, "Putin Should Have Known His Invasion Would Fail," *Foreign Policy*, February 24, 2023, https://foreignpolicy.com/2023/02/24/ukraine-russia-putin-war-invasion-military-failure/.

88 On this acute problem, see Ronald Wintrobe, *The Political Economy of Dictatorship* (Cambridge: Cambridge University Press, 1998). For an account of personalist authoritarian regimes, see Charles Crabtree, Holger L. Kern and David A. Siegel, "Cults of Personality, Preference Falsification, and the Dictator's Dilemma," *Journal of Theoretical Politics*, 32, no. 3 (2020), 409–34.

89 For a critical reassessment of this argument, see Archie Brown, *The Myth of the Strong Leader: Political Leadership in the Modern Age* (New York: Basic Books, 2014).

90 See Georgy Egorov and Konstantin Sonin, *Why Did Putin Invade Ukraine? A Theory of Degenerate Autocracy* (Chicago, IL: Becker Friedman Institute, University of Chicago, Working Paper no. 2023-52), https://bfi.uchicago.edu/wp-content/uploads/2023/04/BFI_WP_2023-52.pdf.

91 For some accounts in a comparative perspective, see Jennifer Gandhi, *Political Institutions under Dictatorship* (Cambridge: Cambridge University Press, 2008); Thomas Pepinsky, "The Institutional Turn in Comparative Authoritarianism," *British Journal of Political Science*, 44, no. 3 (2011), 631–53.

Chapter 3. The Well-Oiled Machine, Out of Control

1 For details of this episode, see Oleg Rubnikovich, "Antenny u nikh ne toi sistemy," *Kommersant*, June 22, 2023, https://www.kommersant.ru/doc/6056099.

2 See "Voina i pir. Glamurnaya zhizn' zamestitelya ministra oborony Timura Ivanova," https://www.youtube.com/watch?v=dSHMow8Ijl8.

NOTES TO P. 61

3 For the scholarly dataset, see Jan Teorell, Aksel Sundström, Sören Holmberg, Bo Rothstein, Natalia Alvarado Pachon and Cem Mert Dalli, *The Quality of Government Standard Dataset*, January 2023 version (Gothenburg: Quality of Government Institute, 2023), https://www.gu.se/en/quality-government/qog-data/data-downloads/standard-dataset.

4 The most prominent examples are presented in a series of investigative reports produced by the Anti-Corruption Foundation, led by the key figure of the Russian opposition, Alexei Navalny. See, in particular, "Dvorets Putina – istoriya samoi bol'shoi vzyatki," https://www.youtube.com/watch?v=ipAnwilMncI. In 2021, the Russian courts jailed Navalny and labeled the Anti-Corruption Foundation an "extremist" organization.

5 Among numerous journalist investigations, one of the most impressive is the Panama Papers, a series of reports about global high-profile corruption and money laundering provided by the Organized Crime and Corruption Reporting Project, https://www.occrp.org/en/. For evidence on Russia, see Paul Radu, "Russia: The Cellist and the Lawyer," April 26, 2016, https://www.occrp.org/en/panamapapers/russia-the-cellist-and-the-lawyer/; Roman Anin, "Russia: Banking on Influence," June 9, 2016, https://www.occrp.org/en/panamapapers/rossiya-putins-bank/.

6 For the comprehensive dataset, see *Worldwide Governance Indicators* (Washington, DC: World Bank, 2023), http://info.worldbank.org/governance/wgi/.

7 For the recent annual report, see *World Justice Project Rule of Law Index 2023* (Washington, DC: World Justice Project, 2023), https://worldjusticeproject.org/rule-of-law-index/global.

8 For the recent annual report, see *Corruption Perception Index 2022* (Berlin: Transparency International, 2023), https://www.transparency.org/en/cpi/2022.

9 See Vladimir Gel'man, *The Politics of Bad Governance in Contemporary Russia* (Ann Arbor, MI: University of Michigan Press, 2022).

10 For a discussion on the link between state secrecy and quality of governance, see Dennis Thompson, "Democratic Secrecy," *Political Science Quarterly*, 114, no. 2 (1999), 181–93; Dorota Mokrosinska, "Democratic Authority and State Secrecy," *Public Affairs Quarterly*, 33, no. 1 (2019), 1–20. For an alternative perspective, see Craig Scott and Daniel P. Fata, "Secrecy and Good Governance," *Global Brief* (Winter 2011), https://globalbrief.ca/2011/02/secrecy-is-a-necessary-condition-for-good-governance/.

11 See Pavel Baev, "Special Services Aggravate Bad Governance in Russia," *Eurasia Daily Monitor*, 18, no. 42 (2021).

12 On the "dictator's dilemma," see Ronald Wintrobe, *The Political Economy of Dictatorships* (Cambridge: Cambridge University Press, 1998), especially chapter 2.
13 For an analysis of the legalization of the status and wealth of Russian elites in the West, see Gulnaz Sharafutdinova and Karen Dawisha, "The Escape from Institution-Building in a Globalized World: Lessons from Russia," *Perspectives on Politics*, 15, no. 2 (2017), 361–78. See also Anders Åslund, *Russia's Crony Capitalism: The Path from Market Economy to Kleptocracy* (New Haven, CT: Yale University Press, 2019), especially chapter 6.
14 For various analyses, see Theodoros Rakopoulos, "The Golden Passport 'Russian' EUtopia: Offshore Citizens in a Global Republic," *Social Anthropology/Anthropologie Sociale*, 30, no. 2 (2022), 161–78; Ho-Chun Herbert Chang, Brooke Harrington, Feng Fu and Daniel N. Rockmore, "Complex Systems of Secrecy: the Offshore Networks of Oligarchs," *PNAS Nexus*, 2, no. 3 (2023), 1–12.
15 See Christopher J. Coyne and Rachel L. Mathers, *The Handbook on the Political Economy of War* (Cheltenham: Edward Elgar, 2011).
16 See Gel'man, *The Politics of Bad Governance in Contemporary Russia*, 10.
17 Among the literature on good governance, see, in particular, Bo Rothstein and Jan Teorell, "What Is Quality of Government? A Theory of Impartial Government Institutions," *Governance*, 21, no. 2 (2008), 165–90; Sören Holmberg and Bo Rothstein (eds.), *Good Government: The Relevance of Political Science* (Cheltenham: Edward Elgar, 2012).
18 On "rules-in-use," see Elinor Ostrom, *Governing the Commons: The Evolution of Institutions for Collective Action* (Cambridge: Cambridge University Press, 1990), 53.
19 On "power pyramids," see Henry E. Hale, *Patronal Politics: Eurasian Regime Dynamics in Comparative Perspective* (Cambridge: Cambridge University Press, 2014), especially chapter 6.
20 See Gel'man, *The Politics of Bad Governance in Contemporary Russia*, 12.
21 On types and causes of corruption, see Andrei Shleifer and Robert W. Vishny, "Corruption," *Quarterly Journal of Economics*, 108, no. 3 (1993), 599–617; Daniel Treisman, "The Causes of Corruption: A Cross-National Study," *Journal of Public Economics*, 76, no. 3 (2000), 399–457.
22 See Margit Cohn, "Fuzzy Legality in Regulation: The Legislative Mandate Revisited," *Law and Policy*, 23, no. 4 (2001), 469–97.
23 See Guillermo A. O'Donnell, "Polyarchies and the (Un)Rule of Law in Latin America: A Partial Conclusion," in Juan E. Mendez, Guillermo

A. O'Donnell and Paulo Sergio Pinheiro (eds.), *The (Un)Rule of Law and the Underprivileged in Latin America* (Notre Dame, IN: University of Notre Dame Press, 1999), 303–37.

24 "Institutions ... are created to serve the interests of those with the bargaining power to devise new rules," Douglass C. North, *Institutions, Institutional Changes, and Economic Performance* (Cambridge: Cambridge University Press, 1990), 16.

25 On Central Asia, see Alisher Ilkhamov, "Neopatrimonialism, Interest Groups and Patronage Networks: the Impasses of the Governance System in Uzbekistan," *Central Asian Survey*, 26, no. 1 (2007), 65–84; Alexander Cooley and John Heathershaw, *Dictators without Borders: Power and Money in Central Asia* (New Haven, CT: Yale University Press, 2017). On sub-Saharan Africa, see Kempe Ronald Hope and Bornwell C. Chikulo (eds.), *Corruption and Development in Africa* (London: Palgrave Macmillan, 2000); Robert Klosowicz, "The Problem of Bad Governance as a Determinant of State Dysfunctionality in Sub-Saharan Africa," *Politeja*, 56 (2018), 9–22.

26 See Nicole Krome, "State Corporate Governance in Russia," *Europe-Asia Studies*, 74, no. 8 (2022), 1350–74; Gel'man, *The Politics of Bad Governance in Contemporary Russia*, chapter 2.

27 See, in particular, Barbara Geddes, *Politician's Dilemma: Building State Capacity in Latin America* (Berkeley, CA: University of California Press, 1994); Michael Roll (ed.), *The Politics of Public Sector Performance: Pockets of Effectiveness in Developing Countries* (London: Routledge, 2014), especially chapter 1.

28 See Hilary Appel, *Tax Politics in Eastern Europe: Globalization, Regional Integration, and the Democratic Compromise* (Ann Arbor, MI: University of Michigan Press, 2011), especially chapter 6.

29 See Juliet Johnson, *Priests of Prosperity: How Central Bankers Transformed the Postcommunist World* (Ithaca, NY: Cornell University Press, 2016), especially chapter 6.

30 See, in particular, Neil Robinson, "Russia's Response to Crisis: The Paradox of Success," *Europe-Asia Studies*, 65, no. 3 (2013), 450–72.

31 For a critical account of the role of technocrats in economic policy-making in Russia, see Ilya Matveev, "From the Chicago Boys to Hjalmar Schacht: The Trajectory of the (Neo)liberal Economic Expertise in Russia," *Problems of Post-Communism*, 71, no. 6 (2024), 508–17.

32 See Alexandra Prokopenko, "Vkhod – kopeika, vykhod – zhizn': chto sdelal god voiny s rossiiskoi elitoi," *Carnegie Endowment for International Peace*, March 7, 2023, https://carnegieendowment.org/politika/89212.

33 For a detailed account, see Andras Toth-Czifra, *The War as an*

Accelerator (Philadelphia, PA: Foreign Policy Research Institute, 2023), https://www.fpri.org/article/2023/05/war-as-an-accelerator/.

34 For a critical account from the former official of the Russian Ministry of Foreign Affairs, see Boris Bondarev, "The Sources of Russian Misconduct," *Foreign Affairs*, 101, no. 6 (2022), 36–55.

35 For various accounts, see Ian Bremmer and Samuel Charap, "The Siloviki in Putin's Russia: Who They Are and What They Want," *The Washington Quarterly*, 30, no. 1 (2007), 83–92; Brian D. Taylor, "The Russian Siloviki & Political Change," *Daedalus*, 146, no. 2 (2017), 53–63; Michael Rochlitz, "The Return of Siloviki," *Russian Politics*, 4, no. 4 (2019), 493–8.

36 For a detailed analysis, see Andrei Yakovlev, "Composition of the Ruling Elite, Incentives for Productive Use of Rents, and Prospects for Russia's Limited Access Order," *Post-Soviet Affairs*, 37, no. 5 (2021), 417–34.

37 For excellent analyses of performance of Russian criminal justice and related state agencies, see Ella Paneyakh, "Faking Performance Together: Systems of Performance Evaluation in Russian Enforcement Agencies and Production of Bias and Privilege," *Post-Soviet Affairs*, 30, nos. 2–3 (2014), 115–36; Ella Paneyakh, Kirill Titaev and Mariya Shklyaruk, *Traektoriya ugolovnogo dela: institutstional'nyi analiz* (Saint Petersburg: European University at Saint Petersburg Press, 2018).

38 For various accounts, see Peter Rutland, "Petronation? Oil, Gas, and National Identity in Russia," *Post-Soviet Affairs*, 31, no. 1 (2015), 66–89; Veli-Pekka Tynkkynen, *The Energy of Russia: Hydrocarbon Culture and Climate Change* (Cheltenham: Edward Elgar, 2019), especially chapter 2; Adnan Vatansever, *Oil in Putin's Russia: The Contests over Rents and Economic Policy* (Toronto: University of Toronto Press, 2021).

39 See Maria Snegovaya, "What Factors Contribute to the Aggressive Foreign Policy of Russian Leaders?" *Problems of Post-Communism*, 67, no. 1 (2020), 93–110.

40 For a detailed account and policy recommendations, see Vadim Volkov et al., *Kontseptsiya kompleksnoi organizatsionno-upravlencheskoi reformy pravookhranitel'nykh organov RF* (Saint Petersburg: European University at Saint Petersburg, Institute for the Rule of Law, 2013), http://www.enforce.spb.ru/images/Issledovanya/IRL_KGI_Reform_final_11.13.pdf. For a more recent analysis, see Ruslan Kuchakov and Dmitry Skugarevskii, *Kontrol' i nadzor v 2022 g.: za predelami normy* (Saint Petersburg: European University at Saint Petersburg, Institute for the Rule of Law, 2022), https://inspections.enforce.spb.ru.

41 For analyses of the impact of this policy on sub-national governance in the Soviet Union, see Yoram Gorlizki and Oleg Khlevniuk, *Substate*

Dictatorship: Networks, Loyalty, and Institutional Change in the Soviet Union (New Haven, CT: Yale University Press, 2020); Saulius Grybkauskas, *Governing the Soviet Union's National Republics: The Second Secretaries of the Communist Party* (Abingdon: Routledge, 2021).

42 For various accounts of Russian elites in the 2010s, see Sharon Werning Rivera and David W. Rivera, "Are Siloviki Still Undemocratic? Elite Support for Political Pluralism during Putin's Third Presidential Term," *Russian Politics*, 4, no. 4 (2019), 499–519; Dmitry Gorenburg, *The Political Elite under Putin* (Garmisch Partenkirchen: George C. Marshall Center for Security Studies, 2020), https://www.marshallcenter.org/sites/default/files/files/2020-04/SecurityInsights_53.pdf. See also Maria Snegovaya and Kirill Petrov, "Long Soviet Shadows: the Nomenklatura Ties of Putin Elites," *Post-Soviet Affairs*, 38, no. 4 (2022), 329–48.

43 See Brian Taylor, "The Police Reform in Russia: Policy Process in a Hybrid Regime," *Post-Soviet Affairs*, 30, nos. 2–3 (2014), 226–55.

44 For a detailed account, see Alexander Golts, *Military Reform and Militarism in Russia* (Boulder, CO: Lynne Rienner, 2018), especially chapter 2.

45 For accounts, see "Crisis in the Caucasus, Russia, Georgia, and the West," *Small Wars and Insurgencies*, 20, no. 2 (2009): special issue; Alexander Astrov (ed.), *The Great Power (Mis)management: The Russian-Georgian War and Its Implications for Global Political Order* (Aldershot: Ashgate, 2011).

46 For a detailed account of Serdyukov's reforms and resistance to them, see Kirill Shamiev, "Against a Bitter Pill: The Role of Interest Groups in Armed Forces Reform in Russia," *Armed Forces and Society*, 47, no. 2 (2021), 319–42. See also Golts, *Military Reform and Militarism in Russia*, chapter 2.

47 For accounts of the effects of the military reforms initiated by Serdyukov, see Dmitry Gorenburg, "The Russian Military under Sergei Shoigu: Will the Reform Continue?," *PONARS Eurasia Policy Memos*, no. 253 (2013), www.ponarseurasia.org/memo/russian-military-under-sergei-shoigu-will-reform-continue; Pavel Baev, *Ukraine: A Test for Russian Military Reforms* (Paris, IFRI, 2015), https://www.ifri.org/sites/default/files/migrated_files/documents/atoms/files/ifri_rnr_19_pavel_baev_russian_military_reform_eng_may_2015_4.pdf.

48 See Golts, *Military Reform and Militarism in Russia*, chapter 2.

49 For an account of Shoigu's performance, see Jörgen Elfving, "Five Years with Russian Defense Minister Shoigu – Only Successes?," *Eurasian Daily Monitor*, 14, no. 151 (2017). See also Andrew Monaghan, *Power in Modern Russia: Strategy and Mobilisation* (Manchester: Manchester University Press, 2020), especially chapter 5.

50 For a detailed account, see Anika Binnendijk et al., *Russian Military Personnel Policy and Proficiency: Reforms and Trends, 1991–2021* (Santa Monica, CA: Rand Corporation, 2023), www.rand.org/t/RRA1233-6.

51 See Irina Dolinina, "A Family Affair: How the Relatives of a Russian State Company's CEO Got Rich," October 8, 2021, https://www.occrp.org/en/the-pandora-papers/a-family-affair-how-the-relatives-of-a-russian-state-companys-ceo-got-rich; Gaspard Sebag and Stephanie Baker, "Superyacht Seized in Spain as Sanctioned Owner Stops Paying Fees," *Bloomberg*, November 3, 2022, https://www.bloomberg.com/news/articles/2022-11-03/sanctioned-superyacht-seized-in-spain-as-owner-stops-paying-fees.

52 See Vladimir Gel'man, "Bad Governance in Times of Exogenous Shocks: The Case of the COVID-19 Pandemic in Russia," in Margarita Zavadskaya (ed.), *The Politics of the Pandemic in Eastern Europe and Eurasia: Blame Game and Governance* (Abingdon: Routledge, 2024), 80–94.

53 See Anton Troianovski, "'You Can't Trust Anyone': Russia's Hidden Covid Toll Is an Open Secret," *The New York Times*, April 10, 2021, https://www.nytimes.com/2021/04/10/world/europe/covid-russia-death.html; Henry Meyer, "Experts Question Russian Data on COVID-19 Death Toll," *Bloomberg.com*, May 13, 2020, https://www.bloomberg.com/news/articles/2020-05-13/experts-question-russian-data-on-covid-19-death-toll.

54 See Paneyakh, "Faking Performance Together."

55 See Bondarev, "The Sources of Russian Misconduct."

56 See https://svop.ru.

57 See https://valdaiclub.com.

58 See https://eng.globalaffairs.ru.

59 See Sergey Karaganov, "Tyazhkoe, no neobkhodimoe reshenie," *Rossiya v global'noi politike*, June 13, 2023, https://globalaffairs.ru/articles/tyazhkoe-no-neobhodimoe-reshenie/.

60 See Joachim Zweynert, *When Ideas Fail: Economic Thought, the Failure of Transition and the Rise of Institutional Instability in Post-Soviet Russia* (Abingdon: Routledge, 2018).

61 For a critical account, see Marina Khmelnitskaya, "Socio-economic Development and the Politics of Expertise in Putin's Russia: The 'Hollow Paradigm' Perspective," *Europe-Asia Studies*, 73, no. 4 (2021), 625–46.

62 See Matthew Frear and Honorata Mazepus, "Security, Civilisation and Modernisation: Continuity and Change in the Russian Foreign Policy Discourse," *Europe-Asia Studies*, 73, no. 7 (2021), 1215–35.

63 For an overview of Russian international relations and foreign policy

thought, see, for example, Maria Lagutina, Natalia Tsvetkova and Alexander Sergunin (eds.), *The Routledge Handbook of Russian International Relations Studies* (Abingdon: Routledge, 2023).
64 See Bondarev, "The Sources of Russian Misconduct."
65 For a detailed journalist account, see Ilya Zhegulev, "Kak Putin voznenavidel Ukrainu," *Verstka*, April 26, 2023, https://verstka.media/8964-2. See also Mikhail Zygar, *War and Punishment: Putin, Zelensky, and the Path to Russia's Invasion of Ukraine* (New York: Simon and Schuster, 2023).
66 On denial of Ukrainian statehood and nationhood, see Vladimir Putin, "Ob istoricheskom edinstve russkikh i ukraintsev," *Kremlin.ru*, July 12, 2021, http://kremlin.ru/events/president/news/66181.
67 For accounts of this proposal, see Steven Pifer, *Russia's Draft Agreements with NATO and the United States: Intended for Rejection?* (Washington, DC: Brookings Institution, 2021), https://www.brookings.edu/articles/russias-draft-agreements-with-nato-and-the-united-states-intended-for-rejection/; Igor Gretskiy, *Putin's Ultimatum: A High Stakes Poker or a Chess Gambit* (Tallinn: International Center for Defense and Security, 2022), https://icds.ee/en/putins-ultimatum-a-high-state-poker-or-a-chess-gambit/.
68 For a detailed account of the role of the Security Council, see Ekaterina Shulmann and Mark Galeotti, "A Tale of Two Councils: the Changing Roles of the Security and State Councils during the Transformation Period of Modern Russian Politics," *Post-Soviet Affairs*, 37, no. 5 (2021), 453–69.
69 For an account of Patrushev's political views, see Martin Kragh and Andreas Umland, "Putinism beyond Putin: the Political Ideas of Nikolai Patrushev and Sergei Naryshkin in 2006–20," *Post-Soviet Affairs*, 39, no. 5 (2023), 366–89.
70 See Julian E. Barnes, "Russia Steps Up Propaganda War Amid Tensions with Ukraine," *The New York Times*, January 25, 2022, https://www.nytimes.com/2022/01/25/us/politics/russia-ukraine-propaganda-disinformation.html. For a detailed and persuasive account of the overestimation of Russia's military might before the assault on Ukraine, see Bettina Renz, "Western Estimates of Russian Military Capabilities and the Invasion of Ukraine," *Problems of Post-Communism*, 71, no. 3 (2024), 219–31.
71 See Michael Kofman and Jeffrey Edmonds, "Russia's Shock and Awe: Moscow's Use of Overwhelming Force Against Ukraine," *Foreign Affairs*, February 22, 2022, https://www.foreignaffairs.com/articles/ukraine/2022-02-21/russias-shock-and-awe.
72 See Liam Collins, Michael Kofman and John Spencer, "The Battle of Hostomel Airport: A Key Moment in Russia's Defeat in Kyiv," *War on

the Rocks, August 10, 2023, https://warontherocks.com/2023/08/the-battle-of-hostomel-airport-a-key-moment-in-russias-defeat-in-kyiv/.

73 See Sinead Baker, "Ukraine Said Russian Troops Brought Parade Uniforms to Kyiv, Expecting a Quick Triumph That Never Came," *Business Insider*, April 7, 2022, https://www.businessinsider.com/ukraine-said-found-russian-parade-uniforms-left-behind-in-kyiv-2022-4; "How Putin's War in Ukraine Became a Catastrophe for Russia," *New York Times*, December 16, 2022, https://www.nytimes.com/interactive/2022/12/16/world/europe/russia-putin-war-failures-ukraine.html.

74 See Leonid Ivashov, "Obrashchenie predsedatelya OOC," *Obshcherossiiskoe ofitserskoe sobranie*, January 31, 2022, https://www.km.ru/v-rossii/2022/02/06/otnosheniya-rossii-i-ukrainy/895037-obrashchenie-obshcherossiiskogo-ofitserskogo. See also Ivashov's detailed interview: Olga Vandysheva and Vitalli Bersenev, "Rossiya prekratit svoe sushchestvovanie: general Ivashov o gotovyasheisya voine," *Biznes-gazeta*, February 13, 2022, https://www.business-gazeta.ru/article/539470.

75 Mikhail Khodarenok, "Prognozy khrovozhadnykh politologov," *Nezavisimoe voennoe obozrenie*, February 3, 2022, https://nvo.ng.ru/realty/2022-02-03/3_1175_donbass.html.

76 See Gel'man, *The Politics of Bad Governance in Contemporary Russia*, chapter 6.

77 See Mark F. Cancian, *What Does Russia's "Partial Mobilization" Mean?* (Washington, DC: Center for Strategic and International Studies, 2022), https://www.csis.org/analysis/what-does-russias-partial-mobilization-mean; Mark Schrad, "Putin's Military Draft Is Unpopular. So What?" *Politico*, September 28, 2022, https://www.politico.com/news/magazine/2022/09/28/putins-military-draft-is-unpopular-so-what-00059145.

78 For assessments of the performance of the Russian military, see Dara Massicot, *Russian Military Operations in Ukraine in 2022 and the Year Ahead* (Santa Monica, CA: Rand Corporation, February 28, 2023), https://www.rand.org/content/dam/rand/pubs/testimonies/CTA2600/CTA2646-1/RAND_CTA2646-1.pdf; Chels Michta, *Russia's Military Has Improved — The West Should Take Note* (Washington, DC: Center for European Policy Analysis, 2023), https://cepa.org/article/russias-military-has-improved-the-west-should-take-note/. For an analysis in a broader perspective, see Zoltan Barany, "Armies and Autocrats: Why Putin's Military Failed," *Journal of Democracy*, 34, no. 1 (2023), 80–94.

79 See Kimberly Marten, "Russia's Use of Semi-State Security Forces: The Case of the Wagner Group," *Post-Soviet Affairs*, 35, no. 3

(2019), 181–204; Candace Rondeaux, *Decoding the Wagner Group: Analyzing the Role of Private Military Security Contractors in Russian Proxy Warfare* (Center for the Future of War, Arizona State University, 2019), https://www.ohchr.org/sites/default/files/Documents/issues/Mercenaries/WG/OtherStakeholders/candace-rondeux-submission-1.pdf.

80 See Nathaniel Reynolds, *Putin's Not-So-Secret Mercenaries: Patronage, Geopolitics, and the Wagner Group* (Washington, DC: Carnegie Endowment for International Peace, 2019), https://carnegieendowment.org/files/GlobalRussia_NateReynolds_Vagner.pdf; Elena Pokalova, "The Wagner Group in Africa: Russia's Quasi-State Agent of Influence," *Studies in Conflict and Terrorism* (2023), https://www.tandfonline.com/doi/full/10.1080/1057610X.2023.2231642.

81 See Shaun Walker and Pjotr Sauer, "Yevgeny Prigozhin: the hotdog seller who rose to the top of Putin's war machine," *The Guardian*, January 24, 2023, https://www.theguardian.com/world/2023/jan/24/yevgeny-prigozhin-the-hotdog-seller-who-rose-to-the-top-of-putin-war-machine-wagner-group; Vitaly Shevchenko, "Yevgeny Prigozhin: From Putin's Chef to Rebel in Chief," *bbc.com*, June 25, 2023, https://www.bbc.com/news/world-europe-64976080.

82 See Douglas Almond, Xinming Du and Alana Vogel, "Reduced Trolling on Russian Holidays and Daily US Presidential Election Odds," *PLOS One*, 17, no. 3 (2022), e0264507; Gregory Eady et al., "Exposure to the Russian Internet Research Agency Foreign Influence Campaign on Twitter in the 2016 US Election and Its Relationship to Attitudes and Voting Behavior," *Nature Communications*, 14 (2023), 62.

83 See Reynolds, *Putin's Not-So-Secret Mercenaries*.

84 See Anton Mukhin, *Prigozhin vs. Petersburg Governor: What a Feud Reveals About Russia's Power Vertical* (Washington, DC: Carnegie Endowment for International Peace, 2022), https://carnegieendowment.org/politika/88572.

85 See Elian Peltier and Abdi Latif Dahir, "Who are the Rapid Support Forces, the Paramilitaries Fighting Sudan's Army?," *The New York Times*, April 17, 2023, https://www.nytimes.com/2023/04/17/world/africa/paramilitary-rsf-explainer.html; Majak D'Agoot, "How the Rise of Rapid Support Forces Sparked Sudan's Meteoric Descent," *Middle East Policy*, 30, no. 3 (2023), 107–19.

86 See Ellen Nakashima, John Hudson and Paul Sonne, "Mercenary Chief Vented to Putin over Ukraine War Bungling," *Washington Post*, October 25, 2022, https://www.washingtonpost.com/national-security/2022/10/25/putin-insider-prigozhin-blasts-russian-generals-ukraine/.

87 See Daniel D. Petris, "Infighting Has Bedeviled Russia's War on Ukraine Since It Started," *msnbc.com*, May 21, 2023, https://www

.msnbc.com/opinion/msnbc-opinion/know-wagner-groups-role-russias-war-ukraine-rcna85406.

88 See Alexander Golts, *The Ghost of Civil War in Russia?* (Stockholm: Stockholm Centre for East European Studies, 2023), https://www.ui.se/globalassets/ui.se-eng/publications/sceeus/the-ghost-of-civil-war-in-russia.pdf.

89 See Nic Robertson, "Why Prigozhin's Short-lived Russian Rebellion Failed," *CNN International*, June 27, 2023, https://edition.cnn.com/2023/06/26/europe/prigozhin-putin-wagner-rebellion-analysis-intl/index.html; Melissa Morgan, *Understanding Prigozhin's Mutiny and What Is – and Isn't – Happening in Russia* (Stanford, CA: Freeman Spogli Institute for International Studies, 2023), https://fsi.stanford.edu/news/understanding-prigozhins-mutiny-and-what-and-isnt-happening-russia. On the effects of Prigozhin's mutiny on the Russian state, see Tatiana Stanovaya, "Putin's Age of Chaos: Dangers of Russian Disorder," *Foreign Affairs*, 102, no. 5 (2023), 44–59.

90 See Jędrzej Czerep and Agnieszka Legucka, "Putin Begins Dismantling Prigozhin's 'Empire'," *PSIM Bulletin*, July 17, 2023, https://www.ceeol.com/search/gray-literature-detail?id=1162829; Oxford Analytica, "Russian Information Management Is Unlikely to Change," *Expert Briefings*, August 21, 2023, https://doi.org/10.1108/OXAN-DB281356.

91 See Matthew Mpoke Bigg, "What to Know about the Plane Crash That Killed Yevgeny Prigozhin," *The New York Times*, August 24, 2023, https://www.nytimes.com/2023/08/24/world/europe/prigozhin-plane-crash-russia-wagner.html.

92 For a thoughtful analysis, see Kimberly Marten, "Whither Wagner? The Consequences of Prigozhin's Mutiny and Demise," *Survival*, 65, no. 5 (2023), 45–64.

93 For various accounts, see Milan Svolik, *The Politics of Authoritarian Rule* (Cambridge: Cambridge University Press, 2012); Barbara Geddes, Joseph Wright and Erica Frantz, *How Dictatorships Work: Power, Personalization, and Collapse* (Cambridge: Cambridge University Press, 2018).

94 See Gel'man, *The Politics of Bad Governance in Contemporary Russia*, chapter 6.

95 Charles Tilly, "Reflections on the History of European State-making," in Charles Tilly (ed.), *The Formation of National States in Western Europe* (Princeton, NJ: Princeton University Press, 1975), 42.

96 See Charles Tilly, "War Making and State Making as Organized Crime," in Peter B. Evans, Dietrich Rueschemeyer and Theda Skocpol (eds.), *Bringing the State Back In* (Cambridge: Cambridge University Press, 1985), 169–91; Charles Tilly, *Coercion, Capital, and European States: AD 990–1992* (Oxford: Basil Blackwell, 1992).

97 On the role of international conflicts in elite turnover, see Michael Colaresi, "When Doves Cry: International Rivalry, Unreciprocated Cooperation, and Leadership Turnover," *American Journal of Political Science*, 48, no. 3 (2004), 555–70. See also John Higley and Michael Burton, *Elite Foundations of Liberal Democracy* (Lanham, MD: Rowman and Littlefield, 2006).

98 See Ilia Nadporozhskii, "Influence of Elite Rotation on Authoritarian Resilience," *Democratization*, 30, no. 5 (2023), 794–814.

Chapter 4. The Great Self-Deception

1 Apart from the wide media coverage of the Capitol Hill attack, for some scholarly assessments, see, in particular: Jorge Heine, "The Attack on the US Capitol: An American Kristallnacht," *Protest*, 1, no. 1 (2021), 126–41; S. Alexander Haslam et al., "Examining the Role of Donald Trump and His Supporters in the 2021 Assault on the U.S. Capitol: A Dual-agency Model of Identity Leadership and Engaged Followership," *The Leadership Quarterly*, 34, no. 2 (2023), 101622. See also Adebowale Akande (ed.), *U.S. Democracy in Danger: The American Political System under Assault* (Cham: Springer, 2023).

2 Apart from the wide media coverage of the US withdrawal from Afghanistan, for some scholarly assessments, see, in particular, Laurel Miller, "The Unwinnable War: America's Blind Spots in Afghanistan," *Foreign Affairs*, 101, no. 6 (2022), 174–80; Robert S. Snyder, "The Fall of Afghanistan: An American Tragedy," *Small Wars and Insurgencies*, 34, no. 4 (2023), 747–58; Donald S. Imbody and Patricia M. Shields, "Perspectives on the Afghanistan War: Commentaries on a Misadventure," *Armed Forces and Society*, 49, no. 4 (2023), 883–92.

3 Apart from the wide media coverage of the Taliban takeover in Afghanistan, for some scholarly assessments, see, in particular, Nilofar Sakhi, "The Taliban Takeover in Afghanistan and Security Paradox," *Journal of Asian Security and International Affairs*, 9, no. 3 (2022), 383–401; Thomas Ameyaw-Brobbey, "The US Withdrawal, Taliban Takeover, and Ontological Insecurity in Afghanistan," *World Affairs*, 186, no. 1 (2023), 105–34.

4 For some recent discussions, see Thomas Carothers, "Rejuvenating Democracy Promotion," *Journal of Democracy*, 31, no. 1 (2020), 114–23; Anna M. Meyerrose, "The Unintended Consequences of Democracy Promotion: International Organizations and Democratic Backsliding," *Comparative Political Studies*, 53, nos. 10–11 (2020), 1547–81; Matthew Alan Hill, *Democracy Promotion in US Foreign Policy: From Carter to Biden* (Abingdon: Routledge, 2022).

5 See, for example, Fyodor Lukyanov, "Farewell to Hegemony," *Russia in Global Affairs*, 19, no. 3 (2021), 5–8.
6 See, for example, Lev Sokol'shchik, "Zakat Ameriki: Spaset li SShA strategiya Baidena?," *Russian Council of International Affairs*, April 27, 2021, https://russiancouncil.ru/analytics-and-comments/analytics/zakat-ameriki-spaset-li-ssha-strategiya-baydena/?sphrase_id=112408670.
7 For a detailed account, see Sharon Werning Rivera (ed.), *Survey of Russian Elites 2020: New Perspectives on Domestic and Foreign Policy* (Clinton, NY: Hamilton College, 2020), https://hamilton.edu/documents/SRE2020ReportFINAL.pdf.
8 See Noah Buckley and Joshua A. Tucker, "Staring at the West through Kremlin-tinted Glasses: Russian Mass and Elite Divergence in Attitudes toward the United States, European Union, and Ukraine Before and After Crimea," *Post-Soviet Affairs*, 35, nos. 5–6 (2019), 365–75; Sharon Werning Rivera and James D. Bryan, "Understanding the Sources of Anti-Americanism in the Russian Elite," *Post-Soviet Affairs*, 35, nos. 5–6 (2019), 376–92.
9 On the impact of conspiracy theories on Russian politics, see Ilya Yablokov, *Fortress Russia: Conspiracy Theories in Post-Soviet Russia* (Cambridge: Polity Press, 2018); Scott Radnitz, *Revealing Schemes: The Politics of Conspiracy in Russia and the Post-Soviet Region* (Oxford: Oxford University Press, 2021).
10 See Robert Jervis, *Perception and Misperception in International Politics* (Princeton, NJ: Princeton University Press, 1976).
11 Ibid., 143.
12 See Amos Tversky and Daniel Kahneman, "Judgment under Uncertainty: Heuristics and Biases," *Science*, 185, no. 4157 (1974), 1124–31; Daniel Kahneman and Amos Tversky, "Prospect Theory: An Analysis of Decision under Risk," *Econometrica*, 47, no. 2 (1979), 263–92.
13 See Karen Dawisha, *Putin's Kleptocracy: Who Owns Russia?* (New York: Simon and Schuster, 2014); Anders Åslund, *Russia's Crony Capitalism: The Path from Market Economy to Kleptocracy* (New Haven, CT: Yale University Press, 2019).
14 See Angela Stent, *The Limits of Partnership: U.S.-Russian Relations in the Twenty-First Century* (Princeton, NJ: Princeton University Press, 2014), chapter 3.
15 See Andrew Wilson, *Ukraine's Orange Revolution* (New Haven, CT: Yale University Press, 2005); Paul D'Anieri, *Ukraine and Russia: From Civilized Divorce to Uncivil War*, 2nd edn (Cambridge: Cambridge University Press, 2023), chapters 4 and 5; Serhii Plokhy, *The Russo-Ukrainian War* (London: Allen Lane, 2023), chapters 3 and 4.
16 On the Kremlin's approach to socio-economic policy-making in Russia and its evolution over time, see Andrei Yakovlev, "Composition

of the Ruling Elite, Incentives for Productive Use of Rents, and Prospects for Russia's Limited Access Order," *Post-Soviet Affairs*, 37, no. 5 (2021), 417–34. See also Marek Dabrowski, "Russia's Two Transitions (1992–2003 and 2003–2022)," in Marek Dabrowski (ed.), *The Contemporary Russian Economy: A Comprehensive Analysis* (Cham: Palgrave Macmillan, 2023), 383–98.

17 See Georgy Egorov and Konstantin Sonin, *Why Did Putin Invade Ukraine? A Theory of Degenerate Autocracy* (Chicago, IL: Becker Friedman Institute, University of Chicago, Working Paper no. 2023-52), https://bfi.uchicago.edu/wp-content/uploads/2023/04/BFI_WP_2023-52.pdf.

18 See Leandro Prados de la Escosura, Joan R. Roses and Isabel Sanz-Villarroya, "Economic Reforms and Growth in Franco's Spain," *Revista de Historia Economica, Journal of Iberian and Latin American Economic History*, 30, no. 1 (2011), 45–89.

19 See Vladimir Gel'man, "Politics versus Policy: Technocratic Traps of Russia's Policy Reforms," *Russian Politics*, 3, no. 2 (2018), 284–302; Vladimir Gel'man, *The Politics of Bad Governance in Contemporary Russia* (Ann Arbor, MI: University of Michigan Press, 2022), chapter 5.

20 See Sergei Guriev and Daniel Treisman, "Informational Autocrats," *Journal of Economic Perspectives*, 33, no. 4 (2019), 100–27; Sergei Guriev and Daniel Treisman, *Spin Dictators: The Changing Face of Tyranny in the 21st Century* (Princeton, NJ: Princeton University Press, 2022), especially chapter 1.

21 See Rivera, *Survey of Russian Elites 2020*.

22 See Buckley and Tucker, "Staring at the West through Kremlin-tinted Glasses."

23 See Martin Kragh and Andreas Umland, "Putinism beyond Putin: the Political Ideas of Nikolai Patrushev and Sergei Naryshkin in 2006–20," *Post-Soviet Affairs*, 39, no. 5 (2023), 366–89.

24 On this problem in autocracies, known as the "dictator's dilemma," see Ronald Wintrobe, *The Political Economy of Dictatorship* (Cambridge: Cambridge University Press, 1998).

25 See Martin K. Dimitrov, *Dictatorship and Political Information: Authoritarian Regime Resilience in Communist Europe and China* (Oxford: Oxford University Press, 2023).

26 See "SMI: sovetniki boyatsya rasskazyvat' Putinu plokhie novosti. Eto i est' prichina voiny?" *Postimees*, April 24, 2022, https://rus.postimees.ee/7507359/smi-sovetniki-boyatsya-rasskazyvat-putinu-plohie-novosti-eto-i-est-prichina-voyny.

27 For various accounts of the KGB's legacy in post-Soviet Russia, see Amy Knight, *Spies without Cloaks: The KGB's Successors* (Princeton, NJ: Princeton University Press, 1997); Andrei Soldatov and Irina

Borogan, *The New Nobility: The Restoration of Russia's Security State and the Enduring Legacy of the KGB* (New York: PublicAffairs, 2010).

28 On the trap of groupthink, see Irving Lester Janis, *Groupthink: Psychological Studies of Policy Decisions and Fiascos* (Boston, MA: Houghton Mifflin, 1982).

29 See Sharon Werning Rivera and David W. Rivera, "Are *Siloviki* Still Undemocratic? Elite Support for Political Pluralism during Putin's Third Presidential Term," *Russian Politics*, 4, no. 4 (2019), 499–519.

30 See Mark Harrison, *Secret Leviathan: Secrecy and State Capacity under Soviet Communism* (Stanford, CA: Stanford University Press, 2023).

31 For biographical accounts, see, in particular, Steven Lee Myers, *The New Tsar: The Rise and Reign of Vladimir Putin* (New York: Knopf Doubleday, 2015); Fiona Hill and Clifford Gaddy, *Mr. Putin: Operative in the Kremlin* (Washington, DC: Brookings Institution Press, 2015).

32 See Soldatov and Borogan, *The New Nobility*, especially chapter 2. For an overall account of the traits of the post-Soviet coercive apparatus in Russia, see Brian D. Taylor, *State Building in Putin's Russia: Policing and Coercion after Communism* (Cambridge: Cambridge University Press, 2011).

33 See Yablokov, *Fortress Russia*, especially chapter 2.

34 See Yevgenia Albats, *The State Within a State: The KGB and its Hold on Russia – Past, Present, and Future* (London: I.B. Tauris, 1995); Amy Knight, "The KGB, Perestroika, and the Collapse of the Soviet Union," *Journal of Cold War Studies*, 5, no. 1 (2003), 67–93.

35 For an account of representatives of this generation, see Vladimir Gel'man, Dmitry Travin and Otar Marganiya, *Reexamining Economic and Political Reforms in Russia, 1985–2000: Generations, Ideas, and Changes* (Lanham, MD: Lexington Books, 2014), especially chapters 4 and 5. See also Vladimir Gel'man and Dmitry Travin, "Fathers versus Sons: Generation Changes and the Ideational Agenda of Reforms in Late Twentieth-Century Russia," in Vladimir Gel'man (ed.), *Authoritarian Modernization in Russia: Ideas, Institutions, and Policies* (Abingdon: Routledge, 2016), 22–39.

36 See Alexei Yurchak, *Everything Was Forever, Until It Was No More: The Last Soviet Generation* (Princeton, NJ: Princeton University Press, 2005).

37 See Petr Aven and Alfred Kokh, *Gaidar's Revolution: The Inside Account of the Economic Transformation of Russia* (London: I.B. Tauris, 2015).

38 See Boris Sokolov, Ronald F. Inglehart, Eduard Ponarin, Irina Vartanova and William Zimmerman, "Disillusionment and Anti-Americanism in Russia: From Pro-American to Anti-American Attitudes, 1993–2009," *International Studies Quarterly*, 62, no. 3 (2018), 534–47.

39 See Janis, *Groupthink*, especially chapter 10.
40 See Rivera, *Survey of Russian Elites 2020*.
41 On the professional credentials of the Central Bank of Russia, see Juliet Johnson, *The Priests of Prosperity: How Central Bankers Transformed the Postcommunist World* (Ithaca, NY: Cornell University Press, 2016), especially chapter 6. On discussions among post-Soviet economists in Russia, see Joachim Zweynert, *When Ideas Fail: Economic Thought, the Failure of Transition, and the Rise of Institutional Instability in Post-Soviet Russia* (Abingdon: Routledge, 2018). For a critical account of economic expertise in Russia, see Marina Khmelnitskaya, "Socio-Economic Development and the Politics of Expertise in Putin's Russia: The 'Hollow Paradigm' Perspective," *Europe-Asia Studies*, 73, no. 4 (2021), 625–46.
42 See, for example, Gregory O. Hall, *Authority, Ascendancy, and Supremacy: China, Russia, and the United States' Pursuit of Relevancy and Power* (London: Routledge, 2013); Judit Trunkos, "Comparing Russian, Chinese and American Soft Power Use: A New Approach," *Global Society*, 35, no. 3 (2021), 395–418.
43 For an in-depth anthropological account, see Alena Ledeneva, *Russia's Economy of Favours: Blat, Networking, and Informal Exchange* (Cambridge: Cambridge University Press, 1998).
44 For Obama's initial comment on Russia as a "regional power," made in March 2014, soon after the annexation of Crimea, see https://www.youtube.com/watch?v=PkQUzeZbLEs. On the US–Russia clash over Syria, see Richard Sokolsky and Perry Cammack, "Parsing Putin on Syria," *Carnegie Endowment for International Peace*, October 2, 2015, https://carnegieendowment.org/publications/61502; Angela Stent, "Putin's Power Play in Syria: How to Respond to Russia's Intervention," *Foreign Affairs*, 95, no. 1 (2016), 106–13.
45 For Putin's comment, see https://www.youtube.com/watch?v=YbT2RGfBwdE. See also "Obama Calling Russia a Regional Power is 'Disrespectful' – Putin," *The Moscow Times*, January 12, 2016, https://www.themoscowtimes.com/2016/01/12/obama-calling-russia-a-regional-power-is-disrespectful-putin-a51414.
46 For various interpretations of claims of Russia's global power status, see, for example, Dmitry Trenin, "Russia Leaves the West," *Foreign Affairs*, 85, no. 4 (2006), 87–96; Andrei Krickovic and Yuval Weber, "What Can Russia Teach Us about Change? Status-Seeking as a Catalyst for Transformation in International Politics," *International Studies Review*, 20, no. 2 (2018), 292–300; Tuomas Forsberg, "Status Conflicts between Russia and the West: Perceptions and Emotional Biases," *Communist and Post-Communist Studies*, 47, nos. 3–4 (2012), 323–31. See also Julia Gurganus and Eugene Rumer,

"Russia's Global Ambitions in Perspective," *Carnegie Endowment for International Peace*, February 2019, https://carnegieendowment.org/files/RumerGurganus_Perspective_final.pdf.

47 For a summary, see Yevgeny Primakov, "A World without Superpowers," *Russia in Global Affairs*, no. 3 (2003), https://eng.globalaffairs.ru/articles/a-world-without-superpowers/. For assessments, see, for example, Thomas Ambrosio, "Russia's Quest for Multipolarity: A Response to US Foreign Policy in the Post-Cold War Era," *European Security*, 10, no. 1 (2001), 45–67; Martin A. Smith, "Russia and Multipolarity since the End of the Cold War," *East European Politics*, 29, no. 1 (2013), 36–51.

48 See *Memorandum of Conversation: Meeting with Russian President Yeltsin [Istanbul, Turkey]* (Washington, DC: National Security Archive, 1999), https://nsarchive.gwu.edu/document/20592-national-security-archive-doc-06-memorandum.

49 For various accounts of Russia's strategy, see Raphael S. Cohen and Andrew Radin, *Russia's Hostile Measures in Europe: Understanding the Threat* (Santa Monica, CA: Rand Corporation, 2019), https://apps.dtic.mil/sti/pdfs/AD1085532.pdf; Jessica BrandtTorrey Taussig, "Europe's Authoritarian Challenge," *Washington Quarterly*, 42, no. 4 (2019), 133–53. See also Paul N. Hodos, "Playing to Extremes: Russia's Choices to Support Western Political Extremists and Paramilitary Groups," *International Journal of Intelligence and Counter Intelligence*, 36, no. 3 (2023), 847–69.

50 See, for example, Angela Stent, *Putin's World: Russia against the West and with the Rest* (London: Hachette UK, 2019); Kathryn E. Stoner, *Russia Resurrected: Its Power and Purpose in a New Global Order* (Oxford: Oxford University Press, 2020).

51 See Gel'man, *The Politics of Bad Governance in Contemporary Russia*, especially chapter 2; Vladimir Gel'man and Anastassia Obydenkova, "The Invention of Legacy: Strategic Uses of a 'Good Soviet Union' in Elite Policy Preferences and Filmmaking in Russia," *Communist and Post-Communist Studies*, 57, no. 1 (2023), 130–53.

52 For assessments, see Eugene Huskey, "Legacies and Departures in the Russian State Executive," in Mark R. Beissinger and Stephen Kotkin (eds.), *Historical Legacies of Communism in Russia and Eastern Europe* (Cambridge: Cambridge University Press, 2014), 111–27; Brian Taylor, "From Police State to Police State? Legacies and Law Enforcement in Russia," in Mark R. Beissinger and Stephen Kotkin (eds.), *Historical Legacies of Communism in Russia and Eastern Europe* (Cambridge: Cambridge University Press, 2014), 128–51.

53 For an account of Russian coercive agencies, see Ella Paneyakh, "Faking Performance Together: Systems of Performance Evaluation in

NOTES TO PP. 98–101

Russian Enforcement Agencies and Production of Bias and Privilege," *Post-Soviet Affairs*, 30, no. 2–3 (2014): 115–36.
54 See Nicole Krome, "State Corporate Governance in Russia," *Europe-Asia Studies*, 74, no. 8 (2022), 1350–74.
55 See Mark Kramer, "The Soviet Legacy in Russian Foreign Policy," *Political Science Quarterly*, 134, no. 4 (2019), 585–609. For an insider's account, see also Boris Bondarev, "The Sources of Russian Misconduct," *Foreign Affairs*, 101, no. 6 (2022), 36–55.
56 For a detailed account of the controversial practices of authoritarian diffusion in post-Soviet Eurasia, see Stephen G. F. Hall, *The Authoritarian International: Tracing How Authoritarian Regimes Learn in the Post-Soviet Space* (Cambridge: Cambridge University Press, 2023).
57 See Shaun Walker, "Vladimir Putin Offers Ukraine Financial Incentives to Stick with Russia," *Guardian*, December 17, 2013, https://www.theguardian.com/world/2013/dec/17/ukraine-russia-leaders-talks-kremlin-loan-deal; Jamila Trindle, "The Loan That Launched a Crisis," *Foreign Policy*, February 21, 2014, https://foreignpolicy.com/2014/02/21/the-loan-that-launched-a-crisis/.
58 The narrative of the Ukrainian "Revolution of Dignity" as a US-led conspiracy is shared by Putin and his entourage. See Mikhail Zygar, *War and Punishment: Putin, Zelensky, and the Path to Russia's Invasion of Ukraine* (New York: Simon and Schuster, 2023).
59 See Yablokov, *Fortress Russia*.
60 For a detailed account, see Douglas Selvage, "Operation 'Denver': The East German Ministry of State Security and the KGB's AIDS Disinformation Campaign, 1985–1986," *Journal of Cold War Studies*, 21, no. 4 (2019), 71–123. See also Nicoli Natrass, *The AIDS Conspiracy: Science Fights Back* (New York: Columbia University Press, 2012).
61 See Joshua Keating, "Russian Spies Can Read Madeleine Albright's Mind," *Foreign Policy*, November 7, 2007, https://foreignpolicy.com/2007/11/07/russian-spies-can-read-madeleine-albrights-mind/; Paul Roderick Gregory, "The Madeleine Albright Declaration: Origins of a Kremlin Lie," *Forbes*, July 16, 2015, https://www.forbes.com/sites/paulroderickgregory/2015/07/16/the-madeleine-albright-declaration-origins-of-a-kremlin-lie/?sh=3b9cf83f7056.
62 See Egorov and Sonin, *Why Did Putin Invade Ukraine?*
63 See Kragh and Umland, "Putinism beyond Putin."
64 For a detailed account, see Robert Lawless, "Russia's Allegations of U.S. Biological Warfare in Ukraine," *Lieber Institute, West Point*, December 2, 2022, https://lieber.westpoint.edu/russias-allegations-us-biological-warfare-ukraine-part-i/.

65 See, for example, Isabel Keane, "Russia Accuses US of Planning to Drop Malaria Bearing Mosquitoes on Troops," *New York Post*, June 19, 2023, https://nypost.com/2023/06/19/russia-accuses-us-of-planning-to-drop-malaria-bearing-mosquitoes-on-troops/.

66 See, in particular, Ludo Block, "The Long History of OSINT," *Journal of Intelligence History*, 23, no. 2 (2024), 95–109; Devan Leos, "Think Like a Spy: How Open Source Intelligence Can Give You a Competitive Advantage," *Entrepreneur*, February 28, 2023, https://www.entrepreneur.com/growing-a-business/thinking-like-a-spy-how-open-source-intelligence-can-give/444634.

67 See Leonid Kuchma, *Ukraina – ne Rossiya* (Moscow: Vremya, 2003).

68 By 2020, a significant part of the Russian elites accepted the fact that Ukraine is an independent state different from Russia. According to the data from the Survey of Russian Elites, 67% of respondents agreed that Ukraine and Russia should be separate states, and only 5% endorsed their unification. In 1995, only 19% of the Russian elites supported Ukrainian independence and 65% of respondents opposed such a view and preferred the unification of Ukraine with Russia. See Rivera, *Survey of Russian Elites 2020*, 29.

69 See "Stat'ya Vladimir Putina 'Ob istoricheskom edinstve russkikh i ukraintsev,'" *kremlin.ru*, July 12, 2021, http://kremlin.ru/events/president/news/66181.

70 Among the voluminous academic literature on Ukrainian history, see, in particular, Serhii Plokhy, *The Gates of Europe: The History of Ukraine* (New York: Basic Books, 2015).

71 Among the voluminous literature on primordialism, see, in particular, Edward Shils, "Primordial, Personal, Sacred and Civil Ties: Some Particular Observations on the Relationships of Sociological Research and Theory," *British Journal of Sociology*, 8, no. 2 (1957), 130–45; Anthony D. Smith, *Nationalism and Modernism: a Critical Survey of Recent Theories of Nations and Nationalism* (London: Routledge, 1998). For a critique of this approach, see Rogers Brubaker, *Nationalism Reframed: Nationhood and the National Question in the New Europe* (Cambridge: Cambridge University Press, 1996); John Coakley, "'Primordialism' in Nationalism Studies: Theory or Ideology?" *Nations and Nationalism*, 24, no. 2 (2018), 327–47. On the construction of the Ukrainian nation, especially after the Soviet collapse, see, in particular, Andrew Wilson, *Ukrainians: The Unexpected Nation* (New Haven, CT: Yale University Press, 2000).

72 On this experience, see, in particular, Paul D'Anieri, "Elections, Succession, and Legitimacy in Ukraine: Lessons from Six Presidential Transitions," *Communist and Post-Communist Studies*, 2023, https://doi.org/10.1525/cpcs.2023.2001608.

73 On decentralization in Ukraine, see Natalia Rudakiewicz, "Long and Arduous Way to Decentralization: Past, Present and Future of the Reforms of Local Self-government in Ukraine," *Southeast European and Black Sea Studies*, 23, no. 3 (2023), 489–507; Valentyna Romanova and Andreas Umland, "Domestic and International Dimensions of Ukraine's Decentralization: Kyiv's Local Governance Reform and Post-Soviet Democratization," *Demokratizatsiya: The Journal of Post-Soviet Democratization*, 31, no. 3 (2023), 363–89.
74 I am indebted to Ivan Kurilla for this observation.
75 See Igor Burdyga, "The Rise and Fall of Putin's Man in Ukraine," *Open Democracy*, July 26, 2022, https://www.opendemocracy.net/en/odr/medvedchuk-putin-poroshenko-treason-ukraine-russia/.
76 For the data, see Benedict Vigers, "Ukrainians Stand Behind War Effort Despite Some Fatigue," *Gallup*, October 9, 2023, https://news.gallup.com/poll/512258/ukrainians-stand-behind-war-effort-despite-fatigue.aspx; Anna Anisimova, "Ukraine and NATO – Evidence from Public Opinion Surveys," *Free Network Policy Brief*, October 30, 2023, https://freepolicybriefs.org/2023/10/30/ukraine-nato-public-opinion/.
77 See Samuel P. Huntington, "The Clash of Civilizations?" *Foreign Affairs*, 72, no. 3 (1993), 22–49; Samuel P. Huntington, *The Clash of Civilizations and the Remaking of World Order* (New York: Simon and Schuster, 1996).
78 For the results of the survey, see Yurii Agafonov and Mikhail Sokolov, "Rossiiskaya politologiya v 2021 godu: sotsial'nyi i intellektual'nyi landshaft," *Polis*, no. 2 (2023), 54–71.
79 On changing electoral geography in Ukraine, see Ralph S. Clem and Peter R. Craumer, "Orange, Blue and White, and Blonde: The Electoral Geography of Ukraine's 2006 and 2007 Rada Elections," *Eurasian Geography and Economics*, 49, no. 2 (2008), 127–51; Mykola Dobysh and Boris Yatsenko, "Borders, Constituency Politics, and 'Our Man' Voting in Electoral Geography of Ukraine," *Belgeo: Belgian Journal of Geography*, no. 2 (2020), https://doi.org/10.4000/belgeo.38851. See also Ulrich Schmid and Oksana Myshlovska (eds.), *Regionalism without Regions: Reconceptualizing Ukraine's Heterogeneity* (Budapest: Central European University Press, 2019).
80 See Joanna Rohozinska and Vitaliy Shpak, "The Rise of an 'Outsider' President," *Journal of Democracy*, 30, no. 3 (2019), 33–47; Paul D'Anieri, "Ukraine's 2019 Elections: Pro-Russian Parties and the Impact of Occupation," *Europe-Asia Studies*, 74, no. 10 (2022), 1915–36.
81 For a detailed account, see Liana Semchuk, *Oligarchs and Separatist Trajectories: A Comparison of Secessionist Rebellions during 2014*

Crisis in Eastern Ukraine (PhD dissertation, Nuffield College, University of Oxford, 2021), https://ora.ox.ac.uk/objects/uuid:4b2133fe-e6a3-4e6d-b1d3-a7651044e313.

82 See Quentin Buckholz, "The Dogs That Didn't Bark: Elite Preferences and the Failure of Separatism in Kharkiv and Dnipropetrovsk," *Problems of Post-Communism*, 66, no. 3 (2019), 151–60; Silviya Nitsova, "Why the Difference? Donbas, Kharkiv and Dnipropetrovsk after Ukraine's Euromaidan Revolution," *Europe-Asia Studies*, 73, no. 10 (2021), 1832–56.

83 See Lowell Barrington, "A New Look at Region, Language, Ethnicity and Civic National Identity in Ukraine," *Europe-Asia Studies*, 74, no. 3 (2022), 360–81; Lowell Barrington, "Is the Regional Divide in Ukraine an Identity Divide?" *Eurasian Geography and Economics*, 63, no. 4 (2022), 465–90. See also Maria Popova and Oxana Shevel, *Russia and Ukraine: Entangled History, Diverging States* (Cambridge: Polity Press, 2024), especially chapter 6.

84 For a detailed account, see Maria Popova and Daniel Beers, "No Revolution of Dignity for Ukraine's Judges: Judicial Reform after Euromaidan," *Demokratizatsiya: The Journal of Post-Soviet Democratization*, 28, no. 1 (2020), 113–42.

85 See Rohozinska and Shpak, "The Rise of an 'Outsider' President"; Olga Onuch and Henry Hale, *The Zelensky Effect* (Oxford: Oxford University Press, 2023).

86 See Onuch and Hale, *The Zelensky Effect*, especially chapter 2.

87 See Christopher Miller, "Zelenskyy Wants to Replace Ukraine's Top Spy after Security Failures," *Politico*, June 23, 2022, https://www.politico.com/news/2022/06/23/zelenskyy-top-spy-security-failures-00041794; Olexiy Haran, "Why Venediktova and Bakanov Were Removed from Office and How It Will Increase Yermak's Influence," *The Page*, July 18, 2022, https://en.thepage.ua/experts/why-venediktova-and-bakanov-were-removed-from-office.

88 See Ilya Zhegulev, "Kak Putin voznenavidel Ukrainu," *Verstka*, April 26, 2023, https://verstka.media/8964-2.

89 See Andrii Darkovych, Myroslava Savisko and Maryna Rabinovych, "Explaining Ukraine's Resilience to Russia's Invasion: The Role of Local Governance and Decentralization Reform," *PONARS Eurasia Policy Memos*, no. 855 (2023), https://www.ponarseurasia.org/explaining-ukraines-resilience-to-russias-invasion-the-role-of-local-governance-and-decentralization-reform/.

90 See Zhegulev, "Kak Putin voznenavidel Ukrainu."

91 On the fall of Nagorno-Karabagh, see Gabriel Gavin, "'Nobody is Helping Us': Inside the Fall of Nagorno-Karabakh," *Politico*, September 22, 2023, https://www.politico.eu/article/nagorno-karabakh

-armenia-azerbaijan-war-inside/. See also Thomas de Waal, "The End of Nagorno-Karabakh: How Western Inaction Enabled Azerbaijan and Russia," *Foreign Affairs*, September 26, 2023, https://www.foreignaffairs.com/armenia/end-nagorno-karabakh.

92 See Habibe Özdal, "Turkey's Policy towards Russia and Turkey–Russia Relations," *Panorama*, September 8, 2023, https://www.uikpanorama.com/blog/2023/09/08/ho-2/; Christopher S. Chivvis, Alper Coskun and Beatrix Geaghan-Breiner, "Türkiye in the Emerging World Order," *Carnegie Endowment for International Peace*, October 31, 2023, https://carnegieendowment.org/2023/10/31/t-rkiye-in-emerging-world-order-pub-90868.

93 See Jordi Vasquez et al., "Exposed Outpost Russian Threats to Baltic Security and Transatlantic Responses," *European Horizons*, 2018, https://voices.uchicago.edu/euchicago/exposed-outpost-russian-threats-to-baltic-security-and-transatlantic-responses/. See also Mark Galeotti, "The Baltic States as Targets and Levers: The Role of the Region in Russian Strategy," *Marshall Center Security Insight*, no. 27 (2019), https://www.marshallcenter.org/en/publications/security-insights/baltic-states-targets-and-levers-role-region-russian-strategy-0.

94 See Sergei A. Karaganov, "A Difficult but Necessary Decision," *Russia in Global Affairs*, June 13, 2023, https://eng.globalaffairs.ru/articles/a-difficult-but-necessary-decision/.

95 See Pavel K. Baev, "Russia Aspires to the Status of 'Energy Superpower,'" *Strategic Analysis*, 31, no. 3 (2007), 447–65; Peter Rutland, "Russia as an Energy Superpower," *New Political Economy*, 13, no. 2 (2008), 203–10.

96 For a detailed journalistic account, see Valery Panyushkin and Mikhail Zygar, *Gazprom. Novoe russkoe oruzhie* (Moscow: Zakharov, 2008). For official statements and Russian expert assessments, see "Novak: zavisimost' Evropy ot rossiiskogo gaza prodolzhit rasti," *Bfm.ru*, July 19, 2015, https://www.bfm.ru/news/298369; "Evropa obrechena na zavisimost' ot rossiiskogo gaza," *rss.ru*, August 22, 2017, http://rcc.ru/article/evropa-obrechena-na-zavisimost-ot-rossiyskogo-gaza-60603.

97 See Adam N. Stulberg, "Out of Gas? Russia, Ukraine, Europe, and the Changing Geopolitics of Natural Gas," *Problems of Post-Communism*, 62, no. 2 (2015), 112–30; Yusin Lee, "Interdependence, Issue Importance, and the 2009 Russia–Ukraine Gas Conflict," *Energy Policy*, 102 (2017), 199–209.

98 See Szymon Kardas, "Own Goal: How Russia's Gas War Has Backfired," *European Council on Foreign Relations*, July 27, 2023, https://ecfr.eu/article/own-goal-how-russias-gas-war-has-backfired/; James Henderson and Kong Chyong, *Do Future Russian Gas Pipeline Exports to Europe Matter Anymore?* (Oxford: Oxford Institute for

195

Energy Studies, 2023), https://www.oxfordenergy.org/wpcms/wp-content/uploads/2023/07/Insight-131-Do-future-Russian-gas-pipeline-exports-to-Europe-matter-anymore.pdf.

99 See Samet Girgin, "Global Gas Supply Security," *Sustainable Energy Analytics*, December 22, 2023 https://seanalytics.substack.com/p/global-gas-supply-security. On the role of the Russian liquefied gas supply, see Ben McWilliams, Giovanni Sgaravatti, Simone Tagliapietra and Georg Zachmann, "The EU Can Manage without Russian Liquefied Natural Gas," *Breugel*, June 28, 2023, https://www.bruegel.org/policy-brief/eu-can-manage-without-russian-liquified-natural-gas.

100 For assessments, see, in particular, Sergey Valukenko, "Can China Compensate Russia's Losses on the European Gas Market?" *Carnegie Endowment for International Peace*, June 1, 2023, https://carnegieendowment.org/politika/89862.

101 For some Russian expert assessments, see Timofei V. Bordachev, "The European World After 1989," *Russia in Global Affairs*, no. 3 (2007), https://eng.globalaffairs.ru/articles/the-european-world-after-1989/; Timofei V. Bordachev, "Russia and Europe: Between Integration and Diplomacy," *Russia in Global Affairs*, no. 3 (2019), https://eng.globalaffairs.ru/articles/russia-and-europe-between-integration-and-diplomacy/.

102 See Geir Hågen Karlsen, "Divide and Rule: Ten Lessons about Russian Political Influence Activities in Europe," *Palgrave Communications*, no. 5 (2019), https://www.nature.com/articles/s41599-019-0227-8.

103 On Hungary's role, see Helena Ivanov and Marlene Laruelle, "Why Still Pro-Russia? Making Sense of Hungary's and Serbia's Russian Stance," *Centre on Social and Political Risk*, December 2022, https://henryjacksonsociety.org/wp-content/uploads/2023/01/Why-Still-Pro-Russia-FINAL.pdf; Katalin Fabian, "Top Gun: The Orbán Government's Position on the War in Ukraine," *Hungarian Studies Review*, 49, no. 2 (2022), 216–20.

104 On pro-Russian parties in the EU, see Anton Shekhvostov, *Russia and the Western Far Right: A Tango Noir* (Abingdon: Routledge, 2018). See also Maria Snegovaya, "Fellow Travelers or Trojan Horses? Similarities across Pro-Russian Parties' Electorates in Europe," *Party Politics*, 28, no. 3 (2022), 409–18.

105 See Giselle Bosse, "Values, Rights, and Changing Interests: The EU's Response to the War Against Ukraine and the Responsibility to Protect Europeans," *Contemporary Security Policy*, 43, no. 3 (2022), 531–46; Oriol Costa and Esther Barbé, "A Moving Target: EU Actorness and the Russian Invasion of Ukraine," *Journal of European Integration*, 45, no. 3 (2022), 431–46.

106 On the role of pro-Russian parties and politicians in the 2023 Bulgarian

parliamentary elections, see Marton Dunai, "Pro-Russia Party Shakes up Bulgarian Politics," *Financial Times*, April 2, 2023, https://www.ft.com/content/88603542-7f82-4dfd-a4bf-bfd023f96451.

107 See Tuomas Forsberg, "Finland and Sweden's Road to NATO," *Current History*, 122, no. 842 (2023), 89–94. For further analyses, see Eemeli Isoaho, Niklas Masuhr and Fabien Merz, "Finland's NATO Accession," *CSS Analyses in Security Policy*, no. 310 (2022), https://www.research-collection.ethz.ch/bitstream/handle/20.500.11850/563548/2/CSSAnalyse310-EN.pdf; Nicholas Lokker, Jim Townsend, Heli Hautala and Andrea Kendall-Taylor, *How Finnish and Swedish NATO Accession Could Shape the Future Russian Threat: A Report of the Transatlantic Forum on Russia* (January 2023), https://s3.us-east-1.amazonaws.com/files.cnas.org/documents/FinlandSweden_TFR_2023_012423.pdf.

108 See David Arter, "From Finlandisation and Post-Finlandisation to the End of Finlandisation? Finland's Road to a NATO Application," *European Security*, 32, no. 2 (2023), 171–89.

109 On public opinion about Ukraine in the EU countries, see Maria Demertzis, Camille Grand and Luca Lery Moffat, "European Public Opinion Remains Supportive of Ukraine," *Breugel*, June 5, 2023, https://www.bruegel.org/analysis/european-public-opinion-remains-supportive-ukraine. See also Catarina Thomson, Matthias Mader, Felix Munchow, Jason Reifler and Harald Schoen, "European Public Opinion: United in Supporting Ukraine, Divided on the Future of NATO," *International Affairs*, 99, no. 6 (2023), 2485–500.

110 See Jervis, *Perception and Misperception in International Politics*.

111 On misperceptions in Sovietology, see Christopher I. Xenakis, *What Happened to the Soviet Union?: How and Why American Sovietologists Were Caught by Surprise* (Westport, CT: Greenwood Publishing, 2002). On the deficiencies and shortcomings of Russian Studies after 1991, see "Conversations within the Field: Russia's War against Ukraine and the Future of Russian Studies," *Post-Soviet Affairs*, 39, nos. 1–2 (2023), special issue.

Chapter 5. The Victims of Previous Successes

1 In fact, the vicious attacks on the different kinds of opposition were aimed at further monopolization of power by the Kremlin and minimization of domestic challenges to the political status quo. However, the increase in domestic repression, especially since 2012, also paved the way for the weakening of anti-military resistance in February 2022 and thereafter. See Vladimir Gel'man, "The Politics of Fear:

How Russia's Rulers Counter their Rivals," *Russian Politics*, 1, no. 1 (2016), 27–45.
2. On acceptance of Russia's drive to reestablish its sphere of influence, including (but not limited to) Ukraine before February 2022, see, for example, Robert E. Berls, Jr., "Strengthening Russia's Influence in International Affairs," *Nuclear Threat Initiative*, July 13, 2021, https://www.nti.org/analysis/articles/strengthening-russias-influence-in-international-affairs-part-ii-russia-and-its-neighbors-a-sphere-of-influence-or-a-declining-relationship/; Wolfgang Munchau, "In the Pipeline: Would Germany Side with Russia in a Conflict?" *The Spectator*, January 22, 2022, https://www.spectator.co.uk/article/in-the-pipeline-would-germany-side-with-russia-in-a-conflict/.
3. For some assessments, see Keir Giles, "Has the West Fallen for Putin's Tricks in Ukraine?" *The Guardian*, January 25, 2022, https://www.theguardian.com/commentisfree/2022/jan/25/panic-invasion-ukraine-buildup-troops-moscow; "Forecast Series. Putin's Likely Actions in Ukraine," *Institute for the Study of War*, January 27, 2022, https://www.understandingwar.org/forecast-series-putins-likely-courses-action-ukraine.
4. For arguments in favor of appeasement of Russia before its assault on Ukraine, see, for example, Samuel Charap, "The U.S. Approach to Ukraine's Border War Isn't Working. Here's What Biden Should Do Instead," *Politico*, November 19, 2021, https://www.politico.com/news/magazine/2021/11/19/ukraine-russia-putin-border-522989; Remy Carugati, "Ukraine: Why NATO Must Make Concessions," *Network for Strategic Analysis*, January 24, 2022, https://ras-nsa.ca/ukraine-why-nato-must-make-concessions/; Doug Bandow, "Appeasement for a Good Cause," *Cato Institute*, February 3, 2022, https://www.cato.org/commentary/appeasement-good-cause#.
5. For parallels between the Munich agreement of 1938 and Russia's demands to the West before the assault on Ukraine, see Steven Blank, "Ukraine: No Need for a Munich Sell Out," *Center for European Policy Analysis*, November 22, 2021, https://cepa.org/article/ukraine-no-need-for-a-munich-sell-out/; Sophie Gallagher, "Russia-Ukraine crisis: Whiff of Munich in the Air," *BBC News*, February 13, 2022, https://www.bbc.com/news/uk-60366088.
6. For Putin's own statement on the matter, see Nataliya Vasilyeva, "Putin Tells Children Russia is Invincible," *The Telegraph*, September 1, 2023, https://www.telegraph.co.uk/world-news/2023/09/01/vladimir-putin-tells-school-children-russia-invincible/.
7. For a critique of such an approach, see, for example, Ivo Daalder, "The Age of Impunity," *Politico*, March 24, 2023, https://www.politico.eu/article/putin-wanted-international-criminal-court-icc-

ukraine-russia-war/. However, at least as of yet, any ideas of imposing legal responsibility on the Russian leadership remain just wishful thinking.

8 For some critical assessments, see, for example, Peter Dickinson, "The 2008 Russo-Georgian War: Putin's Green Light," *Ukraine Alert*, August 7, 2021, https://www.atlanticcouncil.org/blogs/ukrainealert/the-2008-russo-georgian-war-putins-green-light/. See also Michael Kofman et al., *Lessons from Russia's Operations in Crimea and Eastern Ukraine* (Santa Monica, CA: Rand Corporation, 2017), https://www.rand.org/pubs/research_reports/RR1498.html. For an alternative interpretation, see Rajan Memon and Eugene B. Rumer, *Conflict in Ukraine: The Unwinding of the Post-Cold War Order* (Cambridge, MA: MIT Press, 2015).

9 For one such account, see Andrei Soldatov and Irina Borogan, *The New Nobility: The Restoration of Russia's Security State and the Enduring Legacy of the KGB* (New York: PublicAffairs, 2010).

10 For a detailed analysis, see Andrei Yakovlev, "Composition of the Ruling Elite, Incentives for Productive Use of Rents, and Prospects for Russia's Limited Access Order," *Post-Soviet Affairs*, 37, no. 5 (2021), 417–34.

11 See Sharon Werning Rivera and David W. Rivera, "Are *Siloviki* Still Undemocratic? Elite Support for Political Pluralism during Putin's Third Presidential Term," *Russian Politics*, 4, no. 4 (2019), 499–519.

12 See Brian D. Taylor, *State Building in Putin's Russia: Policing and Coercion after Communism* (Cambridge: Cambridge University Press, 2011), especially chapter 2.

13 See Lilia Shevtsova, *Yeltsin's Russia: Myths and Reality* (Washington, DC: Carnegie Endowment for International Peace, 1999), chapters 2–3; Viktor Sheinis, *Vzlet i padenie pralamenta: perelomnye gody v rossiiskoi politike (1985–1993)* (Moscow: Carnegie Moscow Center, 2005), vol. 2, chapters 16–22.

14 For various accounts of Yeltsin's 1996 re-election bid, see Michael McFaul, *Russia's 1996 Presidential Election: The End of Polarized Politics* (Stanford, CA: Hoover Institution Press, 1997); Yitzhak Brudny, "In Pursuit of the Russian Presidency: Why and How Yeltsin Won the 1996 Presidential Election," *Communist and Post-Communist Studies*, 30, no. 3 (1997), 255–75; Shevtsova, *Yeltsin's Russia*, chapter 9; Timothy J. Colton, *Yeltsin: A Life* (New York: Basic Books, 2008), chapter 12.

15 See Vadim Volkov, *Violent Entrepreneurs: The Role of Force in the Making of Russian Capitalism* (Ithaca, NY: Cornell University Press, 2002), chapter 6; Taylor, *State Building in Putin's Russia*, chapter 4.

16 On the Chechen War of 1994–6 and its impact on Russia's development,

see Anatol Lieven, *Chechnya: The Tombstone of Russian Power* (New Haven, CT: Yale University Press, 1999); Carlotta Gall and Thomas De Waal, *Chechnya: Calamity in the Caucasus* (New York: New York University Press, 1999).

17 See, for example, Olga Kryshtanovskaya and Stephen White, "Putin's Militocracy," *Post-Soviet Affairs*, 19, no. 4 (2003), 289–306. For a critique of this approach, see Bettina Renz, "Putin's Militocracy? An Alternative Interpretation of *Siloviki* in Contemporary Russian Politics," *Europe-Asia Studies*, 58, no. 6 (2006), 903–24. See also Daniel Treisman, "Putin's Silovarchs," *Orbis*, 51, no. 1 (2007), 141–53.

18 For various accounts of the Second Chechen War, see Quentin Hodgson, "Is the Russian Bear Learning? An Operational and Tactical Analysis of the Second Chechen War, 1999–2002," *Journal of Strategic Studies*, 26, no. 2 (2003), 64–91; Paolo Calzini, "Vladimir Putin and the Chechen War," *The International Spectator*, 40, no. 2 (2005), 19–28; Roberto Colombo and Emil A. Souleimanov, *Counterinsurgency Warfare and Brutalisation: The Second Russian-Chechen War* (Abingdon: Routledge, 2022).

19 For a detailed account, see Mark Kramer, "Guerrilla Warfare, Counterinsurgency and Terrorism in the North Caucasus: The Military Dimension of the Russian–Chechen Conflict," *Europe-Asia Studies*, 57, no. 2 (2005), 209–90.

20 For analyses of civil-military relations in personalist regimes and in other types of autocracies, see Jeffrey Pickering and Emizet F. Kisangani, "Diversionary Despots? Comparing Autocracies' Propensities to Use and to Benefit from Military Force," *American Journal of Political Science*, 54, no. 2 (2010), 477–93. See also Abel Escribà-Folch, Tobias Böhmelt and Ulrich Pilster, "Authoritarian Regimes and Civil–Military Relations: Explaining Counterbalancing in Autocracies," *Conflict Management and Peace Science*, 37, no. 5 (2020), 559–79.

21 See Philip Hanson, "Observations on the Costs of the Yukos Affair to Russia," *Eurasian Geography and Economics*, 46, no. 7 (2005), 481–94; William Tompson, "Putting Yukos in Perspective," *Post-Soviet Affairs*, 21, no. 2 (2005), 159–81; Thane Gustafson, *Wheel of Fortune: The Battle for Oil and Power in Russia* (Cambridge, MA: Belknap Press of Harvard University Press, 2012), chapter 7.

22 See Yakovlev, "Composition of the Ruling Elite."

23 On the repressive policies of the Russian state in the 2010s, see Kirill Rogov, "The Art of Coercion: Repressions and Repressiveness in Putin's Russia," *Russian Politics*, 3, no. 2 (2018), 151–74; Mariya Y. Omelicheva, "Repression Trap: The Mechanism of Escalating State Violence in Russia," *Center for Strategic and International*

Studies (July 2021), https://www.jstor.org/stable/pdf/resrep33768.pdf; Timothy Frye, *Weak Strongman: The Limits of Power in Putin's Russia* (Princeton, NJ: Princeton University Press, 2022), chapter 7.
24 Gel'man, "The Politics of Fear."
25 In fact, the degree of domestic resistance to the Russian assault on Ukraine was higher than one might expect given the scope of repressions against protesters. Tens of thousands of Russian citizens from various regions openly expressed their discontent with the military action in one way or another. However, these protests were mostly conducted individually rather than as collective actions, and protesters were subject to severe repression by the Russian state. See Lauren A. McCarthy, Douglas Rice and Aleks Lokhmutov, "Four Months of 'Discrediting the Military': Repressive Law in Wartime Russia," *Demokratizatsiya: The Journal of Post-Soviet Democratization*, 31, no. 2 (2023), 125–60.
26 For the essence of post-Cold War triumphalism, see Francis Fukuyama, *The End of History and the Last Man* (New York: Simon and Schuster, 1992). See also John Lewis Gaddis, "Toward the Post-Cold War World," *Foreign Affairs*, 70, no. 2 (1991), 102–22.
27 See James M. Scott, *After the End: Making US Foreign Policy in the Post-Cold War World* (Durham, NC: Duke University Press, 1998); Barbara J. Falk, "1989 and Post-Cold War Policymaking: Were the 'Wrong' Lessons Learned from the Fall of Communism?" *International Journal of Politics, Culture, and Society*, 22, no. 2 (2009), 291–313.
28 See, for example, Vladislav M. Zubok, *A Failed Empire: the Soviet Union in the Cold War from Stalin to Gorbachev* (Chapel Hill, NC: University of North Carolina Press, 2009). See also Mary Elise Sarotte, *Not One Inch: America, Russia, and the Making of Post-Cold War Stalemate* (New Haven, CT: Yale University Press, 2021).
29 See, for example, James M. Goldgeier and Michael McFaul, *Power and Purpose: US Policy Toward Russia after the Cold War* (Lanham, MD: Rowman & Littlefield, 2003). For an alternative interpretation, see Edward Lucas, *The New Cold War: How the Kremlin Menaces Both Russia and the West* (London: Bloomsbury, 2009).
30 For various accounts, see Angela Stent, *The Limits of Partnership: U.S.-Russian Relations in the Twenty-First Century* (Princeton, NJ: Princeton University Press, 2014); Michael McFaul, *From Cold War to Hot Peace: An American Ambassador in Putin's Russia* (Boston, MA: Houghton Mifflin Harcourt, 2018); Sarotte, *Not One Inch.*
31 For an apologist reflection on the Cold War in present-day Russia, see Sergey Karaganov, "Satanizatsii vopreki: o novoi kholodnoi voine i russkoi idee," *Russia in Global Affairs*, July 26, 2021, https://globalaffairs.ru/articles/satanizaczii-vopreki/; on the link between

Putin's political preferences and late Stalinism, see, for example, Andrei Kolesnikov, "Istoki i smysl russkogo natsional-imperializma: istoricheskie korni ideologii Putina," *Carnegie Endowment for International Peace*, November 1, 2023, https://carnegieendowment.org/2023/11/01/ru-pub-90833.

32 See Oksana Antonenko, "Russia and the Deadlock over Kosovo," *Russie.Nei.Visions*, no. 21 (2007), https://www.ifri.org/sites/default/files/migrated_files/documents/atoms/files/ifri_kosovo_antonenko_ang_july2007.pdf; David Mendeloff, "'Pernicious History' as a Cause of National Misperceptions: Russia and the 1999 Kosovo War," *Cooperation and Conflict*, 43, no. 1 (2008), 31–56.

33 For a detailed account, see Martin Gilman, *No Precedent, No Plan: Inside Russia's 1998 Default* (Cambridge, MA: MIT Press, 2010); for a comparative analysis, see William Easterly, *The Tyranny of Experts: Economists, Dictators, and the Forgotten Rights of the Poor* (New York: Basic Books, 2013).

34 See Andrei Shleifer and Daniel Treisman, "A Normal Country," *Foreign Affairs*, 83, no. 2 (2004), 20–38. See also Andrei Shleifer and Daniel Treisman, "Normal Countries: The East 25 Years after Communism," *Foreign Affairs*, 93, no. 6 (2014), 92–103.

35 See Benjamin Denison, "Where US Sees Democracy Promotion, Russia Sees Regime Change," *Russia Matters*, July 29, 2020, https://www.russiamatters.org/analysis/where-us-sees-democracy-promotion-russia-sees-regime-change.

36 For reflections by Russian experts loyal to the Kremlin, see Alexander Vysotsky, "Russia and the Arab Spring," *Connections*, 14, no. 1 (2014), 41–64; Yulia Nikitina, "The 'Color Revolutions' and 'Arab Spring' in Russian Official Discourse," *Connections*, 14, no. 1 (2014), 87–104.

37 For an early warning call, see Ivan Krastev, *The Crisis of the Post-Cold War European Order: What to Do about Russia's Newfound Taste for Confrontation with the West* (Washington, DC: The German Marshall Fund of the United States, 2008), https://core.ac.uk/download/pdf/11870746.pdf.

38 See Stent, *The Limits of Partnership*, chapter 6.

39 See Ruth Deyermond, "The Uses of Sovereignty in Twenty-first Century Russian Foreign Policy," *Europe-Asia Studies*, 68, no. 6 (2016), 957–84; Dima Kortyukov, "'Sovereign Democracy' and the Politics of Ideology in Putin's Russia," *Russian Politics*, 5, no. 1 (2020), 81–104. For a theoretical account, see Roland Paris, "The Right to Dominate: How Old Ideas about Sovereignty Pose New Challenges for World Order," *International Organization*, 74, no. 3 (2020), 453–89.

40 For various accounts, see Svante E. Cornel and S. Frederick Starr

(eds.), *The Guns of August 2008: Russia's War in Georgia* (Armonk, NY: M.E. Sharpe, 2009); Mike Bowker, "The War in Georgia and the Western Response," *Central Asian Survey*, 30, no. 2 (2011), 197–211; Emmanuel Karagiannis, "The 2008 Russian–Georgian War via the Lens of Offensive Realism," *European Security*, 22, no. 1 (2020), 74–93.

41 For various accounts, see Svante E. Cornell, *Getting Georgia Right* (Brussels: Center for European Studies, 2013); Charles H. Fairbanks, Jr., "Georgian Democracy: Seizing or Losing the Chance?" *Journal of Democracy*, 25, no. 1 (2014), 154–65; Christopher Berglund, "Georgia between Dominant-Power Politics, Feckless Pluralism, and Democracy," *Demokratizatsiya: The Journal of Post-Soviet Democratization*, 22, no. 3 (2014), 445–70.

42 For various accounts, see Paul D'Anieri, *Ukraine and Russia: From Civilized Divorce to Uncivil War* (Cambridge: Cambridge University Press, 2023), chapter 6; Serhii Plokhy, *The Russo-Ukrainian War* (London: Allen Lane, 2023), chapter 4.

43 See Serhiy Kudelia, "The House That Yanukovych Built," *Journal of Democracy*, 25, no. 3 (2014), 19–34; Lucan Way, "Civil Society and Democratization," *Journal of Democracy*, 25, no. 3 (2014): 35–43; D'Anieri, *Ukraine and Russia*, chapter 7.

44 See Robert Horvath, "Putin's Preventive Counter-Revolution: Post-Soviet Authoritarianism and the Spectre of Velvet Revolution," *Europe-Asia Studies*, 63, no. 1 (2011), 1–25. See also Michael McFaul, "Putin, Putinism, and the Domestic Determinants of Russian Foreign Policy," *International Security*, 45, no. 2 (2020), 95–139.

45 See Olena Podolian, "The 2014 Referendum in Crimea," *East European Quarterly*, 41, no. 1 (2015), 111–28. See also John O'Loughlin and Gerard Toal, "The Crimea Conundrum: Legitimacy and Public Opinion after Annexation," *Eurasian Geography and Economics*, 60, no. 1 (2019), 6–27.

46 See Charles K. Bartles and Roger N. McDermott, "Russia's Military Operation in Crimea," *Problems of Post-Communism*, 61, no. 6 (2014), 46–63; Daniel Treisman, "Why Putin Took Crimea: The Gambler in the Kremlin," *Foreign Affairs*, 95, no. 3 (2016), 47–55. See also Ted Hopf, "'Crimea is Ours': A Discursive History," *International Relations*, 30, no. 2 (2016), 227–55.

47 See, in particular, Adam Charles Lenton, "Why Didn't Ukraine Fight for Crimea? Evidence from Declassified National Security and Defense Council Proceedings," *Problems of Post-Communism*, 69, no. 2 (2022), 145–54.

48 For an analysis of "rally around the flag" in Russia after the annexation of Crimea, see Samuel Greene and Graeme Robertson,

"Explaining Putin's Popularity: Rallying around the Russian Flag," *Washington Post*, September 9, 2014, http://www.washingtonpost.com/blogs/monkey-cage/wp/2014/09/09/explaining-putins-popularity-rallying-round-the-russian-flag/. On a similar phenomenon after the Russian assault on Ukraine, see Kseniya Kizilova and Pippa Norris, "'Rally Around the Flag' Effects in the Russian–Ukrainian War," *European Political Science*, 23 (2023), 234–50.

49 On the impact of the ban on food imports from the EU on Russian agricultural producers, see Janetta Azarieva, Yitzhak M. Brudny and Eugene Finkel, *Bread and Autocracy: Food, Politics, and Security in Putin's Russia* (Oxford: Oxford University Press, 2023), especially chapter 6.

50 See Evgenia Pismennaya, Ilya Arkhipov and Brad Cook, "Putin's Secret Gamble on Reserves Backfires into Currency Crisis," *Bloomberg*, December 17, 2014, https://www.bloomberg.com/news/articles/2014-12-17/putin-s-secret-gamble-bet-on-ukraine-backfires-in-ruble-crisis#xj4y7vzkg.

51 See, for example, Keir Giles, "Russia's 'New' Tools for Confronting the West: Continuity and Innovation in Moscow's Exercise of Power," *Chatham House Russia and Eurasia Program*, March 2016, https://www.chathamhouse.org/sites/default/files/publications/2016-03-russia-new-tools-giles.pdf; Tom Casier, "Not on Speaking Terms, but Business as Usual: The Ambiguous Coexistence of Conflict and Cooperation in EU–Russia Relations," *East European Politics*, 36, no. 4 (2020), 529–43.

52 See Marlene Laruelle, "The Three Colors of Novorossiya, or the Russian Nationalist Mythmaking of the Ukrainian Crisis," *Post-Soviet Affairs*, 32, no. 1 (2015), 55–74. See also Taras Kuzio, "Russian Stereotypes and Myths of Ukraine and Ukrainians and Why Novorossiya Failed," *Communist and Post-Communist Studies*, 52, no. 4 (2019), 297–309.

53 See Tetiana Malyarenko and Stefan Wolff, *The Dynamics of Emerging De-Facto States: Eastern Ukraine in the Post-Soviet Space* (Abingdon: Routledge, 2019); Sabine Fischer, "The Donbas Conflict: Opposing Interests and Narratives, Difficult Peace Process," *Stiftung Wissenschaft und Politik Research Papers*, no. 5, April 2019, https://css.ethz.ch/content/dam/ethz/special-interest/gess/cis/center-for-securities-studies/resources/docs/SWP_2019RP05_fhs.pdf.

54 For a detailed overview, see "MH17 Ukraine Plane Crash: What We Know," *BBC News*, February 26, 2020, https://www.bbc.com/news/world-europe-28357880.

55 For various accounts, see David R. Marples (ed.), *The War in Ukraine's Donbas: Origins, Context, and the Future* (Budapest: Central European University Press, 2022); Anna Matveeva, "Donbas: The Post-Soviet

Conflict that Changed Europe," *European Politics and Society*, 23, no. 3 (2022), 410–41; Amos C. Fox, "The Donbas in Flames: An Operational Level Analysis of Russia's 2014–2015 Donbas Campaign," *Small Wars and Insurgencies*, 2022, https://doi.org/10.1080/09592318.2022.2111496.

56 See Kristian Åtland, "Destined for Deadlock? Russia, Ukraine, and the Unfulfilled Minsk Agreements," *Post-Soviet Affairs*, 36, no. 2 (2020), 122–39.

57 See Adam Potočňák and Miroslav Mares, "Donbas Conflict: How Russia's Trojan Horse Failed and Forced Moscow to Alter Its Strategy," *Problems of Post-Communism*, 70, no. 4 (2023), 341–51.

58 For overviews, see Seth G. Jones, *Moscow's War in Syria* (Washington, DC: Center for Strategic and International Studies, 2020); Ohannes Geukjian, *The Russian Military Intervention in Syria* (Montreal: McGill-Queen's University Press, 2022).

59 See Samuel Charap, Elina Treyger and Edward Geist, *Understanding Russia's Intervention in Syria* (Santa Monica, CA: Rand Corporation, 2019); Anna Borshchevskaya, *Putin's War in Syria: Russian Foreign Policy and the Price of America's Absence* (London: I.B. Tauris, 2021).

60 See Kimberly Marten, "Russia's Use of Semi-State Security Forces: The Case of the Wagner Group," *Post-Soviet Affairs*, 35, no. 3 (2019), 181–204; Samuel Ramani, *Russia in Africa: Resurgent Great Power or Bellicose Pretender?* (Oxford: Oxford University Press, 2023).

61 On the rise of Russia's hybrid influence in international arenas, see Mark Galeotti, *Russian Political War: Moving beyond the Hybrid* (Abingdon: Routledge, 2019); Mitchell A. Orenstein, *The Lands in Between: Russia vs. the West and the New Politics of Hybrid War* (Oxford: Oxford University Press, 2019).

62 See Nathan Hodge, "Why Putin Would Want Trump to Win in 2020," *CNN*, February 21, 2020, https://edition.cnn.com/2020/02/21/europe/putin-trump-2020-election-analysis-intl/index.html; Max Boot, "Why Russians Still Prefer Trump," *Washington Post*, February 21, 2020, https://www.washingtonpost.com/opinions/2020/02/21/why-russians-still-prefer-trump/.

63 See, in particular, John J. Mearsheimer, "Bound to Fail: The Rise and Fall of the Liberal International Order," *International Security*, 43, no. 4 (2019), 7–50; Richard Lachmann, *First Class Passengers on a Sinking Ship: Elite Politics and the Decline of Great Powers* (London: Verso Books, 2020); Alexander Cooley and Daniel Nexon, *Exit from Hegemony: The Unraveling of the American Global Order* (Oxford: Oxford University Press, 2020).

64 See John J. Mearsheimer, "Why the Ukraine Crisis is the West's Fault: the Liberal Delusions that Provoked Putin," *Foreign Affairs*, 93, no.

5 (2014), 77–89. See also John J. Mearsheimer, "The Causes and Consequences of the Ukraine War," *Horizons: Journal of International Relations and Sustainable Development*, 21 (2022), 12–27.

65 See, in particular, Katrina Vanden Heuvel and Stephen F. Cohen, "Cold War against Russia – Without Debate," *The Nation*, May 1, 2014, https://www.thenation.com/article/archive/cold-war-against-russia-without-debate/; Stephen F. Cohen, *War with Russia? From Putin & Ukraine to Trump & Russiagate* (New York: Simon and Schuster, 2018).

66 See Jim Garamone, "Russian Forces in Initial Phase of Invasion of Ukraine, Official Says," US Department of Defense, February 24, 2022, https://www.defense.gov/News/News-Stories/Article/Article/2945254/russian-forces-in-initial-phase-of-invasion-of-ukraine-official-says/; Jim Sciutto and Katie Bo Williams, "US Concerned Kyiv Could Fall to Russia Within Days, Sources Familiar with Intel Say," *CNN*, February 25, 2022, https://edition.cnn.com/2022/02/25/politics/kyiv-russia-ukraine-us-intelligence/index.html.

67 For a discussion, see Phillips Payson O'Brien, "How the West Got Russia's Military So, So Wrong," *The Atlantic*, March 31, 2022, https://www.theatlantic.com/ideas/archive/2022/03/russia-ukraine-invasion-military-predictions/629418/; Alan Cunningham, "Overestimation in Intelligence: The Overestimation of Russia's Armed Forces," *Modern Diplomacy*, April 26, 2022, https://moderndiplomacy.eu/2022/04/26/overestimation-in-intelligence-the-overestimation-of-russias-armed-forces/.

68 See Bettina Renz, "Western Estimates of Russian Military Capabilities and the Invasion of Ukraine," *Problems of Post-Communism*, 71, no. 3 (2024), 219–31.

69 On parallels between Russia's actions in Ukraine in 2022 and the Soviet invasion of Czechoslovakia in 1968, see Elena Lappin, "The Invasion of Ukraine Brings Back Prague Spring Memories," *Wall Street Journal*, March 2, 2022, https://www.wsj.com/articles/kyiv-brings-back-memories-of-prague-invasion-ukraine-russia-soviet-union-authoritarian-seige-1968-11646257660; Raymond Johnston, "Czechoslovakia's Prague Spring of 1968 and Russia's War against Ukraine," *Kyiv Post*, August 27, 2022, https://archive.kyivpost.com/article/opinion/op-ed/czechoslovakias-prague-spring-of-1968-and-russias-war-against-ukraine.html.

70 See Cedric Pietralunga, "Why Ukraine's Counter-offensive is Failing," *Le Monde*, October 27, 2023, https://www.lemonde.fr/en/international/article/2023/10/27/why-ukraine-s-counter-offensive-is-failing_6206824_4.html; Lewis Page, "Ukraine's Counter-offensive Has Failed for Now – the West Needs a New Plan," *The Telegraph*, November 12, 2023, https://www.telegraph.co.uk/business/2023/11/12/ukraine-counteroffensive-failed-russia-putin-war-plan/.

71 See Jakub M. Godzimirski (ed.), *Russian Energy in a Changing World: What is the Outlook for the Hydrocarbons Superpower?* (Abingdon: Routledge, 2013); Veli-Pekka Tynkkynen, *The Energy of Russia: Hydrocarbon Culture and Climate Change* (Cheltenham: Edward Elgar, 2019).

72 See Thane Gustafson, *The Bridge: Natural Gas in a Redivided Europe* (Cambridge, MA: Harvard University Press, 2020).

73 See Maria Snegovaya, "What Factors Contribute to the Aggressive Foreign Policy of Russian Leaders?," *Problems of Post-Communism*, 67, no. 1 (2020), 93–110.

74 For country-level perspectives, see Kirsten Westphal, "German–Russian Gas Relations in Face of the Energy Transition," *Russian Journal of Economics*, no. 6 (2020), 406–23; Andrea Prontera, "Winter is Coming: Russian Gas, Italy and the Post-war European Politics of Energy Security," *West European Politics*, 47, no. 2 (2024), 382–407.

75 See Brian Whitaker, "Nord Stream Sabotage: A Look at the Evidence So Far," *Medium*, June 20, 2023, https://brian-whit.medium.com/nord-stream-sabotage-a-look-at-the-evidence-so-far-311a615171d; Emma Ashford, "Who Blew Up the Nord Stream Pipeline?" *Foreign Policy*, June 23, 2023, https://foreignpolicy.com/2023/06/23/who-blew-up-the-nord-stream-pipeline/.

76 For a discussion, see Ben McWilliams, Giovanni Sgaravatti, Simone Tagliapietra and Georg Zachmann, "How Would the European Union Fare without Russian Energy?" *Energy Policy*, 174 (2023), 113413; Aura Sabadus, "Russian Gas Imports: More Pain Than Gain?" *Center for European Policy Analysis*, May 30, 2023, https://cepa.org/article/russian-gas-imports-more-pain-than-gain/.

77 See Philip Oltermann, Jon Helney, Angelique Chrisafis, Sam Jones and Shaun Walker, "How Putin's Plans to Blackmail Europe over Gas Supply Failed," *The Guardian*, February 3, 2023, https://www.theguardian.com/world/2023/feb/03/putin-russia-blackmail-europe-gas-supply-ukraine; Szymon Kardas, "Conscious Uncoupling: Europeans' Russian Gas Challenge in 2023," *European Council of Foreign Relations*, February 13, 2023, https://ecfr.eu/article/conscious-uncoupling-europeans-russian-gas-challenge-in-2023/.

78 See Daniel Kahneman and Amos Tversky, "The Psychology of Preferences," *Scientific American*, 246, no. 1 (1982), 160–73; Daniel Kahneman and Amos Tversky, "Choices, Values, and Frames," *American Psychologist*, 39, no. 4 (1984), 341–50.

79 Dostoevsky, *Crime and Punishment*, part V, chapter 4.

80 See Gary S. Becker, "Crime and Punishment: An Economic Approach," *Journal of Political Economy*, 76, no. 2 (1968), 169–217.

Chapter 6. Lost Illusions, Dashed Hopes, and Unlearned Lessons

1 See Anna Chernova, Christian Edwards and David Shortell, "Jailed Russian Opposition Figure Alexey Navalny Dies, Prison Service Says," *CNN*, February 16, 2024, https://edition.cnn.com/2024/02/16/europe/alexey-navalny-dead-russia-prison-intl/index.html; Guy Faulconbridge and Felix Light, "Putin Foe Alexei Navalny Dies in Jail, West Holds Russia Responsible," *Reuters*, February 17, 2024, https://www.reuters.com/world/europe/jailed-russian-opposition-leader-navalny-dead-prison-service-2024-02-16/.

2 See Alexandra Prokopenko, "Putin's Unsustainable Spending Spree: How the War in Ukraine Will Overheat the Russian Economy," *Foreign Affairs*, January 8, 2024, https://www.foreignaffairs.com/russian-federation/putins-unsustainable-spending-spree; Arthur Sullivan, "Ukraine War: Russia's Economy Beats the Odds – Can it Last?," *DW*, February 19, 2024, https://www.dw.com/en/ukraine-war-russias-economy-beats-the-odds-can-it-last/a-68268264.

3 See, in particular, Pavel Luzin and Alexandra Prokopenko, "Russia's 2024 Budget Shows It's Planning for a Long War in Ukraine," *Carnegie Politika*, October 11, 2023, https://carnegieendowment.org/politika/90753; Volodymyr Ishchenko, Ilya Matveev and Oleg Zhuravlev, "Russian Military Keynesianism: Who Benefits from the War in Ukraine?" *PONARS Policy Memos*, no. 865 (2023), https://www.ponarseurasia.org/russian-military-keynesianism-who-benefits-from-the-war-in-ukraine/.

4 See, for example, Courtney Weaver and Anastasia Stognei, "Russia's Surprising Consumer Spending Boom," *Financial Times*, July 25, 2024, https://www.ft.com/content/3e2b2e63-082e-4058-ba92-dea580d4f40c.

5 On Russian elites, see Isaac Chotiner, "Why Russian Elites Think Putin's War is Doomed to Fail," *New Yorker*, May 3, 2023, https://www.newyorker.com/news/q-and-a/why-russian-elites-think-putins-war-is-doomed-to-fail; for mass survey data, see "Konflikt s Ukrainoi: otsenki kontsa 2023 – nachala 2024 goda," *Levada-Center*, February 6, 2024, https://www.levada.ru/2024/02/06/konflikt-s-ukrainoj-otsenki-kontsa-2023-nachala-2024-goda/.

6 On the failure of the Ukrainian counter-offensive in 2023, see, for example, Chris Panella, "How Ukraine's Counteroffensive Went Sideways," *Business Insider*, December 7, 2023, https://www.businessinsider.com/how-the-ukrainian-counteroffensive-ran-into-trouble-2023-11?r=US&IR=T; Mariano Zafra and John McClure,

"Four Factors that Stalled Ukraine's Counteroffensive," *Reuters*, December 21, 2023, https://www.reuters.com/graphics/UKRAINE-CRISIS/MAPS/klvygwawavg/#four-factors-that-stalled-ukraines-counteroffensive.

7 See Guy Faulconbridge and Darya Korshunskaya, "Exclusive: Putin's Suggestion of Ukraine Ceasefire Rejected by United States, Sources Say," *Reuters*, February 13, 2024, https://www.reuters.com/world/europe/putins-suggestion-ukraine-ceasefire-rejected-by-united-states-sources-say-2024-02-13/.

8 See, for example, Pavel Baev, "Russia's New Challenges in the Baltic/Northern European Theater," *Russie. Eurasie. Visions IFRI*, no. 130 (November 2023), https://www.ifri.org/en/papers/russias-new-challenges-balticnorthern-european-theater; Laura Husselman, "Putin could attack Baltics and Moldova Next," *Politico*, December 19, 2023, https://www.politico.eu/article/belgian-army-chief-hofman-putin-attack-after-ukraine-baltics-moldova-next-russia/.

9 For different accounts, see Philippe de Lara, "A Geopolitical Mirage: the 'De-westernization' of the World," *Desk Russie*, May 13, 2023, https://desk-russie.info/2023/05/13/a-geopolitical-mirage.html; Kadri Liik, "From Russia with Love: How Moscow Courts the Global South," *European Council of Foreign Relations*, December 2023, https://ecfr.eu/wp-content/uploads/2023/12/From-Russia-with-love-How-Moscow-courts-the-global-south.pdf.

10 See Daniel Byman and Kenneth M. Pollack, "The Persian–Russian Connection," *Lawfare*, October 26, 2023, https://www.lawfaremedia.org/article/the-persian-russian-connection; Rupal Mishra and Ankur Dixit, "Decoding Russia's Position in the Israel–Hamas Conflict," *Australian Outlook*, February 9, 2024, https://www.internationalaffairs.org.au/australianoutlook/decoding-russias-position-in-the-israel-hamas-conflict/. See also Kimberly Marten, "Upsetting the Balance: Why Russia Choose Hamas over Israel", *Washington Quarterly*, 47, no. 3 (2024), 79–102.

11 See, in particular, Andrei Yakovlev, "Will Russian Business be Sacrificed to Build a New Economic Model?," *Russia.Post*, January 9, 2024, https://russiapost.info/economy/new_economic_model. See also "As cases of asset seizures rise, Vladimir Putin's tycoons seek safeguards," *Business Standard*, March 30, 2024, https://www.business-standard.com/world-news/as-cases-of-asset-seizures-rise-vladimir-putin-s-tycoons-seek-safeguards-124033000047_1.html.

12 See, for example, Bijan Khajehpour, "Decoding Iran's 'Resistance Economy,'" *Al Monitor*, February 24, 2014, https://www.al-monitor.com/originals/2014/02/decoding-resistance-economy-iran.html; Ray Takeyh, "Iran's 'Resistance Economy' Debate," *Council of Foreign*

Relations, April 7, 2016, https://www.cfr.org/expert-brief/irans-resistance-economy-debate.

13 See, in particular, William Taubman, *Khrushchev: The Man and His Era* (New York: W.W. Norton, 2003), chapter 20; Paul Du Quenoy, "The Role of Foreign Affairs in the Fall of Nikita Khrushchev in October 1964," *The International History Review*, 25, no. 2 (2003), 334–56.

14 "The proletarians have nothing to lose but their chains," Karl Marx and Frederick Engels, *Manifesto of the Communist Party*, https://oll.libertyfund.org/pages/marx-manifesto.

15 See Heather Mongilio, "A Brief Summary of the Battle of the Black Sea," US Naval Institute, November 15, 2023, https://news.usni.org/2023/11/15/a-brief-summary-of-the-battle-of-the-black-sea; Igor Delanoe, "Russia's Black Sea Fleet in the 'Special Military Operation' in Ukraine," *Foreign Policy Research Institute*, February 7, 2024.

16 See, in particular, Karen Dawisha, *Putin's Kleptocracy: Who Owns Russia?* (New York: Simon and Schuster, 2014); Anders Åslund, *Russia's Crony Capitalism: The Path from Market Economy to Kleptocracy* (New Haven, CT: Yale University Press, 2019).

17 See Steven Levitsky and Lucan Way, *Revolution and Dictatorship: The Violent Origins of Durable Authoritarianism* (Princeton, NJ: Princeton University Press, 2022), especially chapter 2.

18 For various accounts, see Ken Jowitt, *New World Disorder: The Leninist Extinction* (Berkeley, CA: University of California Press, 1992), especially chapter 4; Yegor Gaidar, *Collapse of an Empire: Lessons for Modern Russia* (Washington, DC: Brookings Institution Press, 2007).

19 See Vladimir Sorokin, *Day of the Oprichnik* (New York: Farrar, Straus, and Giroux, 2012).

20 For typologies of authoritarian regimes, see Milan Svolik, *The Politics of Authoritarian Rule* (Cambridge: Cambridge University Press, 2012); Barbara Geddes, Joseph Wright and Erica Frantz, *How Dictatorships Work: Power, Personalization, and Collapse* (Cambridge: Cambridge University Press, 2018).

21 On the persistence of authoritarian politics in Cameroon, see, for example, Jean-Germain Gros, "The Hard Lessons of Cameroon," *Journal of Democracy*, 6, no. 3 (1995), 112–27; Nicolas G. Emmanuel, "'With a Friend Like This': Shielding Cameroon from Democratization," *Journal of Asian and African Studies*, 48, no. 2 (2012), 145–60.

22 On these issues, see Maria Snegovaya, Michael Kimmage and Jade McGlynn, "Putin the Ideologue: The Kremlin's Potent Mix of Nationalism, Grievance, and Mythmaking," *Foreign Affairs*, November

16, 2023, https://www.foreignaffairs.com/russian-federation/putin-ideologue.
23 For advocacy of this perspective, see Alexander Etkind, *Russia against Modernity* (Cambridge: Polity Press, 2023).
24 For a critical assessment, see Alexander Kynev, "No Putin, No Russia? Why Losing the War Wouldn't Destroy the Russian Federation," *World Crunch*, December 1, 2022, https://worldcrunch.com/will-russia-collapse-if-it-loses. For a theory-driven argument, see Henry E. Hale, "The Makeup and Breakup of Ethnofederal States: Why Russia Survives Where the USSR Fell," *Perspectives on Politics*, 3, no. 1 (2005), 55–70.
25 For a detailed historical account, see Konrad Jarausch, *After Hitler: Recivilizing Germans 1945–1995* (Oxford: Oxford University Press, 2006). See also Nikolay Vlasov, "Novoe nachalo? Zapadnye nemtsy v pervoe poslevoennoe desyatiletie," *Preprint M-101/23* (St. Petersburg: Center for Modernization Studies, European University at St. Petersburg, 2023), https://eusp.org/m-center/publications.
26 See Vladimir Gel'man, *The Politics of Bad Governance in Contemporary Russia* (Ann Arbor, MI: University of Michigan Press, 2022), 159.
27 See, in particular, Andreas Schedler, *The Politics of Uncertainty: Sustaining and Subverting Electoral Authoritarianism* (Oxford: Oxford University Press, 2013); Michael K. Miller, "The Strategic Origins of Electoral Authoritarianism," *British Journal of Political Science*, 50, no. 1 (2020), 17–44.
28 For these arguments, see Vladimir Gel'man, *Authoritarian Russia: Analyzing Post-Soviet Regime Changes* (Pittsburgh, PA: University of Pittsburgh Press, 2015), chapter 3; Vladimir Gel'man, "Escape from Political Freedom. The Constitutional Crisis of 1993 and Russia's Political Trajectory," *Russian History*, 50, nos. 1–2 (2024), 1–20.
29 See Gel'man, *Authoritarian Russia*, chapter 4.
30 For data on elite surveys in Russia since the 1990s, see Sharon Werning Rivera (ed.), *Survey of Russian Elites 2020: New Perspectives on Domestic and Foreign Policy* (Clinton, NY: Hamilton College, 2020), https://hamilton.edu/documents/SRE2020ReportFINAL.pdf.
31 For an overview and case studies, see Mark Beissinger and Stephen Kotkin (eds.), *Historical Legacies of Communism in Russia and Eastern Europe* (Cambridge: Cambridge University Press, 2014).
32 See Brian D. Taylor, "From Police State to Police State? Legacies and Law Enforcement in Russia," in Beissinger and Kotkin (eds.), *Historical Legacies of Communism in Russia and Eastern Europe*, 128–51.
33 For a detailed account, see Vladimir Gel'man and Anastassia Obydenkova, "The Invention of Legacy: Strategic Uses of a 'Good

Soviet Union' in Elite Policy Preferences and Filmmaking in Russia," *Communist and Post-Communist Studies*, 57, no. 1 (2024), 130–53.
34 For revealing evidence of US policy towards Russia in the 1990s, presented by an advisor to Bill Clinton, see Strobe Talbott, *The Russia Hand: A Memoir of Presidential Diplomacy* (New York: Random House, 2003). On the limited impact of Western leverages of democracy promotion in post-Soviet Eurasia, see Steven Levitsky and Lucan Way, *Competitive Authoritarianism: Hybrid Regimes after the Cold War* (Cambridge: Cambridge University Press, 2010), especially chapter 3.
35 For a similar account, see Kathryn E. Stoner, *Russia Resurrected: Its Power and Purpose in a New Global Order* (Oxford: Oxford University Press, 2021).
36 For this argument, see Andrei Shliefer and Daniel Treisman, "A Normal Country: Russia after Communism," *Journal of Economic Perspectives*, 19, no. 1 (2005), 151–74.
37 For Putin's highly critical statement, see https://www.youtube.com/watch?v=YbT2RGfBwdE.
38 For this argument, see Etkind, *Russia against Modernity*.
39 See, in particular, Ronald Inglehart and Christian Welzel, *Modernization, Cultural Change, and Democracy: The Human Development Sequence* (Cambridge: Cambridge University Press, 2005).
40 For a thoughtful account of Russia's past historical trajectories vis-à-vis European historical developmental paths, see Dmitry Travin, *Pochemu Rossiya otstala* (St. Petersburg: European University at St. Petersburg Press, 2021); Dmitry Travin, *Russkaya lovushka* (St. Petersburg: European University at St. Petersburg Press, 2023).
41 See Francis Fukuyama, *The End of History and the Last Man* (New York: Free Press, 1992).
42 *Matthew*, 23:12.

INDEX

Afghanistan
  failure of the government of 15
  Soviet-Afghan war 54
  Soviet invasion of 10, 54, 138
  withdrawal of the US from 86, 88, 110–11, 135
Allison, Graham 22–3
Andropov, Yuri 51, 54, 93
Annexation of Crimea 1, 4, 6, 11, 15–16, 32, 46, 68, 117, 132, 155
  elite perceptions of 94, 131–2, 140
  as a "pre-emptive response" 28
  and Putin 41–3, 57, 131
  in relation to the "special military operation" 25, 27, 136–7
  response to 107, 115–16, 130–2, 140, 155
Anti-Corruption Foundation 60, 175 n.4
anti-Westernism 27, 45, 54, 71, 73, 76, 94, 119
Arab Spring 122, 128
Armenia 110
authoritarian regime(s)
  classification of 37
  "degenerate autocracy" 38, 57, 88–9, 113
  electoral 38, 153
  information flows in 25, 31, 52, 55–6, 58, 61, 70; *see also* dictator's dilemma; veil of secrecy
  "informational autocracy" 89–90, 100, 114; *see also* spin dictatorship
  longevity 66
  military 37–9, 150
  monarchies 37–9, 149–50
  as a norm 30
  party-based 31, 36–7, 39, 48–9, 56, 146, 150
  performance of 37, 57
  personalist 24, 31 40, 48–9, 56–7, 66, 84, 89, 94, 98, 104, 146, 150
    collapse of 82
    consolidation 24, 40–1, 122, 127
    dynamics 38
    effectiveness 39–40, 131
    performance 38–40
  personalist trap 24–5, 36–7, 57, 146–7, 150
  transition to 40–2, 153–5
Avtomatika, company 59–61, 69
Azerbaijan 110–11

bad governance 24, 61–6, 69, 76–8, 81, 117, 147, 150

bad governance (*cont.*)
  definition of 61–3
  government ineffectiveness 61–2, 99
  negative consequences 64, 66, 71, 73, 84, 86, 107
  as a norm 30
  paradox of 64, 77; *see also* "pockets of efficiency"
  role of, in the Russian military assault 83–4
  trap of 24–5, 99, 147, 150
Bakanov, Ivan 108
Belarus 82, 99–100, 103
Bil'ak, Vasil' 53, 56
Bortnikov, Alexander 66, 91
Brexit 90, 97, 135
Brezhnev, Leonid 50–1, 54, 66

ceasefire
  attempts of, in Russia's military assault on Ukraine 18, 144
  in Georgia 129
  in the Minsk agreement(s) 34, 132–3
Central Bank of Russia 21, 22, 43, 64, 78, 139
centralization of governance 41, 145, 154; *see also* decentralization
Chechnya 32, 120–1
checks and balances 12, 30, 43; *see also* constraints
  authoritarian 42–3
Chemezov, Sergey 70, 91
Chernenko, Konstantin 54
China 14, 29, 37, 39, 59–60, 90, 96–7, 136, 145, 150
Clausewitz, Carl von 29
client state(s) 1, 14, 74, 86, 97, 113
Clinton, Bill 97, 127
Cold War 7, 8, 29, 50, 56, 98, 100, 124–5, 143, 161 n.21
  Russia as a loser of 124
  victors of 125, 155

Collective Security Treaty Organization 110
color revolutions 122, 127
  Orange Revolution 1, 104, 108–9
  Rose Revolution 129
Communism 49, 122, 124, 149
  post-Communist development 21
  post-Communist disappointment 94
  post-Communist experience 144
Communist Party 50, 52, 92, 99, 119
  leadership 50
  of Ukraine 51
  of Czechoslovakia 51, 53, 56
comparative perspective 21, 28, 82
confirmation bias(es) 87–8, 89, 95, 102
conspiracy theories 87, 90, 95, 100–2, 147
  among Russian elites 147, 101
constraints 57–8, 63, 117, 153; s*ee also* checks and balances
  on behavior of states 6, 8–10, 29–30, 32, 36–7, 61, 135
  classification 9
  lack of 57, 61
  on elites 47, 119
  international 132, 134, 155
  political and institutional 61, 112
  on presidential power 40–1
  process of diminishing 115
  structural 101
corruption 24, 31, 40, 46, 60–2, 69–70, 83–4
Crimea 17, 130
Cuban Missile Crisis 23
Czechoslovakia 31, 137
  German occupation of 52
  leadership of 51, 53
  "normalization" 49, 53
  "Prague Spring" in 49–50, 137
  resistance in 53
  Soviet invasion of 36, 48–50, 52–4, 56, 58, 75

INDEX

decentralization 108, 119; *see also* centralization of governance
deinstitutionalization 42–5, 55–7; *see also* institutionalization
"demilitarization" 16
democratization 40, 148, 152–6
"denazification" 16
determinism 27
"dictator's dilemma" 31; *see also* authoritarian regime(s), information flows in
disinformation 70, 89–90, 135
Donbas 4, 19, 133, 142, 144
  conflict in 4, 28, 133
  future of 109
  "people's republics" 18, 33–5, 132–3
  plebiscite in the region of 18–19
  separatism 4, 55, 79, 106–9, 132–3
  war in 79, 115, 132–4
Dubček, Alexander 51, 53

elites 5, 11–12, 29; *see also* constraints, on elites
of the Communist Party 66
Czechoslovak elites 49
definition of 11
Eurasian elites 99
European elites 112
Finnish elites 113
in personalist autocracies 38, 73
post-Soviet elites 126, 149, 155
rotation of 66, 84
Russian elites 1, 5, 96, 103, 109, 112–14, 120–2, 126–7, 129, 143, 145–7, 151, 153–7; *see also* Annexation of Crimea, elite perceptions of; conspiracy theories, among Russian elites; impunity, feeling of impunity among Russian elites; misperceptions, of Russian elites
after the military assault 4, 7, 12, 101, 145, 156
attitudes of 11, 13, 27, 45, 89, 91, 94; *see also* Survey of Russian Elites
concerns of 42
discontent 7
focus of analysis on 26–8
intra-elite conflicts 44
loyalty of 4, 35–6, 42, 58, 66–7, 76, 92, 100, 146
mistakes of 3
perceptions of 5, 81, 99, 140–1, 154
preferences 26–7, 36, 87
pro-Western 27, 94
rent-seeking practices of 15–16, 61–2, 99
resentment of 31, 93–4
role models of 47
rotation 89, 148
security elites 91–5, 100
  background of 87, 91–2
  homogeneity of 94–5
self-deception 87
"seventiers" 92–3, 107, 113
siloviki 11, 43–5, 55, 65, 67, 118–23, 142–3, 145, 147, 149–50
status-seeking of 6, 93, 145
undermining international order 1–2
worldviews of 25, 87, 102, 113
Soviet elites 7, 15, 50, 96
Ukrainian elites 17, 55, 106–8
Western elites 110
Eurasian Economic Union 99–100
European Union (EU) 12, 14, 97, 100, 112, 125, 130, 139

G8 96, 126, 131
Gaidar Forum 72
Gazprom 111, 138–40

215

INDEX

Georgia 4, 16, 32, 127–9, 155
  five-day war in 4, 67–8, 115–16, 129
Gerasimov, Valery 75, 81–2
Girkin, Igor 132
Glaziev, Sergey 104
global stakeholders 12–14
good governance 30, 62
Gorbachev, Mikhail 26
Gromyko, Andrei 52, 54
groupthink 91, 94–5, 101
Gulag 99

Hungary 3, 51, 53, 112–13
Huntington, Samuel P. 105–6
hybrid warfare 135

impunity 6, 58, 134
  feeling of impunity among Russian elites 25, 94, 110, 116, 134–6, 120, 123, 130, 132, 134–6, 139–40, 148
  spiral of impunity 117–18
  trap of impunity 24–5, 32, 136, 141, 148, 151
  development of 117–18
institutionalization
  high 39, 50, 52, 56, 58, 122, 146
  low 36–9, 64, 73, 99, 146, 150
  see also deinstitutionalization
International Criminal Court in Hague 20
invincibility 116
  illusory invincibility 135–8, 140–1
  spiral of invincibility 117, 129, 133–6
Iran 144–5, 150
Iraq 5, 127
Ivanov, Timur 60–1, 69–70
Ivashov, Leonid 76

Jervis, Robert 87–8

Kadyrov, Akhmad 121

Kadyrov, Ramzan 121
Karaganov, Sergey 71–2, 110
Kazakhstan 41, 99, 144
Kennan, George F. 6–8, 11, 160–1 n.21
KGB 44, 51, 70, 91–3
Khodarenok, Mikhail 76–7
Khrushchev, Nikita 146
Kosygin, Alexei 51
Kovalchuk, Yuri 54–5
Kozak, Dmitry 35, 105
Kramer, Mark 50
Kravchuk, Leonid 106
Kremlin 3, 6–7, 16, 25–6, 33–4, 97–8, 128, 130–4, 138, 142, 145–6, 150–1, 158 n.1
  expectations of the 16, 99, 102–3, 110–12, 117–18, 135
  information leaks from the 52
  "Kremlin's cues" 27, 89
  misperceptions of 107–9, 111–12, 114, 116–17, 137–8
  preferences 49, 66, 100, 102
  propaganda 28, 71–2, 89, 99, 104, 126
  resistance to 5, 145
Kuchma, Leonid 103, 105–6
Kyrgyzstan 99, 127

Lavrov, Sergey 15, 24, 35, 52, 66, 74
Lenin, Vladimir 26, 34, 103, 106
liberalization 27, 49, 56, 138, 145, 148–9
Lukashenko, Alexander 82, 99

Mearsheimer, John 28, 136
Medinsky, Vladimir 105
Medvedchuk, Viktor 16, 55–6, 105, 108
Medvedev, Dmitry 41, 45, 67–8
militarism 119, 122, 143, 145, 151, 153

military aggression 8–10, 153; see also war
military coup(s) 9, 21, 82
Ministry of Defence of the Russian Federation 45, 55, 60, 68–9, 80–2
Ministry of Foreign Affairs of the Russian Federation 65, 71, 74
Minsk agreement(s) 34, 109, 132–3
  Minsk II in 2015 133
misinformation 24, 69, 83, 102, 148
misperceptions 25–6
  among policymakers 87–9
  of Russian elites 6, 24–5, 31, 87, 89–90, 93–5, 98, 100–2, 104–5, 109, 112–14, 147
    regarding Ukraine 87, 104
  trap of misperceptions 24–5, 147, 150
  see also Kremlin, misperceptions of
Moldova 16, 99
multi-polarity (doctrine) 97–8

Nabiullina, Elvira 43, 95
Naryshkin, Sergey 35, 91, 101
NATO 16, 18, 28, 34, 74, 76, 98, 102, 110, 113, 116, 125–8
Navalny, Alexei 60, 122, 142
negative equilibrium 146, 150–1
Nemtsov, Boris 122
Nord Stream 138–9
"Novorossiya" (New Russia) 106, 132
nuclear weapons 8, 26, 72, 75, 96, 110, 116, 118, 124, 148

Obama, Barack 86, 97, 127, 135
"offensive realism" 28–9
open-source intelligence 53, 102
"Operation Danube" 49–52, 75

patronage
  informal 79

of leadership 46, 64, 68, 70, 77–8, 83, 89
networks 42–3, 119
personalization of 42–5, 47–8, 56–7
Patrushev, Nikolai 33, 74, 91, 101
Pavlovsky, Gleb 104
peace 20, 143
  as an exception 8, 29–30
  negotiations 17–18, 25, 33–4, 74, 144
  rational choice theory of democratic 9
  in Ukraine 20, 133
perestroika 93, 125
"pockets of efficiency" 64, 77–8, 83
Poland 17, 72, 113, 139
Politburo 50–4, 56; see also Communist Party
political institutions 24, 155
  under authoritarianism 57–8
Poroshenko, Petro 55, 107–8
post-Soviet political hangover in 156
Prigozhin, Yevgeny 79–83, 123, 142, 150
Primakov, Yevgeny 97, 126
primordialism 104
propaganda 5, 72–3, 80, 89–90, 100, 142
Putin, Vladimir
  background 91–2
  decision-making 1, 21–2, 24, 36, 41–2, 77, 115, 119, 131, 140
  entourage 28, 33, 35, 43–5, 54–5, 68–70, 79–82, 88, 93, 95, 105, 121–3, 148, 156
  international reputation 57
  order for the arrest of 20
  presidency 6, 22, 40, 45–6, 143
  "putinology" 26–8, 88
  rule 3–4, 12, 36, 44, 65, 89, 97, 127–8, 143, 147

Putin, Vladimir (*cont.*)
  support 7, 57, 70, 131, 147
  understanding of Ukraine 88, 103–5; *see also* Ukraine, as anti-Russia

rally around the flag 17, 27
regional power(s) 14, 97, 127, 135
rent-seeking 16, 24, 29, 31, 45, 47, 61–6, 68–9, 73, 83–4, 99, 119, 123
Renz, Bettina 137
Revolution of Dignity 100, 105, 108–9, 191 n.58
rule of law 46, 61–3, 67
Russia 4, 95–6
  coercion 116, 118
  COVID-19 pandemic in 46, 64, 70
  decision-making in 30, 52–3, 140
    personalist nature of 36, 56, 117, 150
  diplomacy 71, 74
  economy 20, 64–5, 72, 98, 111, 117, 121, 127, 131, 142–3, 145, 154
  "energy superpower" 138, 140
  failure of the 20, 149, 152
  foreign policy 12–14, 15, 61, 71–4, 79, 97, 102, 116, 118, 124, 138, 154–6, 161–2 n.33
  future scenarios 151–2, 157
  global influence 29
  governance in 31, 84
    mechanisms 31; *see also* corruption; rent-seeking
    quality 31, 61
  information control in 52
  in the international arena 142
    international behavior 3, 6–7, 8, 11–12, 29–30, 143, 156
    reputation 20, 52, 155–6
    status 12, 96–7
  leadership 97, 116–17, 127, 145, 151
  mass public in 5, 27, 46–7, 81, 93, 100–1, 121
  military of 60, 75–6, 78, 99, 116, 132, 137
  military performance 78
  military reform in 67–9, 130
  military policy 69–70, 83, 99, 102
  mobilization in 19, 78
  as a personalist autocracy 12, 40
  police reform in 67
  regime personalization in, 40–2, 46, 48
    four pillars of 42
  repression(s) 123, 142, 151, 160 n.16, 197 n.1
  resistance to 115–17, 122
  sanctions against 2, 16–17, 20–1, 34, 43, 110, 117, 131–2, 139, 142
  security apparatus 119
  security policy 24, 31, 52, 58, 62, 66, 73, 76–7, 89
  socio-economic policy 46, 66, 68, 72–3, 83, 88–9, 95, 145, 150
  state performance 64, 69
  state-owned companies 64
  technological sovereignty of 59–60
Russian Academy of Science 71
Russian military assault
  consequences 21, 32, 77, 107, 112–13, 123, 142–3, 147–8, 152
  description of 1–4, 26–7, 35–6, 44, 75, 78, 94, 102, 105, 115
  explanations for 28–9, 47, 152–3
  factors contributing to 10–11, 15–17, 24, 31–2, 83, 95, 103
  failure 22, 57–8, 62, 73, 75, 84, 87, 95, 136, 118, 136, 141
  international response to the 17, 25

INDEX

resistance to 5, 76
see also "special military operation"
Russian National Guard 82
Russian Revolution in 1917 149
Russian Security Council 33–5, 41–2, 55, 60, 74, 94

Saakashvili, Mikheil 129–30
Sarkozy, Nicolas 129
SBU (Ukraine's national security service) 108
Serdyukov, Anatoly 45, 67–9, 130
Shelest, Petro 51, 53
Shoigu, Sergei 45, 54–5, 60, 69, 81–2, 101
South Ossetia 129
Soviet Union 6–8, 96, 149, 154
   collapse of the 11, 23, 93, 103, 119, 124, 126, 149, 152–5
   compared with Russia 48, 55–6, 96, 126, 143, 151
   dominance 49
   energy 138
   foreign policy of the 7, 14, 48, 56, 99, 125, 138
   "the Good Soviet Union" 47–8, 98–100, 102
   higher education 92
   leaders of the 52, 54, 90
   legacy 107, 154
   one-party regime of the 54
   post-Soviet bureaucrats 119
   post-Soviet Eurasia 97, 99, 134, 138, 152, 156
   post-Soviet institution building 98, 119, 154
   post-Soviet public 100
   post-Soviet resentment 94
   post-Soviet trauma 93
   satellites of the 50
   security apparatus 91–3, 113
   status of the 126
"special military operation" 21, 25, 32; *see also* Russian military assault
   aims of the 1–2, 142
   comparison of Ukraine and Czechoslovakia 31, 48–57, 75, 137; *see also* "Operation Danube"
   continuation 3, 26, 143
   description 16–20, 35
   duration 7, 26
   effects 84, 114
   explanations for the 24, 26–8, 61–2, 87
   failure of the 2–3, 5–6, 10, 21, 76, 83, 118, 137, 141–2, 146
   Kremlin's preferences regarding the 49
   launch 35–6, 73–4, 80, 87, 101, 137, 141
   legitimation 53
   losses 2, 20, 47, 146
   planning 54–5, 73, 75
   preparedness for 31, 76, 81, 83, 102, 115
   resistance 5, 123, 136
   term 92
spin dictatorship 5, 31, 89–90; *see also* authoritarian regime(s), "informational autocracy"
Stalin, Joseph 8, 50, 92
Survey of Russian Elites 11, 13, 27, 89, 91–2, 94, 192 n.68; *see also* elites
Syria 15, 69, 79, 97, 115, 134–5

technocrats 22, 31, 43–4, 46, 55, 64, 66, 73, 89, 95, 122
Telegram 81
Thaw 56, 93
think tanks 15, 71–2; *see also* Valdai Club
Timoshenko, Yulia 106
Trump, Donald 80, 85–6, 135, 147

INDEX

Turkey 14, 18, 90, 96, 110, 113

Ukraine 1, 15–17, 34, 54–5, 102–3, 106–8, 127, 131; see also Revolution of Dignity; West, and Ukraine
  as "anti-Russia" 104
  division in 105–6
  military 17, 132
  narrative about non-existence of 105
  politics in 106–7, 130
  resistance of 4–5, 17–19, 55, 78
  security guarantees for 18
  Soviet Ukraine 51
  support for 5, 17
United States 3, 12, 14, 16, 23, 29, 34, 37, 51, 69, 74, 86, 124, 127
UN Security Council 96, 126
Ustinov, Dmitry 54
Utkin, Dmitry 79, 82

Valdai Club 15, 71–2
veil of secrecy 24, 31, 52, 65, 70, 76; see also authoritarian regime(s), information flows

Wagner Group 19, 77, 79–83, 134–5
war(s) 8–10, 83–4, 143; see also Cold War; Georgia, five-day war in; military aggression
  of attrition 19, 78
  in Chechnya 121
  civil 79, 97, 126, 149
  constraints 8–9
  crimes 79
  definition of 29–30
  "gas wars" 111
  impact on state-building of 84
  large-scale inter-state 29
  misperceptions contributing to 87–8
  political economy of 62
  probability of 9
  "small victorious" 9, 17, 121
  "war against terrorism" 134
  World War I 9, 19, 125
  World War II 1–2, 8, 28–9, 52, 124
Warsaw Pact 10, 49–52, 56
West 1, 21, 88, 112, 124, 126, 128, 135, 155–6; see also anti-Westernism
  "collective West" 4, 8, 11, 16, 26, 28, 32, 98, 111, 117, 124–31, 135–6, 138, 144, 147–8, 155–6
  Russia's hostility towards the 6, 28, 88, 116, 135
  and Ukraine 1, 4, 34, 102–3, 105–6, 109, 115, 117, 137
  underestimating the 25, 112

Xi, Jinping 37, 147

Yakovlev, Andrei 43
Yanukovych, Viktor 15, 49, 55–6, 94, 100, 104–7, 130–2
Yeltsin, Boris 26, 40–1, 44, 97, 120–1, 125–7, 154
Yugoslavia 126
the Yukos affair 41, 44, 122
Yushchenko, Viktor 106, 111

Zelensky, Volodymyr 15, 55, 74, 107–9